MADHVA'S UNKNOWN LITERARY SOURCES

MADHVA'S UNKNOWN LITERARY SOURCES

Some Observations

ROQUE MESQUITA
University of Vienna

ADITYA PRAKASHAN
New Delhi

First published: 2000

ISBN 81-7742-028-3

Published by Aditya Prakashan, Delhi – 110 009
and printed at Rajkamal Electric Press, Delhi – 110 033.

TABLE OF CONTENTS

कान्तायै कुमारकुमारीभ्यश्चस्नेहात् समर्पितम्

PREFACE TO THE ENGLISH EDITION

The present English edition of my original German monograph on Madhva: 'Madhva und seine unbekannte Quellen. Einige Beobachtungen', which was published in the Publications of the De Nobili Research Library, Vienna 1997, contains slight changes, minor additions and indices. The main aim of this translation is to make the results of this monograph accessible to English speaking scholars.

The study sheds light on a neglected chapter of Madhva's philosophy, although his 'unknown sources' were already a subject of general discussion at his time and stirred up heated controversies which developed into an open hostility that even affected the Purāṇic literature. Thus Madhva has been target of sharp and unfair criticism in three interpolated chapters of the Saura Purāṇa.[1]

In this sense the present study clears out some misconceptions of 'friends and foes', which so far hindered the passing of a correct judgement on Madhva's unknown sources. For instance, that „The attempt to discredit the sources of Madhva is of much later origin, springing from the days of Appaya Dīkṣita. He was the first to raise the cry which was assiduously taken up by others like Bhaṭṭoji and Veṅkaṭanātha." As a matter of fact, Veṅkaṭanātha lived three centuries before Appayadīkṣita! And the criticism against Madhva has been already uttered by his contemporary, the Viśiṣṭādvaita author Varadaguru.[2] Another misconception was that the authenticity of Madhva's sources is

---

1 Cf. below n 141.

2 Cf. below n 31f.

attested by independent quotations of the same by the later authors: „. . . but one quotation of three verses beginning *sarvābhimānino devās tatrāpi* is not anywhere in Madhva's works. It must be a quotation taken by Trivikrama direct from the Brahma Tarka. If this view is correct, at once it concludes the matter." The three *śloka*s alluded here are mentioned in fact by Madhva himself under *iti ca*-quotation.[3]

In the same way, the charge levelled by the 'foes' against Madhva that he is quoting 'fabricated Vedic and other texts in support of his doctrines'[4] can by no means stand up to the theological and philosophical frame wherein Madhva's unknown sources are embedded, as shown in the course of this study. Strange enough, that no one so far even took notice of a crucial statement by Madhva in his MBhTN, which would have helped to make a critical appraisal of the real position of Madhva, namely:

> *ānandatīrthākhyamuniḥ supūrṇa-*
> *prajñābhidho grantham imaṃ cakāra /*
> *nārāyaṇenābhihito badaryāṃ*
> *tasyaiva śiṣyo jagadekabhartuḥ //*
> *yas tatprasādād akhilāṃś ca vedān*
> *sapañcarātrān sarahasyasaṅgrahān /*
> *vedetihāsāṃś ca purāṇayuktān*
> *yathāvad anyā api sarvavidyāḥ //*[5]

„The sage called Ānandatīrtha, [also] with the name Supūrṇaprajña – who has been named [so or taught] by Nārāyaṇa himself in Badarī [and therefore Viṣṇu] alone is his teacher, the sole Lord of the world – composed the present work in verse. He composed also (*ca*) by the grace of Viṣṇu all the Vedas together

---

[3] Cf. below n 162.

[4] Cf. below n 27; 31.

[5] Cf. below n 105f.

with the Pañcarātrasaṃhitās, summarizing the secret doctrines [of the Vedas], as well as the [fifth] Veda with Itihāsas and Purāṇas and also all other Vidyās in a very exact way."

I wish to express my gratitude to pupils and friends of mine who helped me in various way, specially by reading the last draft of this translation. I have adopted many of their suggestions and stylistic revisions. For any mistakes, which may have remained, I alone shoulder the responsibility for them.

PREFACE TO THE GERMAN EDITION

Madhva's sources were always a puzzling question and they remained up to now a mystery to Indologists, although Veṅkaṭanātha raised serious doubts about their authenticity already in the 13th century. For Madhva's followers the genuineness of the sources was a question of faith and therefore they saw no reason to inquire into this subject. On the contrary, they viewed such an inquiry as an inexcusable offence against the credibility of Madhva. They felt confirmed in their defence reaction, since the critics such as Appayadīkṣita and others accused Madhva of 'literary forgery' without having taken into consideration the teaching of Madhva in its totality.

The European Indologists in general had left aside the question of Madhva's sources. In principle, they were of the opinion that Madhva by no means would have dared to falsify his sources, since Madhva's contemporaries would have challenged him and made fun of his new philosophical system. The first Western scholar who tried to prove the authenticity of Madhva's sources was the french Indologist, Mme. S. SIAUVE. Unfortunately, she based her rather hypothetical arguments and risky interpretations mostly on the hagiographical work Sumadhvavijaya, (a work mixing facts with legends), and did not take into consideration the factual assertions of Madhva and other redactional arguments in his several works. The present study is the very first attempt to solve the problem of these unknown sources on the basis of authentical statements of Madhva himself, which allow us to reconstruct the theological and literal frame in which the sources of Madhva are embedded.

As the results of this study sharply contrast with the opinion of Mme. SIAUVE, a detailed discussion about her ways and process of reasoning has become an imperative. This has been carried out deliberately in the footnotes, in order to avoid an interruption in the continuity of the exposition. My critical remarks do by no means intend to belittle the excellent studies of Mme. SIAUVE. On the contrary, I owe her several stimulating suggestions and in many cases the present exposition leans on the results of her research.

The materials collected by me over the years and put forward in this book for the first time have been analysed and evaluated only in relation to the unknown sources. A thorough discussion of these materials would have gone beyond the scope of this study.

The results of my inquiry may somehow be surprising for Indian local tradition, as Madhva for the first time in the history of philosophical and religious systems of India claims to be an *avatāra*, through the taking possession (*āveśa*) of him by Viṣṇu. He is absolutely convinced to be entitled to speak for Viṣṇu on account of his divine charisma (*viṣṇuprasādāt*) and to proclaim in His name (*bhagavatkāryasādhaka*) the canonical books (*sadāgamāḥ*) in the *kali* age.

The findings of this investigation have revealed that the unknown sources of Madhva are neither ancient works which got lost, as the followers of Madhva maintain, nor a literary forgery (*svamātrakalpita/svakapolakalpita*), as Madhva's adversaries claim, but 'texts' Madhva himself produced in sincere obedience to the impelling force of Viṣṇu and which in a special way can be attributed to Viṣṇu himself as their author. For this reason Madhva ascribes not only these text quotations but also the titles of these texts, as well as his established doctrines (*bhagavatrāddhānta*) and even the logical conclusive arguments for this doctrine formulated by Madhva himself, directly to Viṣṇu (*yuktayo nirṇayasyaiva svayaṃ bhagavatoditāḥ*). It is remarkable that this teaching of taking possession (*āveśa*) of Madhva by Viṣṇu is in many respects very similar to the Christian concept of inspiration.[6] However, this does not imply that Madhva is drawing from Christian thought patterns. In the past some scholars have maintained that Madhva's teaching of predestination and of *vāyu*, as son of God and mediator of salvation has been developed under the influence of Christian thoughts.[7] The fact is that all of Madhva's teachings are based on original Indian concepts.

I wish to thank all persons who helped me in various ways to complete this monograph. Prof. Dr. Gerhard Oberhammer for his willingness to include it in the „Publications of the De Nobili Research Library". Prof. Dr. Walter Slaje who suggested many valuable improvements and corrections to my earlier version of this monograph. Dozent Dr. Utz Podzeit and Eberhard Guhe, M.A. who improved my German diction. Joachim Prandstetter for his technical help in the electronic data processing. Sibylla Hoffmann for her careful lay-out and Alexandra Böckle for proof-reading and for checking the correctness of the quotations. Last but not least my sincere thanks to my wife and my children, Sushila, D. Avinash and Sunanda, for their fullest understanding for my research work. As my modest present I want to dedicate this study to them.

---

6 Cf. K. RAHNER/H.VORGRIMLER, Concise Theological Dictionary, translated by R. STRACHAN. London 1983, p. 231, *s. v.* inspiration: „As distinguished from divine revelation to and by a prophet, inspiration is that charismatic divine influence upon the writers of the OT and NT whereby (without these writers ceasing to be the authors of their work) God becomes the author of these books in a special sense and the books become the infallible word of God (2 Tim 3; 16 . . .). This charismatic divine influence instigates and guides the composition of these books in all their aspects, internal and external, so that they contain what God himself wishes to say by their means – the genuine expression, free of all error . . ."

7 Cf. G.A. GRIERSON, Encyclopedia of Religion and Ethics. Ed. by J. HASTINGS, [2]1967, Vol. 8, *s.v.* Mādhvas, Madhvachāris, pp. 232-235, also SIAUVE 1971: 99-111.

INTRODUCTION

Madhva *alias* Ānandatīrtha and Pūrṇaprajña, names used by him very often,[8] was a shimmering personality among the intellectuals in India at the beginning of the 13th century,[9] not only because he developed a new Vedāntic school as an unified whole system,[10] which had no links to any existing Vedānta tradition, but also owing to the uniqueness of his appearance as an *avatāra* Vāyus, 'son of Viṣṇu', as the divinely appointed teacher with a clear sense of a mission,[11] to fight off false doctrines, to annihi-

---

[8] Cf. MBhTN I 136-137: . . . *viduṣā* . . . / *ānandatīrthamuninā pūrṇaprajñābhidhāyujā* / *tātparyaṃ śastrāṇāṃ sarveṣāṃ uttamaṃ mayā proktam* ; *ibid.* III 8cd: *ānandatīrtha varanāmavatī tṛtīyā bhaumī tanur marutaḥ*; cf. below n 106; 107; 115; 374. According to the Dvaita-*guruparaṃparā* these names have been conferred on him by his teacher Acyutaprekṣa at the Saṃnyāsa-ordination. Madhva is also known under Madhyamandira (cf. SDS p. 262,16; 294,27-28; below n 32), which should be a reference to his father's family name (cf. Sumadhvavijaya II 9; B.N.K. SHARMA, ABORI 13 [1931-32]: 56 n 3; below n 141). It is conspicuous that Madhva does not name his human teacher. Viṣṇu is his only *guru* (cf. below n 106). Nowhere in the works of Madhva did I find a corroboration for the opinion in Sumadhvavijaya, which has been upheld by many authors (cf. SHERIDAN 1992: 109ff.), that Madhva acknowledges Vyāsa as his teacher. In all places where Viṣṇu is praised as *guru*, he does not appear in the form of Vyāsa! (*vyāsarūpiṇā*); cf. n 75f.; 12; 84f.

[9] Madhva reports his birth year in MBhTN (XXXII 120) as 4300 of *kaliyuga* (= 1199 A. D.):

> *catuḥsahasre triśatottare gate saṃvatsarāṇāṃ tu kalau pṛthivyam* /
> *jātaḥ punar vipratanuḥ sa bhīmo daityair nirgūḍhaṃ haritattvam āha* //

The date of birth given in the different lists of Maṭhas deviates from the date in MBhTN, cf. SHARMA 1960: 101f.; BHANDARKAR 1913: 58f.; GLASENAPP 1992: 9f.; SIAUVE 1968: 2f.

[10] Cf. GLASENAPP 1992: 28f.; SIAUVE 1968: 33.

[11] Cf. above n 9; below n 115; KANE V/II 1962: 1220: „It is remarkable that great ācāryas like Śaṅkara and Rāmānuja never claimed in their own

late the reign of terror of *asurāḥ/daityāḥ* and to proclaim the ultimate supremacy (*sarvottamatva*) of Viṣṇu. The special feature of the Dvaita school, distinguishing it from all other Vedānta systems is therefore the originality of its teaching which does not depend on a *guruparaṃparā*, but goes back to the outworldly authority of Madhva.[12] In this sense the doctrine or the message of Madhva appears like a revealed religion. This fact did not prevent the rapid and wide dissemination of the Madhva school followed by the establishment of several communities and Maṭhas, despite the severe opposition of the existing Vedāntic

---

works that they were the avatāras of some deity. It was left to their disciples to say so, if at all"; CHANDRAVASU (1910: xv) [a Madhvite]: „Other authors have been more modest, and left it to their disciples to deify them, but Madhva, like Jesus, boldly lays claim to be the incarnation of Vāyu, the son of God"; PH. GRANOFF [Scholars and Wonder-Workers: Some Remarks on the Role of the Supernatural in Philosophical Contests in Vedānta Hagiographies, JAOS (FS Daniel H. H. Ingalls) 103 (1985), p. 462:] „The subject of the biography is regarded as an *avatāra* or incarnation of a major deity, come to earth at the request of the Gods to destroy heretical demons who are propagating the wrong faith."; cf. also J. BRONKHORST, The two Sources of Indian Asceticism. Delhi 1998: 69f. „In the classical Sāṃkhya texts he [Kapila] is more than just a sage; he is an incarnation of God (*īśvara*). The *Yuktidīpikā* describes him as *īśvaramaharṣi* 'great seer who is [an incorporation of] God'. The *Māṭharavṛtti* speaks of „the great seer called Kapila, an incarnation of the exalted old Self, the son of Prajāpati Kardama" . . . ; in other words, God is the self of Kapila, and Kapila an incarnation of God. This interpretation is supported by the *Yoga Bhāṣya* . . . Vācaspati Miśra's *Tattvavaiśāradī* on Yoga sūtra 1. 25, finally, calls Kapila an *avatāra* of Viṣṇu, and adds that Kapila is identical with the self-existent Hiraṇyagarbha, and with God (*īśvara*)."

12 Cf. SIAUVE 1968: 1 „A la différence de ses deux grands prédecesseurs *vedāntin*, Śaṅkara et Rāmānuja, Madhva ne fait référence au début de ses ouvrages à aucune lignée de *guru*."; SHARMA 1960: 79f.; 100f. Madhva is of the opinion, that all systems are beginningless: *anādikālato vṛttāḥ samayā hi pravāhataḥ / na cocchedo 'sti kasyāpi samayasya* (Anuv p. 71, 24; cf. below n 176). The Guruparamparā, referred to in the 'Dvaita-Catechism', is of later date. According to this Guruparamparā Viṣṇu appearing as Haṃsa announced the Dvaita-Doctrine first to god Brahmā at the creation of the world, which has been handed down through ten different teachers up to Madhva, cf. GLASENAPP 1992: 22f.

schools. And through its inclusion in Sāyana Mādhava's Sarvadarśanasaṅgraha, the Madhva school gained a full fledged acceptance as equal orthodox system of Vedānta, which is even presented having a superior rank than the Rāmānuja school in the hierarchical scheme of Sāyana's doxographical work. So he attributes the refutation of this school to Madhva.

However, the sources of the Madhva school are not primarily the Veda-Texts, which he quotes very often and interprets them in a rather artificial, risky and coercive way,[13] but a huge quantity of texts which belong to the so-called 'fifth Veda'. Judging from their titles we could assign them to the Āgama literature. And Madhva's commentaries to the texts of Prasthānatraya are nothing more than a long chain of verse quotations from the *śruti* and specially from the *smṛti* literature. The short prose explanations in between serve to link the quotations with one another. Generally, Madhva's commentaries begin and end with citations.[14] By the way, Madhva uses the texts of Prasthānatraya as a mere outer frame to put forward his original views. In this sense, *e.g.* his commentary to the Brahmasūtras deviates from the different traditions of Vedānta.[15]

---

[13] Cf. for instance Madhva's interpretation of ChUp VI 8,7: *sa ātmā / tat tvam asi* as *sa ātmā atat tvam asi* (cf. below n 183f. and HEIMANN 1922: 6; GHATE 1981: 30f.).

[14] Cf. RAO 1960: 64 „The second feature that every reader of Madhva's works notices is the abundance of quotations . . . They range over a wide field, of śruti and smṛti literature . . . Often times the entire meaning of the text is found in the quotation and in such cases, Madhva contents himself by making the quotation without adding any words of his own." Exception to this rule are the shorter works of Madhva as Mithyātvānumānalakṣaṇa, Tattvasaṅkhyāna, Tattvaviveka, which has no quotations at all, or other works as MBhTN and Anuv comparatively with fewer quotes.

[15] In this sense, for instance Appayadīkṣita noted in his autocommentary to MTM, that in several BSū (*katipayeṣv api sūtreṣu*) different interpretations have been put forward, as Saguṇa-Nirguṇa-Bheda-Abheda etc. whereas the BSū-Interpretation of Madhva nowhere in the BSū is included (*tathāpy ānandatīrthīyaṃ yojanam anupādeyam eva*), and that his explanation deviates absolutely from the other teachers of Vedānta (*ānandatīrthīye tu yojane*

We could assign Madhva's abundant quotations to five different groups, namely (1) Quotations out of *śruti* and *smṛti* literature which can be identified, (2) Quotations of the same literature, which however cannot be located,[16] (3) Quotations from

---

prāyas sarvatraiva prakārabhedaḥ); cf. below n 32f.; BHANDARKAR 1913: 58 „All the Sūtras of Bādarāyaṇa. . . have been interpreted by him in an entirely different way. Probably he would have set aside the Brahmasūtras altogether, but he could not do so, since the work had acquired an uncontested authoritativeness as regards religious truth before his time. He had therefore to show that his system did not go against the Brahmasūtras and therefore accepted them and interpreted them in almost a fantastic manner"; GHATE 1981: 30 „Madhva denies even Brahman's being the material cause of the universe, a point clearly established in the Brahmasūtras and the very fantastic and forced manner in which he interprets many of the sūtras leaves no doubt about the fact that he would have even set aside the sūtras altogether, but that their uncontested authoritativeness prevented him from doing so" (cf. below n 27). The remark of Prof. SHERIDAN (1992: 110), that the above mentioned critical evaluation is a „distortion by reliance on nonindigenous philosophical categories", fails to recognize the fact, that the critical assessment of Madhva's dealing with the sources has a long indigenous tradition behind it, which goes back to the time Madhva lived; cf. below n 30f.

[16] Cf. VENKATASUBBIAH 1933:190 „The passages cited by Madhva from the *Harivaṃśa, Mahopaniṣad,* and *Bṛhatsaṃhitā* are not found in the books mentioned bearing those names, and are evidently fabrications of Madhva. So are, likewise, the citations from *Prakaṭaśruti* and other mythical books; and to judge from these, it is also very probable that his citations from the *Pādma, Gāruda* and other Purāṇas are likewise fabrications"; cf. below n 150ff., 270ff. Even Madhvite scholars, who translated works of Madhva into English, did in fact locate several *śruti* quotations, but they were unable to identify the overwhelming majority of them, specially from *smṛti* literature. Nevertheless, one should admit that Madhva has an excellent and comprehensive knowledge of *śruti* and *smṛti* literature. A good many citations I checked Madhva quoted correctly, sometimes with slight deviations. There are, however, some slips, for instance Madhva falsely replaces *pañcarātram* by *pāśupatam* when he quotes Mokṣadharma (MBh XII 337,1ab), teaching the unity of Veda and Pañcarātra (*vedapañcarātrayor aikya* ; cf. BSūBh p. 10,11-12). There are also other deviations (GīBh p. 42,6): '*kṛtsnaṃ śatapathaṃ cakre*' iti instead of *kṛtsnaṃ śatapatham caiva praṇeṣyasi dvijarṣabha* (MBh XII 306,11ab). Sometimes citations from MBh (XII 337,67; XII 233,7) are referred to as *iti gītā* or *iti bhagavadvacanam* (cf. Anuv p. 88,23-24; BSūBh p.162,22-23). On the other hand excerpts from Gītā appear as *iti bhārate* (MuUBh p. 490,21-22 = Gī XV 25cd). Elsewhere, (VTN p. 38,21-

unknown *śruti* texts, (4) Quotations from unknown Āgama/Saṃhitā literature and finally a good number of citations which are quoted in a rather vague way, merely as *iti, iti ca* etc.[17]

The *lacunae* in the quotations of Madhva do not confine to a few excerpts (these kind of *lacunae* are to be found also in the works of other Vedānta-Commentators), but they comprise a whole class of literary works with countless different titles.[18] It is

---

22) Madhva ascribes a quote from Rāmāyaṇa (crit. ed. App. I No. 19,81f.) to MBh. It is noteworthy, that *śruti* quotations, which Madhva refers to in a general way merely as *śruti*, could be identified. This is valid also for the citations from Bhagavadgītā (also refered to as Bhagavadvacana), as well as for quotations from BhāgP. However, I was unable to identify several quotations from this Purāṇa, which sometimes is referred to as *śruti* (cf. below n 258).

[17] While analysing this type of citations in different works of Madhva I made following observations. Madhva quotes in this way, when he puts together several excerpts from different *śrutis* (without naming them, *e.g.* GīBh p. 88,16f.: BĀU III 7,16; 17;18; ChU IV 15,1; MahānārU XVI 5); or when he quotes many passages of one and the same text (as in KN p. 99,24-100,4: Gī VI 37, 16-20; VI 26,33ab); or when he adduces passages from an unknown text together with a passage from a known text (as in BĀUBh p. 305,25-306,17: Brahmatarka [unknown] and Gī XV 16-17; in BhāgTN p. 3,1-4,5: Tantrabhāgavata [unknown] and BSū II 2,28); or when he quotes an unknown text (= Sattattva and Sāmasaṃhitā) followed by other not identified citations (cf. GīT p.73, 23-26; ChUBh p. 384,27ff.). Very often a chapter of a commentary ends with '*iti ca* ' reference followed by similar references in the new chapter ahead (as in BhāgTN p. 454,10ff.; 474,10ff.; 490,4ff.). Sometimes we find a quotation in another quotation with '*iti* ', *e.g.* the citation from the Paiṅgiśruti (= BSūBh p. 28,1-2) in the excerpt from Bhāllaveyaśruti (as in BhāgTN p.11,6-9, cf. below n 145.; MBhTN I 50ab; from the MahānārU XVII 14 in GīBh p. 53,1-3; cf. below n 22 and SIAUVE 1968: 25). In the same way, some unknown sources are mentioned in other unknown works, *e.g.* Brahmatarka (cf. GīT p. 23,24-28; BĀUBh p. 323,20-23; n 150). Occasionally, one single quotation reaches to several pages, (as in AiUBh p. 165+175; 233,21+237,12; TaiUBh p. 529,19+535,22! cf. also SHARMA 1960: 110).

[18] Appayadīkṣita names in his MTM (cf. below n 33) altogether 40 unknown works. Out of these 29 titles are from *śruti* literature and 11 titles from *smṛti* literature. Since he ends this enumeration in both cases with *ityādi*, it does mean that his count is incomplete. Cinnasvāmi Śastri adds in his

a very striking fact that Madhva quotes from the unknown or anonymous sources only when he puts forward his original teaching.[19] In the same way, it is also remarkable that these sources were unknown not only to his predecessors but also to his contemporaries, and even to his own pupils.[20] It is noteworthy, that these anonymous quotations under different titles are not identical in all their contents, although they are adduced as a proof for a particular teaching. Apart from some common features these quotations have sometimes complementary, also contrary or even contradictory elements, so that they necessarily

---

Ṭippaṇa eight other titles to this number. One should bear in mind that the here collected titles of unknown works are to be found only in Madhva's BSūBh. If we take into account that Madhva has written altogether 36 works the total number of these works should be much higher; cf. RAO 1960: 59: „We find that Madhva quotes, in round figures, from fifty Śrutis, forty Saṃhitas, twenty five Purāṇas, ten Tantras, five dictionaries, two works on logic, one grammar and hundred forty miscellaneous works." It is striking that these unknown works are named after well known old Vedic teachers and sometimes they have also very strange names (cf. below n 33).

[19] Cf. GLASENAPP 1992: 27; HEIMANN 1922: 6; SIAUVE 1968: 25ff.; 1971: 9ff.; SHARMA 1960: 112. and (The sacred Books of the Hindus, translated by various Sanskrit Scholars, Vol. 1: Isa, Kena etc. ed. by B.D.BASU. Allahabad 1911: 2): „Madhva always quotes some Purāṇic authority for his apparently strange interpretations. It is clear from these apt quotations, that the school of thought which he represents existed long before him."

[20] Cf. SIAUVE 1968: 24 „Un des traits assez déconcertants de son oeuvre est le fait qu'il cite un nombre considérable de Śruti inconnues qui, à de rares exceptions prés, ne sont utilisées par aucun auteur antérieur ni postérieur à lui, pas même à l'intérieur de son école . . . Il reste que le nombre de telles citations données par Madhva est immense." Elsewhere (p. 32) SIAUVE withdraws somehow from this remark when she notes: „Que ses disciples n'utilisent pas ces mêmes ouvrages ne prouve pas qu'ils les ignoraient"; cf. (1971:15; 74n 8 also without this withdrawal; cf. below n 26). VENKATA-SUBBIAH (1933: 190n 24) makes a clear statement in this connection: „The only alternative is to believe that copies of those works existed in a library to which Madhva had access, that these copies were unique, and that no other writer except Madhva (whether anterior, posterior or contemporary to him) had access to that library. This is impossible, and hence one cannot but conclude that Madhva fabricated evidence on large scale."

give the impression that by no means one single person could be the author of these quotations.[21] It is also strange that some *śruti* quotations contain citations of other *śruti* texts and some texts from the Saṃhitā literature refer to other similar texts, which are expressly attributed to Viṣṇu himself (*svayaṃ bhagavatā kṛtāḥ*).[22]

In view of these various and serious problems in regard to the unknown sources which Madhva freely quotes, the reader is on the horns of a dilemma. If we regard Madhva's teaching as a mere synthesis of the doctrine found in his unknown sources, this would contradict not only his genius as a sagacious and original thinker but also his philosophico-theological system as an organic whole unit. If we on the other hand presume that Madhva himself was the secret author of his unknown sources, then his system would be in the eyes of his contemporaries a mere human creation and therefore extremely suspicious, since it is not grounded in the eternal knowledge, handed down through long generations and accepted as such by wise and learned men (*śiṣṭāḥ*).

---

[21] A small illustration to make it clear: ChUBh (p. 441,16) declares: *viṣṇoḥ paramotkarṣe hi sarvapramāṇānāṃ mahātātparyaṃ bhagavatābhihitam*. In contradiction to it we find a quote from Paramasaṃhitā (not identified) in connection with Viṣṇu as the highest God that not everywhere in Veda Viṣṇu's paramount supremacy is taught (MuUBh p. 490,13f.):

> *ṛgādyā aparā vidyā yadā viṣṇor na vācakāḥ |*
> *tā eva paramā vidyā yadā viṣṇor tu vacakāḥ |*
> iti paramasaṃhitāyām.

Immediately after we find another contradictory statement: *vede . . . ādav ante ca madhye ca viṣṇuḥ sarvatra gīyate* (cf. below n 59). For other similar examples cf. specially below n 51; 88f.; 71; 110; 169; 185; 192; 201; 204; 257; 258; 269; 325; 330.

[22] Cf. SIAUVE 1968: 25 „Il peut paraître étrange que des textes dits de Śruti citent d'autres Śruti puisque les uns et les autres font partie du même Veda éternel"; also above n 17 and below n 143.

All scholars who were engaged in the research of Madhva's Philosophy as well as his ardent followers[23] were conscious of this paradox. But they were not aware of how Madhva positively declared his position on this matter. In fact, there are several statements of Madhva which make his point of view clear. Showing a high degree of imagination and innovation he makes use of traditional thought patterns, where the unknown sources are firmly established, as will be argued below.

Hitherto, no effort has been made to unlock this strange world of ideas. So, it is somehow surprising that the Indologists in Europe without ever having any direct knowledge of Madhva's statements on the concerned matter were rather inclined to accept that Madhva did not 'fabricate' his sources. According to them he could not dare to quote from imaginary sources known only to him. This opinion was put forward by HEIMANN and GLASENAPP.[24] Much more categorical in her statement was SIAUVE, who was not only convinced of the genuiness of Madhva's sources,[25] but thought that she had reasons ('preuve décisive') to prove the authenticity at least of one unknown source.[26] Consequently, she applied this evidence to all other unknown sources of Madhva.

---

[23] Cf. SHARMA 1960: 112 „The inaccessibility of many of these sources, at the present time and difficulty of tracing many of these quotations in the extant sources also, raises a problem as to the genuineness of these passages and the degree and extent of their reliability and the acceptability of the new line of interpretation of the Vedānta, based on them."

[24] Cf. HEIMANN 1922: 8n 6; GLASENAPP 1992: 27f.; also PUTHIADAM 1985: 5f.

[25] Cf. SIAUVE 1968: 25 „une fraude peu vraisemblable, . . . s'il avait forgé ses sources il aurait été plus habile"; 1971: 14; 75 n 8.

[26] Cf. SIAUVE 1971: 13ff.; SIAUVE's considerations are based in a high degree on Sumadhvavijaya. Many legendary details in this book find their way into the otherwise excellent and accurate studies of SIAUVE. In accordance with this hagiography she maintains that Madhva was acquainted with these sources during his two lengthy journeys in northern India: „ . . . nous trouvons des citations d'un bon nombre des textes, Śruti, Saṃhitā,

Otherwise, many Indian scholars not belonging to the Madhva school simply turned down the genuineness of Madhva's sources. For instance, VENKATASUBBIAH refering to Appayadīkṣita (16th century) and to Vīraśaivite Nirvāṇa (18th century?) remarks: „The charge has often been brought against Madhvācārya that he is addicted to the fabrication of evidence, and that he very frequently cites passages from books which do not, and did not at any time, exist."[27]

Tantra, qui ne nous sont connus que par lui" (p. 15). „Tout ce que nous savons c'est que plusieurs siècles après Madhva, au seizième siècle, les textes qu'il avait cites n'etaient plus en possession des siens. Il se peut d'ailleurs qu'une partie d'entre eux n'ait jamais éte en possession de Madhva lui-même, mais qu'il en ait seulement puisé des extraits dans des manuscripts consultés au cours de ses voyages, ce qui expliquerait son souci d'en donner des citations complètes et souvent étendues" (1968: 32; 25). Elsewhere, she speaks of Madhva's 'mémoire remarquable' (1968: 25) which allowed him to cite the texts from memory. She declares that the loss of these sources at a later date was due to moslem vandalism: „Peu de temps après Madhva, le Nord de l'Inde subissait bien des destructions, et il'est pas étonnant que rien n'ait subsisté de ses sources, et que même ses plus anciens commentateurs soient silencieux sur l'existence de textes auxquels ils n'eurent vraisemblablement jamais accès" (1971: 15). As I already remarked, SIAUVE's judgement leaning on Sumadhvavijaya and based – according to her – also on some textual observations comprise several conjectures which is in contradiction to the over-abundant evidence I collected in scrutiny of clear statements of Madhva (cf. below n 28; 120; 125; 147; 161; 176; 178).

[27] Cf. VENKATASUBBIAH 1933: 189f.; above n 16; and KANE 1962 V/II: 1218ff.: „ . . . he was roughly handled by eminent writers like Appaya-Dikṣita who charges Madhva with citing fabricated Vedic and other texts in support of his doctrines"; BHANDARKAR 1913: 58ff.; cf. also the pejorative judgement of GHATE (1981:30; 156) on Madhva's commentary of Brahmasūtra: „To begin with, the commentary of Madhva is evidently inferior in character and is a performance of little or no merit. His interpretations differ from those of the rest very widely and in a very large number of cases, but the reader has seen that in a majority of instances, his explanations are far-fetched, fantastic and too sectarian in character; the scriptural passages he refers to for discussion more often belong to the Saṃhitās than to the Upaniṣads, a procedure which can be easily explained by the fact that it is very difficult for him to find in the Upaniṣads a support for his own doctrine."; also above n 21.

MADHVA AND HIS CRITICS

Madhva's unknown sources gave rise to very strong criticism. Its starting point was not the 16th century, when Appayadīkṣita launched an attack on Madhva, as it is claimed, but already at the time of Madhva himself. As admitted by the followers of Madhva Veṅkaṭanātha (13th century) was one of his outspoken critics.[28] In his Śatadūṣaṇī [65: *alepakamatabhaṅgavāda*] Veṅkaṭanātha criticizes in connection with the dharma of Saṃnyāsin, authors who manipulate sources and calls them sinful people (*pāpiṣṭhāḥ*):

> *yāni cānyāni vākyāni saṃpratipannaśrutismṛtiṣv adṛśyamānāni svācārānurūpamataparicaryayā keṣucid aprasiddheṣu vā naṣṭakośeṣu vānirūpitamūlāgreṣu vā purāṇeṣu prakṣipya paṭhanti pāpiṣṭhāḥ, tāni pratyakṣaśrutyādipariśīlanaśālinīṣu gariṣṭhagoṣṭhīṣu nāvakāśaṃ labhante.*

„There are other passages which are not found in acknowledged Vedas and smṛtis. Sinful people, because of their devotion to opinions that accord with their conduct, first

---

[28] Cf. SHARMA 1960: 114 „The attempt to discredit the sources of Madhva is of much later origin, springing from the days of Appaya Dīkṣita. He was the first [*sic* !] to raise the cry which was assiduously taken up by others like Bhaṭṭoji and Veṅkaṭanātha." SHARMA is widely mistaken in that he thinks that Veṅkaṭanātha (SINGH 1958: 3f.; 1268-1369) lived after Appayadīkṣita and his pupil Bhaṭṭoji (16th cent.). SIAUVE also follows him in this matter (1968: 24; 32; 1971: 75n 8; recently K.K. RAJA too in his book-review of my publication, cf. Adyar L. B. 61 (1997): 261). SHARMA (and RAO [1960: i] too) unfortunately does not quote the passage where Veṅkaṭanātha conveyed his criticism. I could not locate this critical remark. Most probably he did it in his Maṇipravāla work 'Paramatabhaṅga' or in his 'Śatadūṣaṇī' which is fragmentary. Paramatabhaṅga was available to me in English translation but only in part.

interpolate them and then claim to find them in some Purāṇas that are not well known, or whose collections are lost, or whose beginnings and ends are not determined. These passages are not admitted in venerable assemblies distinguished for their meticulous study of express Vedic and other authoritative texts."[29]

In *yatiliṅgabhedabhaṅga* of the same text [64] Veṅkaṭanātha identifies these authors as some people (*kaiścit*), who quote sentences of Vyāsa and of his pupils (*vyāsādivacana*).[30] Varada-

---

[29] OLIVELLE 1987: 115 [369]; for transl. *ibid.* 153. Cf. similar statement of Madhva himself:

> *kvacid granthān prakṣipanti kvacid antaritān api* /
> *kuryuḥ kvacic ca vyatyāsaṃ pramādāt kvacid anyathā* //

(MBhTN II 3); see below n 131.

[30] OLIVELLE 1987: 75 [102-105]. Unfortunately, I could not identify this passage in the works of Madhva. But Madhva quotes in BSūBh (p. 171,28f.) from an unknown literary work Bhaviṣyatparvan (a fictitious text, see below n 34f.) that the teaching of authors degrading the function of *dharma* or *karman* goes back to Vyāsa himself since they are his pupils:

> . . .
> *iti kecid vidaḥ prāhur vyāsaśiṣyā ime 'khilāḥ* /
> *yasmād vyāsamataṃ sarvaṃ satyam eva tato 'khilam* //

In GīT (p. 59,23-28 = MuUBh p. 492,22-23) Madhva quotes five and half *ślokas* from Vyāsasmṛti. Only the first verse could be located (= Manusmṛti XII 89cd-90cd = KūrP I 2,63f.= GīBh p. 51,15). The last *śloka* of this citation runs:

> *jñānamārgaḥ karmamārga iti bhedas tato na hi* /
> *tasmād āśramabhedo 'yaṃ karmasaṅkocasaṃbhavaḥ* /
> iti vyāsasmṛteḥ.

The fact that only the first *śloka* is tradited, whereas the rest spontaneuosly supplemented, is basically comparable to the remark of Veṅkaṭanātha: „first interpolate them and then claim to find them in some Purāṇas." Similarly, in another fictitious quote from PadP (BSūBh p. 51,4):

> *kṛṣṇadvaipāyanamatād ekadeśavidaḥ pare* /
> *vadanty ete yathāprajñaṃ na virodhaḥ kathaṃcana* /
> iti pādme.

guru, the immediate predecessor of Veṅkaṭanātha and in addition a contemporary of Madhva polemizes in his *yatiliṅgasamārthana* against the very same authors and calls their opinion a 'fantasy' (*svakapolakalpita*), an expression used later also by the Vīraśaivite author Nirvāṇa to describe the anonymous works of Madhva, since – according to him – Madhva's opinion could not be verified either in *śruti* nor in the *smṛti* works.[31]

If this is true, then we can trace back the criticism to the life time of Madhva that his sources are not genuine! Even Sāyana Mādhava (14th cent.) who relates the teaching of Madhva faithfully on basis of quotations found in Madhva's works asserts at the end of his presentation that Madhva pretends to be the third *avatāra* of Vāyu: *etac ca rahasyaṃ pūrṇajñena madhyamandireṇa vāyos tṛtīyāvatāraṃ manyena nirūpitam.*[32] In relation to this short remark Appayadīkṣita's criticism is in detail and plainspoken. Despite its polemical tone it supplies a good basis for a proper appraisal of the unknown sources of Madhva. For this reason, the present discussion begins with the statement of

---

Cf. also GīBh p. 44,6-7: *yathāha bhagavān –*

> *yāni tīrthādivākyāni karmādiviṣayāṇi ca* /
> *stāvakāny eva tāni syur ajñānāṃ mohakāni vā* /
> *bhaven mokṣas tu maddṛṣṭer nānyatas tu kathaṃcana* /
> iti nāradīye.

Since there is a close connection between Vyāsa and Madhva which the latter underlines every now and then in his statements (cf. below n 58ff.) we can be pretty sure that Veṅkaṭanātha was aiming his criticism also at Madhva.

31 OLIVELLE 1987: 47 [79]: *yac ca kenacit tadupajīvinātyantaniṣedhaparatvena vyāsādivacanam ity udāhṛtam, tad api tattatkośeṣv adarśanāt, udāhṛtaśrutismṛtivirodhāt, pūrvavyākhyātṛbhir anudāhṛtatvāc ca svakapolakalpitam iti draṣṭavyam* ; cf. Vīraśaivite author Nirvāṇa in his commentay on Nīlakaṇṭha's Kriyāsāra (cited by VENKATASUBBIAH 1933: 189): *svavacanaprakaṭitavaidikamārgānanuguṇabhāgavatvenābhimatasvakapolakalpita vacane.* One cannot deny that this statement has a strong similarity with the remark of Varadaguru.

32 SDS p. 294,27-28.

Appayadīkṣita. He concedes that there are many different schools in the Vedānta based on different sūtras (*katipayeṣu eva sūtreṣu*) as Nirguṇavāda, Saguṇavāda, Bhedavāda, Abhedavāda and Bhedābhedavāda, but denies at the same time that any of these *sūtras* give support to Madhva's interpretation. For this reason he rejects his system sharply. Appayadīkṣita introduces his rejection in a very clear and concise way in *śloka* two and three of his MTM:

> *tathāpy ānandatīrthīyaṃ matam agrāhyam eva naḥ /*
> *yatra vaidikamaryādā bhūyasyākulatāṃ gatā //*
> *ataḥ pañcādhikaraṇīṃ lakṣyīkṛtyaiva tanmate /*
> *dūṣyasthalāni sarvatra sūcyante sudhiyāṃ mude //*

„Nevertheless, we reject the teaching of Madhva since in that [system] the [clear cut] boundaries of the Veda teaching have been confused in a greater degree. For this reason, he adduces everywhere spurious text passages in support of his teaching to the sheer commotion of the learned people pointing out to the fivefold division (of Veda = Pañcamaveda)."

In his autocommentary he discusses these *ślokas* in detail. But for our purpose the following statements are very significant:

> *ānandatīrthīye tu yojane prāyas sarvatraiva prakārabhedaḥ / so 'py anyeṣām asaṃpratipanneṣu svamātrakalpiteṣv artheṣu / tatra ca tura . . . śrutyādivacanānīti tadanusāriṇy adhyātma . . . bhaviṣyatparvādivacanānīti cātyantāprasiddhānām eva vacanānāṃ sākṣitayopanyāsaḥ / tadupanyāsaprasaktasvānāptatvaśaṅkāparihārāya hanumadbhīmasenakrameṇa vāyoḥ svayaṃ tṛtīyāvatāra ity udghoṣas / tatra ca sākṣitayā*
>
> *prathamo hanumān nāma dvitīyo bhīmasenakaḥ /*
> *pūrṇaprajñas tṛtīyas tu bhagavatkāryasādhakaḥ //*
>
> *iti smṛtivacanam astīti svayam eva tadudāharaṇam / baḷitthā tadvapuṣe dhāyi darśatam ity ādyṛgvedamantrasya svakal-*

pita vāyvavatāratrayaparatayā pradarśakam ityādi prāmāṇikamaryādālaṅghanaṃ bhūyasā dṛśyate /

„The [BSū-] interpretation of Madhva differs almost in every sense [from other Vedānta schools]. This difference appears with regard to the subject [of the doctrine] which is not recognized by other [Vedānta systems], since it has been fabricated by Madhva himself. To that end he adduces passages from the *śruti*, as Tura, Kamaṭha, Māṭhara, Kauṭharavya, Kauṇḍinya, Māṇḍavya, Mārkaṇḍeya, Maudgalya, Pauṣyāyaṇa, Pautrāyaṇa, Sautrāyaṇa, Pārāśaryāyaṇa, Mādhyaṃdināyana, Kauṣārava, Kāṣāyaṇa, Bṛhad, Uddālaka, Auddālakāyana, Kauśika, Sauparṇa, Śāṇḍilya, Vatsa, Gaupavana, Bhāllaveya, Agniveśya, Caturvedasaṃhitā, Caturvedaśikhā, Indradyumna und Parama, as well as passages [out of *smṛti* texts], which follow [the *śruti*] as Adhyātma, Nārāyaṇa, Adhyātmasaṃhitā, Bṛhatsaṃhitā, Mahāsaṃhitā, Nārāyaṇatantra, Bṛhattantra, Puruṣottamatantra, Māyāvaibhava, Brahmatarka und Bhaviṣyatparvan.[33] [In fact] it is unequivocally a quotation of passages which are absolutely unknown. In order to eliminate the doubt of untrustworthiness implied in this quotation he proclaims aloud that he himself is the third *avatāra* of Vāyu after Hanumān and Bhīma. And as evidence he cites a passage from an [unknown] *smṛti* work [namely Bhaviṣyatparvan[34]]: 'The first *avatāra* is Hanumān, the second is Bhīmasena, and the third one is Pūrṇaprajña, who performs deeds of Bhagavān.' In this sense there is also a selfassertion that in the Ṛgvedamantra (II 2,8,1): *baḷitthā tadvapuṣe dhāyi darśatam* etc. the three *avatāras* of Vāyu, which have been invented by [Madhva] himself, have been predicted. It is clear that this and other [statements

[33] This list comprises only quotes from the unknown sources in BSūBh. However, the real number of these quotations in other works of Madhva should be much higher, cf. above n 18.

[34] MBhTN II 112-118: *bhaviṣyatparvagaṃ cāpi vaco vyāsasya sādaram* . . .; cf. above n 30.

of Madhva] transgress in a high degree the boundaries of credibility."

The analysis of this accurate criticism bears evidence to three striking observations. First of all, Appayadīkṣita does not deny that the Madhva school belongs to Vedānta. Secondly, he mantains that there is a close relation between Madhva's teaching and his unknown sources and thirdly, that the credibility of these sources is based on his claim that he is an *avatāra* of Vāyu.

On the other hand, Appayadīkṣita emphasizes that Madhva's doctrine has no footing in an existing Vedānta tradition and that his unknown sources as well as his pretension of being an *avatāra* refering to Baḷitthāsūkta is an innovation or an invention of his (*svakalpitavāyvavatāra*) and the alluded prophecy cannot be but a *post factum* statement by Madhva himself (*vaticinium ex eventu*).[35] Drawing on this fact we could apply this evidence to all other unknown sources of Madhva also, where his pretension as *avatāra* is strongly pronounced.

It is remarkable that the judgement of Appayadīkṣita has been widely confirmed by modern scholars[36] that there is an intimate connection between the unknown sources and Madhva's characteristic teaching. Besides, the opinion expressed by Appayadīkṣita about the *avatāra*-claim, is supported by Madhva, since in his self-understanding this very claim excludes once for all that a forger is behind the unknown sources and that Viṣṇu himself is ultimately author and proclaimer of them. Both these points will be discussed below building upon the concrete statements of Madhva.

The best way to examine carefully the world of Madhva's ideas is to inquire at the very outset into his doctrine of *avatāras*, not only because the unknown sources are grounded on this

---

[35] Madhva refers to this Sūkta in MBhTN (XXXII 124: *ityādisūktāni ca tat pramāṇam*), when he points out his birth year (cf. XXXII 120)! As a matter of fact, in this case, Madhva himself speaks without appealing to the sources.

[36] Cf. above n 19f.; 23f.; below n 150f.

doctrine, but also because it allows us to have an insight into Madhva's methods in dealing with his sources. As a matter of fact, Madhva bases also his doctrine of *avatāra* on unidentified quotations from Purāṇas and other unknown sources.

THEOLOGICAL FOUNDATION OF AVATĀRA-CLAIM

As a every staunch devotee of Viṣṇu, Madhva is convinced that Viṣṇu comes down to earth from time to time in order to protect His devotees, to annihilate His enemies and to reestablish the dharmic order in the world.[37] The divine appearances of Viṣṇu in this world, due to His inconceivable might (*acintyaśakteḥ*) are pure and absolutely identical with the prototype of Viṣṇu (*kṛṣṇarāmādirupāṇi paripūrṇāni sarvadā / na cāṇumātram bhinnāni*).[38] In Anuv he declares that the identity between Viṣṇu and his *avatāras* – taught according to him in KathU (II 1,11) and BĀU (II 5,19) – implies an identity of consciousness, since an identity one is not aware of, says Madhva, cannot be an identity of being. In this sense the consciousness of identity is a clear evidence for the identity of being:

> *anusandhānarahitam aikyaṃ ced ekatā na tat /*
> *cetanaikye 'nusandhānaṃ pramāṇaṃ naiva cāparam //*[39]

---

[37] Cf. Gī IV 7-8. Cf. HACKER 1960 for the historical development of *avatāra*-doctrine.

[38] GīBh p. 37,16-17. Madhva quotes NārP (could not be identified). For the same purpose other unidentified quotations have been adduced, for instance from VarP (BhāgTN p. 15,8-16,1) or from Mahāsaṃhitā (*ibid.* p. 25,4-6). It is striking that one half *śloka* is almost identical with the citation from VarP: *dehidehabhidā cātra neśvare vidyate kvacit = dehidehavibhedaś ca na pare vidyate kvacit*! Cf. also Madhva's self-statement in (MBhTN II 27):

> *ityādyāḥ kevalo viṣṇur naiṣāṃ bhedaḥ kathaṃcana /*
> *na viśeṣo guṇaiḥ sarvaiḥ balajnānādibhiḥ kvacit /*

[39] Anuv p. 136,25-26; 137,12-23. For the explanation of *anusandhāna* cf. SIAUVE 1968: 45f. Jayatīrtha defines it as *svīyatayānubhavamātram*; cf. UKhT p. 338,15; below n 58f.

Whereas Madhva in Anuv puts forward his ideas without the help of quotations[40], in KathUBh he cites an anonymous source (= *iti ca*) preceded by several *iti ca*-quotations. The aforesaid citation expands the identity of consciousness further into a fullsized one: the identity of members of the body, qualities and deeds of the *avatāras*:

yaḥ prādurbhāvagato viṣṇur dehādiṣu ca saṃsthitaḥ |
sa eva mūlarūpaś ca sākṣān nārāyaṇābhidhaḥ ||
mūlarūpaś ca yo viṣṇuḥ prādurbhāvādikaś ca saḥ |
guṇataḥ svarūpato vāpi viśeṣaṃ yo 'tra paśyati ||
atyalpam api mṛtvā sa tamo 'ndhaṃ yāty asaṃśayam |
bhedābhedaṃ cātra tathā tamo yāti na saṃśayaḥ ||
tathaivāvayavānāṃ ca guṇānāṃ ca parasparam |
kriyāṇāṃ tena caiteṣāṃ bhedavic cobhayaṃ viduḥ ||
yānty evāndhaṃ tamo nātra kāryā kācid vicāraṇā |
iti ca.

„God Viṣṇu, who exists in the manifested form [as *avatāra*] and in the bodies etc. [on the earth], is identical with the original form and his personal name is Nārāyaṇa. Viṣṇu in [his] original form is the very same being in the manifested form [as *avatāra*]. One who sees even a slightest difference between them with regard to their attributes or with respect to their essential nature, undoubtedly enters blinding darkness after death.[41] In the same way, one undoubtedly enters darkness if one sees *bhedābheda* [relation] between them. Similarly, those who see mutual difference or *bhedābheda* [relation] between the limbs of his body, attributes and deeds and between these [all] and him (=Viṣṇu) go to blind darkness. There is no slightest doubt about it."[42]

---

40 Cf. SIAUVE 1971: 26f.

41 For this technical expression *tamo 'ndham* (= BĀU IV 4.10; ĪśU IX) cf. SIAUVE 1971: 6f.

42 KathUBh p. 483,27-484,12; cf. *ibid.* line 16f.; ṚgBh p. 11, v. 86; also self-assertion of Madhva in MBhTN I 11:

The far reaching implications of this statement become fully visible only after confronting it with another teaching of Madhva on the relation between essential nature (*svarūpa*) of Viṣṇu and his attributes, as his eternal Body.[43] According to Madhva there is no difference at all between his *svarūpa* and his attributes (*naiva bhedo 'sti kaścana*) in the same way as there is no difference between a jewel and its shine (*ratnasya ca prakāśasya na bhedaḥ kaścid iṣyate*).[44] And he applies exactly this pattern not only to explain the identity between Viṣṇu and his *avatāra*s, but also the identity between these and their attributes. In both cases Madhva denies that there is *parasparabheda* or *bhedābheda* relation.[45] In a further step, Madhva brings this idea of identity into focus when he underlines in the commentary of AiU (II 3) that Viṣṇu never, even in his *avatāra*-forms, loses his divine consciousness: 'I alone am ever free and perfect'(*aham eva svatantraḥ paripūrṇa iti kṛṣṇarāghavādisarvāvatārarūpo 'pi sarvadānubhavaty eva*). In support of it he quotes an unidentified passage from SkaP:

> *nāyaṃ daśarathāj jāto na cāpi vasudevataḥ* /
> *kvāsyājñānaṃ kuto duḥkhaṃ prādurbhāveṣv api prabhoḥ* //
> *prādurbhūtaś cidānandaśarīro rāghavaḥ svayam* /
> *staṃbhād vā naradehād vā naivāsya prākṛtā tanuḥ* //
> *daityānāṃ mohanārthāya so 'jñānādyaṃ prakāśayet* /
> *pūrṇacitsukharūpo 'pi sadā sarvāvatāragaḥ* //
> ityādi skānde.

---

nirdoṣapūrṇaguṇavigraha ātmatantro
niścetanātmakaśarīraguṇaiś ca hīnaḥ /
ānandamātrakarapādamukhodarādiḥ
sarvatra ca svagatabhedavivarjitātmā //

cf. below n 48f.; MBhTN II 27; above n 38.

43 Cf. below n 49.

44 Cf. BĀUBh p. 269,20f., Anuv p. 77, 29-30; below n 220f.;228.

45 Cf. below n 234f.

„He is not born from Daśaratha nor from Vasudeva. How can he, the Lord, be an ignorant of something? How can he suffer even when he descends as *avatāra*? Even when he appears as Rāma, he has a body of intelligence and pure happiness. He has no material body either [coming] out of a pillar,[46] nor out of a human· body. In order to bewilder the demons he manifests ignorance etc. Although he always has a body of pure intelligence and happiness, he exists in all *avatāras*. This and [other teachings] have been delivered in the SkaP.“[47]

A further emphasis on the identity of Viṣṇu with his *avatāras* is laid through another statement that the body of Viṣṇu is not caused by *karma* or that it is not made out of Prakṛti

---

[46] This statement refers to Narasiṃha's coming out of a pillar as it is described, for instance, in BhāgP (VII 8, 18-19; cf. VarP 75,44a):

satyaṃ vidhātuṃ nijabhṛtyabhāṣitaṃ
vyāptiṃ ca bhūteṣv akhileṣu cātmanaḥ |
adṛśyatātyadbhutarūpam udvahan
staṃbhe sabhāyāṃ na mṛgaṃ na mānuṣam ||
sa sattvam evaṃ parito 'pi paśyan
staṃbhasya madhyād anu nirjihānam |
nāyaṃ mṛgo nāpi naro vicitram
aho kim etan nṛmṛgendrarūpam ||

[47] AiUBh p. 215,22-25; BhāgTN p. 142,12f.; cf. VTN p. 42, 14f.

. . .
strīpuṃmalābhiyogātmadeho viṣṇur na jāyate |
kiṃtu nirdoṣacaitanyasukhāṃ nityāṃ svakāṃ tanum |
prakāśayati saiveyaṃ janir viṣṇor na cāparā |
. . .
iti brahmāṇḍe.

In MBhTN (II 74-75) we find a similar passage, which Madhva adduces together with several unidentified *śloka*s from MBh having a special connection to Madhva's peculiar ideas (*ibid.* II 63-111):

vasudevasuto nāyaṃ nāyaṃ garbhe 'vasat prabhuḥ |
nāyaṃ daśarathāj jāto na cāpi jamadagnitaḥ ||
jāyate naiva kutrāpi mriyate kuta eva tu |
na vedhyo muhyate nāyaṃ baddhyate naiva kenacit ||
kuto duḥkhaṃ svatantrasya nityānandaikarūpiṇaḥ |

(*aprākṛtarūpatvāt*),[48] since his eternal body consists of pure Being, Intelligence and Happiness (*sajjñānānanda*).[49]

This small sample out of countless passages and instances on the subject scattered on Madhvas different literary works shows clearly that the *avatāras* are infinitely superior to the mortal men not only because they are identical with Viṣṇu in their essential nature and attributes, but also because their earthly body is essentially different from the mortals. Their body being immaterial is beyond space and time (*na deśakālasāmarthyaiḥ pārāvaryaṃ kathaṃcana*).[50] Human weaknesses, afflictions and

---

Anuv p. 137, 27-28:

sa cāprākṛtarūpatvād arūpaḥ svaguṇātmakaṃ /
rūpam asya śiraḥpāṇipādādyātmakam iṣyate //

cf. MBhTN I 11b: . . . *niścetanātmakaśarīragaṇaiś ca hīnaḥ*, *cf.* II 80:

prādurbhāvā hareḥ sarve naiva prakṛtidehinaḥ /
nirdoṣā guṇasaṃpūrṇā darśayanty anyathaiva tu //

cf. above n 42. This subject-matter is found also in the Pañcarātrasaṃhitās (SCHRADER1973: 55); cf. below n 86.

[49] In ĪśUBh (p. 511,14f.) Madhva quotes from VarP [not located]:

. . .
sajjñānānandaśirṣo 'sau sajjñānānandabāhukaḥ /
sajjñānānandadehaś ca sajjñānāndapādavān /

cf. below n 278). Elsewhere (BĀUBh p. 264,1-2) according to a quote of an unknown Paiṅgiśruti the body of liberated souls has also the same qualities:

. . .
cidānandaśirodehapāṇipādātmakāḥ sadā /
sarvadoṣavinirmuktā muktāḥ krīḍanti nityaśaḥ //

[50] BĀUBh p. 351,20-21; cf. below n 55. One should not interpret these statements in a docetical sense since Madhva strongly rejects the *māyāvāda*. For this reason, he would never accept a position which could bring him in the proximity of *māyāvādins*. On the contrary, the phenomenal world is for him absolutely real, not only because Viṣṇu is aware of it and protects it (*parameśvareṇa jñātatvād rakṣitatvac ca na dvaitaṃ bhrāntikalpitam*, VTN p. 34,15f.), but specially because he is omnipresent in the world as *antaryāmin* and as a creator, being effortless active for mere diversion (Anuv p. 25,24:

other infirmities the *avatāras* share with other beings are intended by Viṣṇu, in order to bewilder the demons. As evidence for this teaching he adduces an unidentified quotation from PadP:

> *svātmānaṃ paramaṃ viṣṇuṃ viditvāpi sa rāghavaḥ /*
> *daityānaṃ mohanārthāya darśayāmāsa mūḍhatām/*
> iti ca pādme.

„Although being aware of his identity with supreme Viṣṇu, Rāma displayed ignorance in order to bewilder the demons."[51]

---

tatra tatra sthito viṣṇus tattacchaktiprabodhakaḥ / dūrato 'py atiśaktaḥ sa līlayā kevalaṃ prabhuḥ; cf. below n 52). In MBhTN (II 79) Madhva compares this play (*līlā*) with real causal facts as a stage-play and magic:

> *ityādyasuramohāya darśayāmāsa nāṭyavat /*
> *avidyamānam eveśaḥ kuhakaṃ tad viduḥ surāḥ //*

[51] ChUBh p. 445, 8-9. In MBhTN II 77 Madhva attributes this view to MBh:

> *nātmānaṃ veda mugdho 'yaṃ duḥkhī sītā ca mārgate /*
> *baddhaḥ śakrajitetyādi līlaiṣāsuramohinī /*

I could not locate this as well as other *śloka*s (cf. above n 47). The motive expressed here, however, as regard to content has been handed down in PadP (VI 236,6):

> *daityānāṃ nāśanārthāya viṣṇunā buddharūpiṇā /*
> *bauddhaśāstram asat proktaṃ nagnanīlapaṭādikam //*

cf. MBhTN II 74-81 and above n 47; below n 95. Madhva quotes also from an unknown source (= Bhaviṣyatparvan, which should go back to Madhva himself, cf. above n 33-35 and below n 102f.) where the human infirmities of the *avatāras* are listed in detail (MBhTN I 37-47):

> *avatāreṣu yat kiñcid darśayen naravad dhariḥ /*
> *tac cāsurāṇāṃ mohāya doṣā viṣṇor na hi kvacit //*
> *ajñatvaṃ pāravaśyaṃ vā vedhabhedādikaṃ tathā /*
> *tathā prākṛtadehatvaṃ dehatyāgādikaṃ tathā //*
> *anīśatvaṃ ca duḥkhitvaṃ sāmyam anyaiś ca hīnatām /*
> *pradarśayati mohāya daityādīnāṃ hariḥ svayam //*
> *na tasya kaścid doṣo 'sti pūrnākhilaguṇo hy asau /*
> *sarvadehastharūpeṣu prādurbhāveṣu ceśvaraḥ // . . .*

The real motive why Viṣṇu takes different *avatāra*-forms is mere sport or diversion (*līlā*). It is likewise a result of Viṣṇu's sovereign power: *aiśvaryayogād bhagavān krīḍaty evam janārdanaḥ.*[52] According to another unknown source, namely Nārāyaṇa-śruti, Viṣṇu's pleasure in this sport is absolutely pure and does

---

tasmād etad viruddhaṃ yan mohāya tadudāhṛtam I
tasmād ye ye guṇā viṣṇor grāhyās te sarve eva tu II
ityādy uktaṃ bhagavatā bhaviṣyatparvaṇi sphuṭam I

Specially interesting is that Madhva in VTN (p. 42,10-43,2) puts forward the same ideas in a fictitious form of a dialogue between Nārada und Brahmā and attributes them to BrāṇP:

nityapūrṇo 'khilaguṇo vidoṣaḥ sarvadaiva yaḥ I
svatantraḥ sa paro viṣṇur janmamṛtyādivarjitaḥ II
śrīnārada uvāca –
nirdoṣaś cet kathaṃ viṣṇur mānuṣeṣūdpadyata I
cintāśramavraṇājñānaduḥkhayug dṛśyate katham II
eṣa me saṃśayo brahman hṛdi śalya ivārpitaḥ I
anuddhāryo 'parair martyaiḥ sūktiśaktyā tam uddhara I
brahmovāca –
strīpuṃmalābhiyogātmadeho viṣṇur na jāyate I
kiṃtu nirdoṣacaitanyasukhāṃ nityāṃ svakāṃ tanum II
prakāśayati saiveyaṃ janir viṣṇor na cāparā I
tathāpy asuramohāya pareṣāṃ ca kvacit kvacit II
duḥkhājñānaśramādīn sa darśayec chuddhasadguṇaḥ I
kva vraṇādi kva cājñānaṃ svatantrācintyasadguṇe II
daurlabhyāyaiva mokṣasya darśayet tāny ajo hariḥ I
mithyādarśanadoṣeṇa tena muktiṃ na yāti ca II
tamo yāti ca tenaiva tasmād doṣavivarjitam I
prādurbhāvagataṃ caiva jānīyād viṣṇum añjasā II
iti brahmāṇḍe.

[52] For support Madhva quotes from an unknown Sāmasaṃhitā (BhāgTN p. 25,4-6); cf. another fictitious citation from PadP (GīBh p. 37,4-5):

. . .
nityānando 'dvayo 'py evaṃ krīḍate moghadarśana I
iti pādme.

The question implied here is that of almight of Viṣṇu touching the outmost mystery of divine nature which remains hidden to human mind and resists all kind of human reasoning (VTN p. 43,7 8: . . . *dustarkyabalato hareḥ*); cf. below n 242.

not impair his nature as perfect happiness.[53] It means that Viṣṇu is free from all kinds of human deficiencies in every respect: *na tasya kaścid doṣo 'sti pūrṇākhilaguṇo hy asau.*[54] After accomplishing his earthly mission the *avatāra* disappears suddenly without leaving any trace or without dying (*adṛṣṭiṃ vinā nānyo layaḥ kṛṣṇādīnāṃ kvacit*), since his body is not made out of Prakṛti.[55]

It is of special interest for the subject matter of unknown sources that Madhva identifies in the very first place Vyāsa-*avatāra* with Viṣṇu, as explained before. It is also noteworthy, that Madhva does not offer any original ideas in this connection. He rather draws inspiration from the Purāṇas that Vyāsa and Nārāyaṇa/Viṣṇu are identical (*bhagavān vyāsaḥ sākṣān nārāyaṇaḥ prabhuḥ*)[56] and that he transmits to mankind all branches of

---

53 GīT 140,28f.:

> *bhuṅkte hariḥ śubhān bhogān indriyeṣu vyavasthitaḥ /*
> *pūrṇānando 'pi bhagavān krīḍayā bhuṅkta eva tu //*

54 Cf. MBhTN I 40 above n 51.

55 As reference serves again an anonymous citation (= *iti ca*) as proof for the infinite perfection of *avatāras* on the ground that they are identical with Viṣṇu (BĀUBh p. 351,19-27):

> *avatārā mahāviṣṇoḥ sarve pūrṇāḥ prakīrtitāḥ /*
> *pūrṇaṃ ca tat paraṃ rūpaṃ pūrṇāt pūrṇāḥ samudgatāḥ //*
> *parāvaratvaṃ teṣāṃ tu vyaktimātraviśeṣataḥ /*
> *na deśakālasāmarthyaiḥ pārāvaryaṃ kathañcana //*
> *pūrvarūpasya pūrṇasya pūrṇaṃ yad avatāragam /*
> *rūpaṃ tad ātmany ādāya pūrṇam evāvatiṣṭhate //*
> *laukikavyavahāro yo bhūbhārakṣapaṇādikaḥ /*
> *tad adṛṣṭiṃ vinā nānyo layaḥ kṛṣṇādināṃ kvacit //* . . .

According to MBh (XVI) a sudden death came upon Kṛṣṇa since he was killed by a hunter named Jarā through his arrow. This took place on 17th of February 3102 B. C. marking the begin of *kali* age; cf. ViṣP IV 24,113.

56 MBhTN II 7cd; Madhva refers here to VāyP (*ibid.* II 51):

> *vāyuprokte 'pi tat proktaṃ bhāratasya praśaṃsanam /*
> *kṛṣṇadvaipāyanaṃ vyāsaṃ viddhi nārāyaṇaṃ prabhum /*
> *ko hy anyaḥ puṇḍarīkākṣān mahābhāratakṛd bhavet /*

knowledge as the author of all canonical texts.[57] In MBhTN Madhva combines these both constituent principles and puts them in one *śloka*:

> *nārāyaṇo vyāsa iti vācyavaktṛsvarūpakaḥ* /
> *ekaḥ sa bhagavān uktaḥ sādhakeśo narottamaḥ* //

I could not identify this *śloka* in VāyP. It is actually a verse from PadP (I 1,43cd-44ab), with slight deviations. It occurs also in ViṣP (III 4,5) and in MBh (XII 334,9); cf. also Gī X 37c; SULLIVAN 1990: 69f. In the Purāṇas Vyāsa is, however, referred to mere as a part (*aṃśa*) of Viṣṇu not as a full *avatāra* (cf. BrāṇP I 2, 34,11; VāyP I 60, 11; BhāgP I 4ff.; II 11; MBh XII 337).

57 MBhTN X 80cd-84 :

> *sa tasmai* (Kāmadeva = Śiva) *jñānam akhilaṃ dadau dvaipāyanaḥ prabhuḥ* //
> *sanatkumārapramukhāṃś cakre yogapravartakān* /
> *bhṛgvādīn karmayogasya jñānaṃ datvāmalaṃ śubham* //
> *jaiminiṃ karmamīmāṃsākartāram akarot prabhuḥ* /
> *devamīmāṃsikādyantaṃ kṛtvā pailam athādiśat* //
> *śeṣaṃ ca madhyakaraṇe purāṇāny atha cākarot* /
> *śaivān pāśupatāc cakre saṃśayārthaṃ suradviṣām* //
> *vaiṣṇavān pañcarātrāc ca yathārthajñānasiddhaye* /
> *brāhmāṃś ca vedataś cakre purāṇagranthasaṅgrahān* //
> *evaṃ jñānaṃ punaḥ prāpur devāś ca ṛṣayas tathā* /
> *sanatkumārapramukhā yogino mānuṣās tathā* //
> *kṛṣṇadvaipāyanāt prāpya jñānaṃ te mumuduḥ surāḥ* /

MBhTN X 57-59:

> *dvaipāyanaḥ so 'tha jagāma meruṃ*
> *caturmukhādyair anugamyamānaḥ* /
> *uddhṛtya vedān akhilān surebhyo*
> *dadau munibhyaś ca yathādisṛṣṭau* //
> *sarvāṇi śāstrāṇi tathaiva kṛtvā*
> *vinirṇayaṃ brahmasūtram cakāra* /
> *tac chuśruvur brahmagirīśamukhyāḥ*
> *surā munīnāṃ pravaraś ca tasmāt* //
> *samastaśāstrārthanidarśanātmakaṃ*
> *cakre mahābhāratanāmadheyam* /
> *vedottamaṃ tac ca vidhātṛśaṅkara-*
> *pradhānakais tanmukhataḥ suraiḥ śrutam* //

(cf. also MBhTN XVIII 28; below n 60f.).

„The adorable [highest God] alone is Nārāyaṇa [and] Vyāsa [at the same time] with the nature of the object to be proclaimed (= Nārāyaṇa) and with the nature of the proclaimer (= Vyāsa) respectively. He, the best of men (= Viṣṇu), is called Lord of the devotees."[58]

With this word pun (*vācyavaktṛsvarūpaka*) Madhva can explain that Vyāsa, as author of all canonical texts, and Viṣṇu, as the main purport (*mahātātparya*) of these texts are closely related. It is of special interest, that Madhva makes this statement the starting point of one of his main doctrine of Sadāgamas. Their striking feature is that they have been proclaimed by Vyāsa (= Nārāyaṇa) and that their purport is Viṣṇu/ Nārāyaṇa. Madhva bases this statement on Gī (XV 15cd:) *vedaiś ca sarvair aham eva vedyo vedāntakṛd vedavid eva cāham* or on another reference from Harivaṃśa:

vede rāmāyaṇe caiva purāṇe bhārate tathā /
ādāv ante ca madhye ca viṣṇuḥ sarvatra gīyate /[59]

In the fact that Madhva identifies Vyāsa as the author of all venerable texts, he follows the teaching of the Purāṇas.

---

[58] MBhTN III 6; cf. *ibid.* 1cd: *svabhaktahārdoccatamonihantā vyāsāvatāro harir ātmabhāskaraḥ*; II 23cd: . . . *vyāsādirūpeṣu jñānakāryas tathā prabhuḥ*.

[59] MuUBh p. 490,17-18; 22-23. Madhva has attributed this *śloka* in (BSūBh p. 7,9-10) correctly to Harivaṃśa (III 132,95, purged! in the crit. ed. cf. below n 266). It has also been handed down, although anonymously, in the commentary of Śaṅkara (?) and Parāśarabhaṭṭa (BGD p. 192) to Viṣṇusahasranāmastotra [v. 104]:

vede rāmāyaṇe puṇye bhārate bharatarṣabha /
ādau madhye tathā cānte viṣṇuḥ sarvatra gīyate //

Cf. also BhāgTN (p. 395,5-6):

vedānāṃ prathamo vaktā harir eva yato vibhuḥ /
ato viṣṇvātmakā vedā ity āhur vedavādinaḥ //
iti śabdanirṇaye (unknown text!).

For a detailed discussion on Sadāgamas cf. VTN (p. 11,6-9), where three and half unidentified *ślokas* from the BrāṇP are quoted (cf. below n 249f.).

Likewise, in accordance with the Purāṇas, Madhva also gives an etymology of Vyāsa as 'arranger and compiler' of the Vedas: *vivyāsa vedān sa vibhuś caturdhā cakre tathā bhāgavataṃ purāṇam.*[60] Another thought pattern adduced by Madhva in this connection is that Viṣṇu in the *dvāpara* age, which is marked by a sudden decay of moral behaviour and of Veda knowledge, descends on request (*arthita/codita*) of Brahmā out of compassion (*kṛpālu*) to those in Saṃsāra (*saṃsāre kliśyamānānāṃ*) and to those who are not entitled to the Vedas as *śūdra*s and women (*vedānadhikāriṇāṃ strīśūdrādīnāṃ ca*) in the form of Vyāsa (*bhagavān vyāso avatatāra*) in order to impart the Veda knowledge in its purity in the form of the fifth Veda.[61] In a similar way, Madhva identifies Vyāsa with Bādarāyaṇa in agreement with an old tradition[62] and attributes to him some known texts like Mahābhārata[63] and Brahmasūtras (*proktaṃ brahmasūtraṃ tu*

---

60 MBhTN X 62cd; BhāgTN p. 112,1-3 (an anonymous source = *iti ca*); cf. also ViṣP III 2,58; III 3,5; III 4,1ff. (for details see WESSLER 1995: 97ff.); BhāgP XII 6,35ff.; MBh I 57,73cd: *vivyāsa vedān yasmāc ca tasmād vyāsa iti smṛtaḥ* ; *ibid.* I 99,14; XII 327,18; I 1,9; Aśvaghoṣa, Buddhacarita I 42; IV 16. About a possible dependence on Brahmā-Mythos see B.M. SULLIVAN, The Epic's two Grandfathers, Bhīṣma and Vyāsa, in: Essays on the Mahābhārata, ed. by A. SHARMA. Leiden 1991: 207f. and U.N. DHAL, Dvaipāyano 'smi vyāsānām, in Purāṇa 34/2 (1992) pp. 23-29.

61 Cf. GīBh 1, 4f.; BSūBh 1,4f.; Anuv p. 2, 19f. Although this topic is amply transmitted in the Indian literature (cf. BrāṇP I 2,34,1ff.; VāyP I 60,2; ViṣP III 3,4ff.; III 4,6f.; BhāgP XII 6,48f.; VājasaneyiS [WEBER Varanasi 1972: 1,5-8]; ParameśvaraS I 74ff.; ĪśvaraS I 40ff.; BGD 4,9f.), Madhva's citations in this respect cannot be traced, since they are either from the unknown texts as Nārāyaṇāṣṭākṣarakalpa (GīBh p. 2, 1-6; cf. below n 305) nor they are found in the known sources referred to by Madhva, as BrāṇP (GīT p.1,12-17), NārP (GīBh 3,2-3); SkaP (BSūBh 2,1f.).

62 Cf. H. NAKAMURA, A History of Early Vedānta Philosophy [Religions of Asia Series 1]. Delhi 1983: 404ff.; ĀP p.102,7f.; also U.N. DHAL, o.c. above n 60.

63 Cf. above n 56.

viṣṇunā vyāsarūpeṇa)[64] and also unknown sources as Brahmatarka, Bhaviṣyatparvan, Lakṣaṇaśāstra, Vyāsasmṛti, etc.[65] In his BĀUBh he quotes anew from an unknown source, namely Pratisaṅkhyāna, which records that Vyāsa is not only the author of Brahmasūtra but also of the Mīmāṃsāsūtra, Saṅkarṣaṇakāṇḍa and of four other commentaries. No further details are given about them.[66]

It is not something incidental that Madhva names here a series of unknown texts together with some well-known texts, whose authenticity is corroborated by the *śiṣṭas*. Definitely, Madhva pursues here a specific purpose. With the help of a traditional scheme he builds a frame which guarantees the genuineness of Madhva's unknown sources on the basis that they are proclaimed by Viṣṇu in the shape of Vyāsa (*vyasarūpeṇa*). That we are on the right path is shown by at least two unknown sources, namely Bhaviṣyatparvan and Brahmatarka. They actual-

---

64 MBhTN I 42ac. As a matter of fact, it is a quotation from the fictitious Bhaviṣyatparvan! (cf. above n 34f.). Viṣṇu also appears as author of the Brahmasūtras: *bhagavān brahmasūtram acīkḷpat* (*ibid.* I 43d); cf. also ṚgBh p.10,22f.; Vāda p. 47,14-15. He is also author of MBh: *viṣṇur bhāratam sa cakāra ha* (unidentified citation from NārP in GīBh p. 3,2); see MBhTN II 66:

> *ādyantayor ity avadat sa yasmād vyāsātmako viṣṇur udāraśaktiḥ |*
> *tasmāt samastā harisadguṇānāṃ nirṇitaye bhāratagā kathaiṣā ||*

65 Cf. Anuv p.7,16f.; MBhTN II 112ab; *ibid.* IX 133ab.

66 BĀUBh p. 323,20-23:

> *sūtraṃ tu brahmasūtrākhyaṃ mahāmīmāṃsikā tathā |*
> *tathā sāṅkarṣaṇaṃ sūtraṃ brahmatarkādayas tathā ||*
> *prakāśikā nirṇayaś ca tattvanirṇaya eva ca |*
> *vyākhyeti kathitāḥ sarvāḥ svayaṃ bhagavatā kṛtāḥ ||*
> *bṛhattarkādayaḥ sarvā anuvyākhyāḥ prakīrtitāḥ |*
> iti pratisaṅkhyāne.

cf. below n 150f. and self-statement Madhva's: MBhTN X 80cd.; 84; 57-59; above n 57.

ly go back to Madhva, as I have argued elsewhere.[67] Both these sources have according to Madhva an intimate connection with Vyāsa and Viṣṇu.[68]

It is noteworthy, that the criticism of Appayadīkṣita did not take into consideration this Vyāsa-context referred to by Madhva to defend the authenticity of his sources. In this regard Appayadīkṣita limits himself exclusively to the *avatāra*-claim of Madhva, that will be dealt with in the following exposition.

The *avatāra*-claim of Madhva starts from completely different presuppositions, since he could not vindicate before his contemporaries the pretension that he himself was a full *avatāra* of Viṣṇu and as such identical with him. On the contrary, he makes use of another traditional thought pattern handed down in Rāmāyaṇa and Mahābhārata[69] that Vāyu is the father of the heroes Hanumat and Bhīma. For this reason they are known in the tradition as Marutsuta.

The features of Vāyu (= Marut/Prāṇa) as recorded in different sources of Madhva and even in the single fictitious text like Brahmatarka[70] are so contradictory that it is not possible to form a coherent and unified picture of him. It is, however, out of question that Vāyu is not identical with Viṣṇu, since he is introduced as son of Viṣṇu.[71]

---

67 Cf. above n 35. and below n 138f.

68 Cf. MBhTN II 112ab; I 47cd; Anuv p. 7,16-18; below n 51; n 88f.

69 Rāmāyaṇa VII 35,20ff.; MBh I 114,9; cf. GLASENAPP 1992: 37.

70 Cf. SIAUVE 1971: 10n 4.

71 Cf. MuUBh p. 493,21f. (unidentified citation from BrāṇP!); ChUBh p. 409,21 (anonymous source). According to another anonymous source Vāyu is originated from Brahmā and Brahmā from Viṣṇu (BĀUBh p. 274, 12f.); In Brahmatarka Vāyu appears as inferior to Brahmā (BĀUBh p. 248,17-18). In the fictitious Ācāryasaṃhitā, however, (ChUBh p. 417,25) it is recorded that Vāyu is above all Gods (*devebhyo vāyur uttamaḥ*); cf. MBhTN III 24, 65; MuUBh p. 500,6f. (= anonymous source). In MBhTN (II 34; 142ab; III 10cd;

The elaboration of the afore-said thought pattern does not take place in an isolated and independent way but in an innermost relation to full *avatāras* of Viṣṇu, namely Rāma, Kṛṣṇa[72] and Vyāsa, each of them entrusted with different tasks in the age of *tretā*, *dvāpara* and *kali* (?)[73] respectively. Whereas the tasks of

I 15ab) on the contrary Vāyu is identical with Brahmā. In MuUBh (p. 497,20ff.) Vāyu is the principal abode of Viṣṇu:

> *pradhānaṃ dhāma viṣṇos tu prāṇa eva prakīrtitaḥ* I
> . . .
> iti ca.

For details see SIAUVE 1971: 10ff. and GLASENAPP 1992: 36f.; 142ff.

72 According to the teaching of Purāṇas the incarnation of Viṣṇu in the shape of Rāma takes place before his incarnation as Kṛṣṇa, cf. M. WINTERNITZ, Geschichte der indischen Litteratur. Leipzig 1920, Bd. III p. 630; MBhTN II 44-47 . . . *paścāttanatvāt kṛṣṇasya* ; cf. above n 55 and H. BRINKHAUS, Early Developmental Stages of the Viṣṇuprādurbhāva Lists, WZKS (Supplement – Proceedings of the VIIIth World Sanskrit Conference. Vienna 1990) 36 (1993 [1992]), p. 101-110.

73 The present arrangement implies a striking inconsequence. According to Tradition and other sources adduced by Madhva (cf. above n 61) Vyāsa is assigned to *dvāpara* age (cf. WESSLER 1995: 97ff.; 135). In the periodical scheme of Madhva he appears in the *kali* age! possibly based (?) on MBh (XII 337,42-44; cf. below). It is remarkable, that Madhva quotes in BhāgTN (p. 45,7f.) an unidentified passage from BrahP teaching that Vyāsa transposes the sequence of the periods in order to bewilder the demons (cf. also MBhTN IX 125):

> *vyāsādayo vartamānam atītānāgate tathā* I
> *vyatyasyāpi vadanty addhā mohanārthaṃ durātmanām* II
> *paurvāparyaṃ yato naiva sadaiva parivartanāt* I
> *ataś ca vyatyayād etad vadanti jñānacakṣuṣaḥ* II
> iti brāhme.

Elsewhere, (BhāgTN p. 19,3f.) it is reported that Vyāsa appears as *avatāra* before Rāma (*rāmāt pūrvam apy asti vyāsāvatāraḥ*). In KūrP (reference not located!) Vyāsa-*avatāra* takes place more than once from *dvāpara* age onwards (*tṛtīyaṃ yugam ārabhya vyāso bahuṣu jajñivān* I iti kaurme), cf. *ibid.* p. 112,1-3. In MBh (XII 337, 42-44) Vyāsa is assigned to the *kali* age! This could be related with the point of view recorded in the tradition, that Vyāsa is endowed with a supernatural gift, not only to peek into future, but also to live beyond *caturyuga* (see WESSLER 1995: 101).

Rāma and Kṛṣṇa are of physical nature (*kṛṣṇarāmādirūpeṣu balakāryo janārdanaḥ*), as far they are involved in fighting the demons and in protecting the earth or in removing the burden of the earth (*bhūbhāraharin*),[74] Vyāsa's duty, consisting in imparting knowledge, lays on the intellectual level (*vyāsādirūpeṣu jñānakāryas tathā prabhuḥ*).[75] Side by side with the first series of three full *avatāras*, Madhva puts a second chain of other three *aṃśāvatāras* originated through the incarnation of Vāyu, who is *prathamam aṅga* of Viṣṇu,[76] namely Hanumat, Bhīma and

---

[74] On the myth of *bhārāvataraṇa* in the doctrine of *avatāra*, see HACKER 1960: 50ff.

[75] MBhTN II 23; 15ab: *bhūbhārahāriṇo viṣṇoḥ pradhānāṅgaṃ hi mārutiḥ*; *ibid.* II 124ab: *martyāvatāras tv iha martyaśikṣaṇaṃ rakṣovadhāyaiva na kevalaṃ vibhoḥ*. As a matter of fact, the point of difference among these tasks is founded in Vāyu's nature itself, because it consists of knowledge and force (*ibid.* III 74a: *vāyur balasaṃvidātmā*). Madhva begins the third chapter of his MBhTN with an eulogy of these *avatāras*:

jayaty ajo 'khaṇḍaguṇorumaṇḍalaḥ sadodito jñānamarīcimālī /
svabhaktahārdoccatamonihantā vyāsāvatāro harir ātmabhāskaraḥ //
jayaty ajo 'kṣīṇasukhātmabimbaḥ svaiśvaryakāntipratataḥ sadoditaḥ /
svabhaktasantāpaduriṣṭahantā rāmāvatāro harir īśacandramāḥ //
jayaty asaṅkhyorubalāmbupūro guṇoccaratnākara ātmavaibhavaḥ /
sadā sadātmajñanadībhir āpyaḥ kṛṣṇāvatāro harir ekasāgaraḥ //

It is interesting that the distribution of the duties is made following the pattern of the caste-classification (MBhTN II 19f.; 22):

pravṛtto duṣṭanidhane jñānakārye tad eva ca /
anyatra brāhmaṇānāṃ tu pramāṇaṃ jñānam eva hi //
kṣatriyāṇāṃ balaṃ caiva sarveṣāṃ viṣṇukāryatā /

[76] MBhTN II 118:

tasyāṅgaṃ prathamaṃ vāyuḥ prādurbhāvatrayānvitaḥ /
prathamo hanumān nāma dvitīyo bhīma eva ca /
pūrṇaprajñas tṛtīyas tu bhagavatkāryasādhakaḥ //

ibid. III 8cd, 65ab: *sa devatānāṃ prathamo guṇādhiko babhūva nāmnā hanumān prabhañjanaḥ* (= Vāyu); *ibid.* II 135ab: *etaddaśātmako vāyus tasmād bhīmas tadātmakaḥ* (quoted from fictitious Vyāsavākya!). Apart from Vāyu, the Bhaviṣyatparvan mentions as second and third *aṅga* of Viṣṇu, Sarasvatī and Śeṣa together with their respective three *avatāras*, namely

Madhva. The fact that they arise from the *prathamam aṅga* of Viṣṇu implies that they are essentially connected (*antaraṅga*) with the members of the first series, as far as these are identical (*abheda*) with Viṣṇu. As a consequence, we have three primary *avatāras* in the first series and three subordinate or secondary in the second series, which are assigned, like the members of the first series, to *tretā*, *dvāpara* and *kali* age respectively.[77] It is noteworthy, that the *aṃśāvatāra*s of the second series are consigned to the same tasks, in the same succession as the primary *avatāras*. Accordingly, we could draw the following diagram[78]:

Rāma/Hanumat – [tretā] – *balakārya*
Kṛṣṇa/Bhīma – [dvāpara] – *balakārya*
Vyāsa/Madhva – [kali] – *jñānakārya*

However, this sketch raises one serious question as to the traditional account ascribing Vyāsa to the *dvāpara* age.[79] In Madhva's assignement Vyāsa belongs to the *kali* age. A clear contradiction is here at hand. A clean break with the tradition implies also the fact that in the presentation of Madhva, Hanumat

---

Draupadī, Kālī und Candrā and Nara, Lakṣmaṇa und Bala(rāma), cf. *ibid.* II 119-121.

77 MBhTN II 119:

tretādyeṣu yugeṣv eṣa saṃbhūtaḥ keśavājñayā /
ekaikaśas triṣu pṛthag . . . /

cf. AiUBh p. 243, 8 and below n 81.

78 MBhTN II 33:

tasmād balapravṛttasya rāmakṛṣṇātmano hareḥ /
antaraṅgaṃ hanūmāṃś ca bhīmas tatkāryasādhakau //

ibid. II 118: *pūrṇaprajñas tṛtīyas tu bhagavatkāryasādhakaḥ* /

MBhTN II 17cd: *anyāveśanimittaṃ ced balam anyātmakaṃ hi tat* /

(cf. n above 76; below n 128).

79 Cf. above n 73.

and Bhīma appear as *aṃśāvatāras*. Nowhere in the literary sources, however, they are introduced as *avatāras*, but as the sons of Vāyu (Marutsuta/sūnu). In fact, Madhva can appeal to the teaching of Pañcarātra for the distinction between primary and secondary *avatāras*. But he deviates from this source when he assigns Vyāsa to the primary *avatāras*.[80]

These discrepancies are altogether very significant. They show that Madhva himself has developed the above mentioned pattern by adapting the existing ideas in order to put forward the original teaching of his *avatāra*-claim. On further consideration, we could win from this fact another criterion to judge Madhva's unknown sources. All unknown sources proclaiming Vyāsa as a primary *avatāra* or Hanumat, Bhīma and Madhva himself as *avatāra* of Vāyu, should be regarded as literary productions of Madhva.

By introducing Vāyu and Vyāsa inbetween, Madhva has shown that he himself cannot be identified with Viṣṇu like the primary *avatāras*, nevertheless he is close enough to Viṣṇu, so that one can say that Madhva, exactly like Hanumat and Bhīma, is effecting the deeds of Viṣṇu: *pūrṇaprajñas tṛtīyas tu bhagavatkāryasādhakaḥ.*[81] This claim enables Madhva to justify that the unknown texts are not fabricated by him but inspired by Viṣṇu himself.

---

[80] Cf. SCHRADER 1973: 55; below n 86.

[81] MBhTN II 118cd. This very statement has also been made about Hanumat and Bhīma (*ibid.* II. 33), cf. above n 78. In the unknown text 'Sadbhāva' (AiUBh p. 243,8; cf. n 77) Viṣṇu is described as the guide or leader of the secondary *avatāras*: *eteṣāṃ paramo viṣṇur netā sarveśvareśvaraḥ*. Madhva attributes this teaching to fictitious sources, cf. BSūBh p. 106,6-9, BhagTN p. 296,7-8:

> *āviṣṭā hariṇā jīvā brahmā dakṣo manuḥ pṛthuḥ /*
> *śakrādyā ṛṣayaś caiva matsyavyāsādayo hariḥ /*
> iti brahmavaivarte.

The subordination of Madhva to Vyāsa, the teacher and author of all canonical texts in the *dvāpara* age, makes it also possible that Madhva himself can appear as the author of the texts in the *kali* age.

The difference between the primary and secondary *avatāras* is – as already mentioned before – that the first ones are absolutely identical with Viṣṇu,[82] whereas the subordinate *avatāras* have only a temporary consciousness of identity with Viṣṇu. Madhva expresses this distinction of rank in a very conspicious way, when he says that Viṣṇu appears in the shape of Vyāsa (*vyāsarūpin*), but he never says that Viṣṇu appears in the shape of Madhva (*madhvarūpin*)! The expressions used in this connection are that Madhva is the third earthly form of Vāyu (*tṛtīyā bhaumī tanur marutas*) or that he is an *antaraṅga* of Vyāsa[83] or that he has a divine appearance (*divyaṃ rūpam*). Besides, Madhva is called disciple (*śiṣya*)[84] and devotee of Viṣṇu (*nārāyaṇasyaiva padaṃ siṣeve*),[85] these particulars are not reported with regard to Vyāsa. Furthermore, the subordinate *avatāras* are subjected to human weaknesses and other infir-

---

[82] MBhTN II 27:

. . .
ityādyāḥ kevalo viṣṇuḥ naiṣāṃ bhedaḥ katañcana |
na viśeṣo guṇaiḥ sarvair balajñānādibhiḥ kvacit ||

Cf. above n 55; n 37ff.

[83] Cf. MBhTN III 8cd; *ibid.* II 33; above n 78.

[84] It is noteworthy, that Madhva has composed the commentary to the MBh on command of Viṣṇu alone (*viṣṇvājñayaiva*; MBhTN I 136a), but on command of Vyāsa (*vyāsājñayā*) he wrote commentaries to the BSū and to the Upaniṣads. (MBhTN XXXII 161; cf. below n 107). I was, however, unable to find a single remark, where Madhva is said to be a disciple of Vyāsa; cf. below n. 106.

[85] MBhTN IX 116f.; cf. below n 122.

mities.[86] But God can make exceptions, exempting some subordinate *avatāras* from human weaknesses. For Viṣṇu, due to his inconceivable (*acintya*) might, nothing is impossible.[87] Certainly, Madhva speaks here about his own person. Madhva makes a very strong statement in this regard in his commentary to BSū (III 2):

> *ityādiśrutimānena*[88] *jīvāṃśāḥ sarva eva ca* /
> *niyamenānusandhānavanto yady ekatā svataḥ* /
> *aṃśino 'śeṣasandhānam atyalpasyāpi vidyate* /
> *bhuvi jātena cāṃśena sukhaduḥkhādi tadgatam* /
> *anubhūyate viśeṣas tu kaścid īśakṛto bhavet* /
> *īśasyācintyaśaktitvān nāśakyaṃ kvāpi vidyate* / [89]

In this valuable assessment Madhva vindicates his claim of being a partial incarnation (*aṃśāvatāra*) of Viṣṇu and in this

---

[86] The Pañcarātrasaṃhitās differentiate between full and subordinate *avatāras*, (cf. SCHRADER 1973: 55): „There the primary *avatāras* only are declared to be like a flame springing from a flame, that is to say Viṣṇu himself with a transcendent (*aprākṛta*) body, while a secondary *avatāra* is a soul in bondage with natural body which, however, is possessed (*āviṣṭa*) or pervaded, for some particular mission or function, by the power (*śakti*) of Viṣṇu." In opposition to Madhva, Vyāsa belongs in the above reference to the subordinate *avatāras*. Madhva differentiates also between *avatāras*, which are *viśeṣāveśino hareḥ* and those which are *kiṃcidāveśino hareḥ* (MBhTN II 32); cf. below n 123f.; n 133.

[87] Cf. above n 52.

[88] KathU II 1,11; BĀU II 5,19.

[89] Anuv p.137,13f.; Transl. SIAUVE (1971:27: „Et d'autres textes de Śruti font autorité pour dire que toutes les incarnations partielles possèdent nécessairement la conscience de l'unité, chaque fois que cette unité existe en soi. Il est admis qu'un être qui s'incarne partiellement, si limité soit-il, possède la conscience de toutes ses incarnations partielles; et l'incarnation partielle née sur cette terre éprouve les plaisirs, douleurs et autres expériences appartenant à l'être dont elle est partie; mais le Seigneur peut parfois produire une exception; il n'existe rien qui soit hors du pouvoir du Seigneur, du fait de sa puissance inconcevable." Cf. above n 52.

quality an authentic bearer of the revelation of Viṣṇu, an attribute ascribed to Vyāsa in the Hindu tradition.[90]

This line of argument is pursued further, when Madhva offers a literary reference to prove his claim. It is very striking, that Madhva quotes from the verifiable Purāṇa sources to establish the identity of Vyāsa with Viṣṇu,[91] but to substantiate his own claim of being a partial incarnation he can put forward only unknown sources, anonymous and unidentifiable references. For instance, a reference based on a prophecy in Baḷitthāsūkta (Ṛgveda I 141,1-3). For illustration I give below a fictitious citation in three parts, which again and again appears with slight variations at the end of Madhva's works. It is beyond doubt, that this quotation is not a later interpolation by the disciples of Madhva, because they occur not only at the end of Madhva's works,[92] where an interpolation could have been easily pos-

---

[90] Cf. SIAUVE (1971:17f.), who has left behind the best studies so far on Madhva had recognized the importance of this statement when she remarked: „après avoir dit que tous les *avatāra* du Seigneur ont nécessairement conscience permanente de leur identité avec lui, Madhva ajoute qu'il n'en est pas même pour les *avatāra* des *deva*. L'incarnation partielle, née en ce monde, ne possède pas toujours toutes le expériences du dieu qu'elle incarne. Ceci se fait par le pouvoir inconcevable de Dieu, ajoute Madhva. Rien n'empêche de concevoir que Madhva ne parle ici de lui-même, et ne réponde à une question intérieure: comment se fait-il que les limitations de la nature humaine puissent obscurcir la lumière spirituelle, même chez celui qui a la certitude de'une mission et d'une destinée divine?." Unfortunately, she failed to see here an intimate relation with the unknown sources of Madhva, because she was convinced, as the followers of Madhva, that these sources did really exist; (cf. above n 26).

[91] Cf. above n 56; 61.

[92] The part A (cf. GīBh; GīT; VTN; TSāS; KhN; BSūBh; Anuv; NyāV) does not appear as a quotation. The contention included therein is that Madhva has a divine appearance/form (*divyaṃ rūpam*), or that he is the third incarnation of Vāyu in harmony with the prophecy in Ṛgveda (I 141,1-5) should be, in fact, a self-statement of Madhva (cf. above n 34f.). The parts B und C are anonymous citations, which carry on the topic of A. Whereas the B-citation has no *iti* at end (but there is v. l. with *iti ca* indicated by the editor! and also in BĀUBh), the C-quotation ends everywhere with *iti ca*. The fact that Madhva in BĀUBh ends the B-quotation with *iti ca*, seems to

sible,[93] but in several places within one and single work of Madhva.[94]

Besides, the idea of divine incarnation is firmly established in the system of Madhva and fits seamless in the doctrine of *avatāras* propounded by Madhva. The following text passage is taken from AiUBh. The Veda quotations have been underlined for easier identification:

A)
yasya trīṇy uditāni
vedavacane rūpāṇi divyāny alaṃ
baṭ taddarśatam itham
eva nihitaṃ devasya bhargo mahat I
vāyo rāmavaconayaṃ
prathamakaṃ pṛkṣo dvitīyaṃ vapur
madhvo yat tu tṛtīyakaṃ
kṛtam idaṃ bhāṣyaṃ hi tena prabhau II

B)
hanaśabdo jñānavācī hanumān matiśabditaḥ I
rāmasya svṛtarūpasya vācas tenānayanta hi II
bhṛtamo bhīma ity ukto vāco mā mātaraḥ smṛtāḥ I
ṛgādyā itihāsaṃ ca purāṇaṃ pañcarātrakam II

---

imply that he wants to connect it with the quotation shortly before (*ibid.* p. 370,21-23) attributed to 'Sadbhāva'. This is corroborated by Madhva in ChUBh (p. 469,15). For this very reason, we should admit that Madhva wants to attribute the C-quotation with *iti ca* to 'Sadbhāva'. The parts A, B, C are transmitted in AiUBh, BĀUBh, TaiUBh; A, B in ChUBh.

93 The fact that these citations are included in the original Palm-MS in Tulu-characters written down by the immediate disciple of Madhva, Hṛṣīkeśatīrtha, and which according to the editor is complete and unimpaired (*samagram avikalaṃ ca*), speaks in favour of their authenticity. This original MS is preserved in the Palimār-Maṭha (SHARMA: 277f.). The authenticity of them is confirmed also by Sāyana Mādhava (SDS p. 265,1f.) when he remarks: *etad evābhipretya tatra tatra granthasamāptāv idaṃ padyaṃ likhyate.*

94 Cf. MBhTN II 144-147; 118-119; III 8; XXXII 120-125ab; 157-165. SIAUVE (1968: 5) also rejects the possibility of an interpolation.

proktāḥ saptaśivās tatra śayo bhīmas tataḥ smṛtaḥ /
madhva ity ānanda uddiṣṭo veti tīrtham udāhṛtam //
madhva ānandatīrthaḥ syāt tṛtīyā mārutī tanuḥ /
iti sūktagataṃ rūpatrayam etan mahātmanaḥ //
yo veda vedavit sa syāt tattvavit tatprasādataḥ /
[iti ca]

C)

sādhako rāmavākyānāṃ tatsamīpagataḥ sadā /
hanumān prathamo jñeyo bhīmas tu bahubhuk pitoḥ //
pṛthanākṣayakārī ca dvitīyas tu tṛtīyakaḥ /
pūrṇaprajñas tathānandatīrthanāmā prakīrtitaḥ //
daśeti sarvam uddiṣṭaṃ sarvaṃ pūrṇam ihocyate /
prajñā pramatir uddiṣṭā pūrnaprajñas tataḥ smṛtaḥ //
ā samantāt patitve tu gūḍhaṃ kaliyuge harim /
asatyam apratiṣṭhaṃ ca jagad etad anīśvaram [95] *//*
vadadbhir gūhitaṃ santaṃ tṛtīyo 'sur mathāyati /
yena viṣṇor hi varṇākhyān guṇān ajñāsiṣuḥ parān //
īśānāsaḥ sūrayaś ca nigūḍhān nirguṇoktibhiḥ /
tretāyāṃ dvāpare caiva kalau caite kramāt trayaḥ //
eteṣām paramo viṣṇur netā sarveśvareśvaraḥ /
svayaṃbhu brahmasaṃjño 'sau paro 'smai brahmaṇe namaḥ //
iti ca.

---

[95] Cf. Gī XVI 8:

asatyam aprathiṣṭhaṃ te jagad āhur anīśvaram /
aparasparasaṃbhūtaṃ kim anyat kāmahaitukam //

cf. VTN p. 29,7f.; MBhTN XXXII 160; ChUBh p. 437,21f. Madhva seems to lean here on PadP (VI 236,6ff.) where Viṣṇu appears in the shape of Buddha in order to announce the doctrine of true and disguised Buddhists for the destruction of demons:

daityānāṃ nāśanārthāya viṣṇunā buddharūpiṇā /
bauddhaśāstram asat proktaṃ nagnanīlapaṭādikam // 6 //
māyāvādam asac chāstraṃ pracchannaṃ bauddha ucyate /
mayaiva kathitaṃ devi kalau brāhmaṇarūpiṇā // 7 //

cf. above n 51.

A literal translation of this passage by a person staying outside of the tradition of Madhva school cannot do justice to the context implied here. For, a 'outsider' to that tradition has not a perceptive faculty for the reference from Ṛgveda[96] as a 'proph-

---

[96] Ṛgveda I 141,1-5:

Baḷ itthā tad vapuṣe dhāyi darśatam
devasya bhargaḥ sahaso yato jani /
yad īm upa hvarate sādhate matir
ṛtasya dhenā anayanta sasrutaḥ // 1 //
pṛkṣo vapuḥ pitumān nitya āśaye
dvitīyam ā saptaśivāsu mātṛiṣu /
tṛtīyam asya vṛṣabhasya dohase
daśapramatim janayanta yoṣaṇaḥ // 2 //
nir yad īm budhnān mahiṣasya varpasa
īśānāsaḥ śavasā kranta sūrayaḥ /
yad īm anu pradivo madhva ādhave
guhā santam mātariśvā mathāyati // 3 //
prayat pituḥ paramān nīyate paryā
pṛkṣudho vīrudho damsu rohati /
ubhāyad asya januṣam yad invata
ād id yaviṣṭho abhavad ghṛiṇā śuciḥ // 4 //
ād in mātrīr āviśad yāsv āśucir
ahiṅsyamāna urviyā vi vāvṛdhe /
anu yat pūrvā aruhat sanājuvo
ni navyasīṣv avarāsu dhāvate // 5 //

Transl. GRIFFITH 1987: I 207: „1.Yea, verily, the fair effulgence of the God for glory was established, since he sprang from strength. When he inclines thereto successful is the hymn: the songs of sacrifice have brought him as they flow. 2.Wonderful, rich in nourishment, he dwells in food; next, in the seven auspicious Mothers in his home. Thirdly, that they might drain the treasures of the Bull, the maidens brought forth him for whom the ten provide. 3. What time from out the deep, from the Steer's wondrous form, the Chiefs who had the power produced him with their strength; When Mātariśvan rubbed forth him who lay concealed, for mixture of the sweet drink, in the days of old. 4. When from the Highest Father he is brought to us, amid the plants he rises hungry, wondrously. As both together join to expedite his birth, most youthful he is born resplendent in his light. 5. Then also entered he the Mothers, and in them pure and uninjured he increased in magnitude. As to the first he rose, the vigorous from of old, so now he runs among the younger lowest ones."

ecy'. The only words in the reference having some relation to the historical Madhva and divine person are *madhva*, *mātariśvā* (=*vāyu*) and they do not give any hint at the context of a prophecy. As a matter of fact, the passage speaks only of the origin of fire out of pieces of wood! In order to read and interpret this passage in the context of Madhva school I have given below a rendering through a madhvite scholar, which is, however, by no means a literal translation but rather an interpretation. (I have put the sanskrit words therein in italics and with diacritical marks).[97]

A)„In the verses of the Veda, there are described three Divine forms [incarnations] of Vāyu [see Rigveda I 141,1-5]. The third of those forms has composed this Commentary, explaining it as describing Hari. The archetypal form of Vāyu, of which these are the various *avatāras,* consists of power and wisdom. By the command of God, these qualities appear fully in the *avatāra*-forms of Vāyu, the mighty, the supporter and mover of the universe. His first form of *avatāra* is as Hanumat, who carried the message of Rāma [to Sītā], or who ever obeys the words of Rāma. The second form is that of the warrior Bhīma, who destroyed the army of the Kurus. His third is that of Anandatīrtha, called also Madhva, who has composed this Commentary."

B)„The word *han* denotes wisdom, therefore, *hanumat* means he who possesses wisdom, the word *matiḥ* also means he who possesses wisdom. Therefore, when the Rigveda uses the words *yad īm upa hvarate sādhate matiḥ,* it refers to Hanumat; similarly, the words *ṛitasya dhenā ananyanta sa* (*su*)*śrutaḥ*, mean he who carries (*anayanta*) the words (*dhenā*) of Rāma, the ever truthful (*suritasya*) to Śītā.

The words *saptaśivavāsu mātṛiṣu* refer to Bhīma. The word Bhīma means, literally, he who supports all authorities, true

[97] CHANDRAVASU 1916: 708ff. and 1910: 591f.

sciences (*bhi bhṛta*: supported, *ma pramāṇāni,* authorities). The word *mataraḥ* means measurer of authoritative words. The word *saptaśivā* refers to the seven authoritative Scriptures, namely the four Vedas, Purāṇa, Itihāsa, and Pañcarātra. He who rests or constantly studies these seven is Bhīma.

The word Madhva in the third verse, is composed of two words, *madhu* meaning sweet or *ānanda*, and *va*, meaning *tīrtha* or the scripture or the teachings. He whose teachings are ever sweet, is called Madhva or Ānandatīrthā. Thus Madhva and Ānandatīrtha literally mean the same thing. This is the third body of Vāyu.

He who knows these three forms of the mighty spirit (Vāyu) as described in this Vedic hymn, understands through His grace all the Vedas and all the truths. [Thus it is in the book called Sadbhāva]."

C) „Of the powerful God Vāyu, the root-form consists of strenght and wisdom, which supports the world and moves through it. He thus for the sake of three-fold forms, was born under the command of the Lord. His first form is called wisdom (Hanumat), who stands near the throne of the Lord and fulfills all his commands, and who carries the life-giving words of the True (Śītā or to mankind). His incarnation, as the destroyer of the hosts; is his second form, rich with food, this eternal one sleeps in the home of the seven measures. The third form of this powerful Vāyu is assumed, in order to give the milk of wisdom to mankind. This is the ten measured form, called the Pūrṇaprajña, which the virgins immaculately conceive.

When Hari, on account of the advent of the *Kaliyuga* becomes hidden from the sight of man, and when men began to assert that the world is false – without any foundation in reality – and that there is no such being as Īśvara, but that Jīva is Brahma, then the third manifestation of Vāyu took place, viz., Madhva came on earth and he established the glory and greatness of

Viṣṇu. He explains that the words 'Brahman being *nirguṇa*' do not mean that God has no qualities but that He has qualities which are *nir* of hidden, that is, not easily known to all. Thus Vāyu has three Avatāras, first, in the Tretā Yuga, the second, in the *dvāpara* and the third, in the *Kali* age. The Lord of all lords – The supreme Viṣṇu – is the guide in all these *avatāras* and their leader; they merely carry out His commands. Viṣṇu is called Svayaṃbhu as well as Brahman, Salutations to that Supreme Brahman."

This translation is not very helpful for our investigation since it has its *sitz im leben* in the religious faith of the Madhva school and not in the philology. Nevertheless, the quoted passage gives us some valuable details in regard to philological, religious and historical perspectives. It supplies at the same time an excellent illustration which is highly suited to deliver a satisfactory answer to unknown sources of Madhva. As we have seen, we have here three different passages with some features in common and others distinct. The common feature is the prophecy in the Vedas in reference to the three *aṃśāvatāras* as divine appearances (*divyāni rūpāṇi*). The divergence is, first of all, in the outer literary form. Whereas the part A is not rendered in a 'quoted form' and for this reason it is clearly a self-statement of Madhva, the other both parts B and C are quotations in disguise, attributed to an unknown source 'Sadbhāva'.[98] They also have a diverging inner structure in regard to the contents. The part A mentions the tasks of the three *avatāras* exactly in the same manner as in the aforesaid diagram of Madhva, namely the tasks of Hanumat und Bhīma are based on the physical force (*bala*) and the task of Madhva is based on knowledge (*jñāna*).[99] As such, Madhva is the author of his independent works and also of

---

[98] Cf. above n 81.

[99] Cf. above n 75f.

commentaries.[100] Curiously, the parts B and C attribute to Hanumat and Bhīma also tasks based on knowledge. In the part B Bhīma is introduced as the bearer of the authentic texts, as Vedas, Itihāsas, Purāṇas and Pañcarātra (= fifth Veda). In the scheme of Madhva this task was reserved only to Vyāsa and Madhva. In opposition to it, Madhva appears in the part C as the Teacher in the *kali* age with a special mission to fight against the doctrine of Advaita. Since all the doctrines mentioned here, as that of *aṃśāvatāra*, etc. have been passionately put forward by Madhva in his different works,[101] we can surmise that Madhva himself is in disguise behind these quotations. This conjecture clears the way for certainty, because the quotations above refer to a *vaticinium ex eventu*, a prophecy after its fulfillment![102] This would imply that the quotations from 'Sadbhāva' are in fact self-statements of Madhva.

As far as I know, this is the only place, where this unknown source is quoted. It seems that Madhva wanted to make it appear as a source belonging to Pañcarātra. Another unknown source heralding the arrival of Madhva as *aṃśāvatāra* is 'Bhaviṣyatparvan', but with the difference that it does not appeal to the prophecy in the Ṛgveda. There are reasons for the assumption that Madhva wanted to introduce it as a Purāṇa text.[103] It is remarkable that these titles are not chosen at random.

---

[100] Cf. AiUBh p. 242,25f. and VTN l. c.: *madhvo yat tu tṛtīyakaṃ kṛtam idaṃ bhāṣyaṃ hi tena prabhau*; *madhvo tu tṛtīyam etad amunā granthaḥ kṛtaḥ keśave* and above n 84.

[101] Cf. above n 76f.; below n 111f.; 118f.; 213f.

[102] This is valid also for MBhTN II 118; 141-147; III 8cd; XXXII 120-125ab; 157-165; cf. above n 35.

[103] Cf. MBhTN XXXII 164ab; II 112-119.; below n 105. Bhaviṣyatparvan is not identical with Bhaviṣyatpurāṇa, since there are separate quotations from these sources, as in BSūBh (respectively 6 against 11 entries), BhāgTN (respectively 13 against 4 entries); BĀUBh (respectively 3 against 1 entry), as well as (only Bhaviṣyatparvan) once in AiUBh; KathUBh and 3 entries in

There is a definite purpose behind them, because they describe the context of prophecy (Bhaviṣyatparvan = a text about future events awaiting their fulfillment!) and the context of coming into being of the *avatāras* (= Sadbhāva). This is a clear indication that many other titles of the texts quoted by Madhva, which in fact never existed and which are in agreement with the particular context of his doctrine, have been coined by Madhva himself. The fact that these unknown sources of Madhva differ in their contents, as explained above, although they refer to the same doctrine, gives the impression that not a single author but many authors were at work.[104]

GīT. Bhaviṣyatparvan has also nothing to do with the last chapter of Harivaṃśa, bearing the title of Bhaviṣyaparvan.

104 Cf. above n 21; 70f.

MADHVA AS A VIṢṆU EMPOWERED AUTHOR OF ALL CANONICAL TEXTS

The findings of our analysis so far are supplemented by a very remarkable statement of Madhva at the end of his MBhTN, where Madhva anew appeals to the doctrine of *avatāra* as found in the texts of Pañcarātra and Purāṇas. With this remark he possibly alludes to his exposition, as put forward above, in harmony with 'Sadbhāva' (= Pañcarātra) and 'Bhaviṣyatparvan' (= Purāṇa).[105] This statement is of particular interest for the present inquiry because it shows in a very impressive manner that there is an innermost connection between Vyāsa, a full *avatāra*, the messenger and the author of all canonical texts in the *dvāpara* age, and Madhva, an *aṃśāvatāra*, and in this quality the messenger of the true doctrine in the *kali* age. It runs as follows:

ānandatīrthākhyamuniḥ supūrṇa-
prajñābhidho grantham imaṃ cakāra /
nārāyaṇenābhihito badaryāṃ
tasyaiva śiṣyo[106] *jagadekabhartuḥ* //
yas tatprasādād akhilāṃś ca vedān
sapañcarātrān sarahasyasaṅgrahān /
vedetihāsāṃś ca purāṇayuktān

---

[105] In (MBhT I 106-126) Madhva again mentions these texts as support while propounding his typical teaching on other topics: *ity etat pañcarātroktaṃ purāṇeṣv anumoditam.*

[106] Madhva calls Viṣṇu his Guru in several places (cf. Maṅgala verse and closing verse) in BSūBh and (Maṅgala verse) in GīBh, BhāgT, Anuv and MBhTN II 1. Prof. SHERIDAN's opinion (cf. above n 8) that Madhva is a disciple of Vyāsa, is not endorsed by Madhva himself, unless we use as evidence his statement in MBhTN III 6, identifying Vyāsa with Nārāyaṇa: *ekaḥ sa bhagavān uktaḥ.* There are also other references, where Vyāsa is mentioned alone, however, without the title of Guru of Madhva. The limitation: *tasyaiva śiṣyaḥ* is also noteworthy!

yathāvad anyā api sarvavidyāḥ ||
samastaśāstrārthavinirṇayo 'yaṃ
viśeṣatobhāratavartmacārī |
granthaḥ kṛto 'yaṃ jagatāṃ janitraṃ
hariṃ guruṃ prīṇayatāmunaiva ||
vinirṇayo nāsty amunā vinā yad
viprasthitānām iva sarvavācām |
tad brahmasūtrāṇi cakāra kṛṣṇo
vyākhyātha teṣām anyathā kṛtānyaiḥ ||
nigūhitaṃ yat puruṣottamatvaṃ
sūtroktam apy atra mahāsurendraiḥ |
jīveśvaraikyaṃ pravadbhir ugrair vyā-
khyāya sūtrāṇi cakāra cāviḥ ||
vyāsājñayā bhāṣyavaraṃ vidhāya
pṛthak pṛthak copaniṣatsu bhāṣyam |
kṛtvākhilān yaṃ puruṣottamaṃ ca
hariṃ vadantīti samarthayitvā ||
tanus tṛtīyā pavanasya seyaṃ
sadbhāratārthapratidīpanāya |
granthaṃ cakāremam udīrṇavidyā
yasmin ramante haripādabhaktāḥ ||
tṛtīyam asya vṛṣabhasya dohase
daśapramatiṃ janayanta yoṣaṇaḥ |
nir yad īm budhnān mahiṣasya varpasa
īśānāsaḥ śavasā kranta sūrayaḥ
yad īm anu pradivo madhva ādhave
guhā santam mātariśvā mathāyati
ityādivākyoktam[107] *idaṃ samastaṃ*
tathāpurāṇeṣu capañcarātre |
atroditā yāś ca kathāḥ samastā
vedetihāsādivinirṇayoktāḥ ||
tasmād ayaṃ granthavaro 'khiloru-
dharmādimokṣāntapumarthahetuḥ |

---

[107] MBhTN XXXII,157-165. This quotation from the Ṛgveda is referred to again by Madhva (MBhTN XXXII 120-125ab), when he indicates his birth year; cf. above n 9; 35.

kim voditair asya guṇais tato 'nyair
nārāyaṇaḥ prītim upaity ato 'lam ||

„The sage called Ānandatīrtha, [also] with the name Supūrṇaprajña[108] – who has been named [so or taught] by Nārāyaṇa himself in Badarī[109] [and therefore Viṣṇu] alone is his teacher, the sole Lord of the world – composed the present work in verse. He composed also (*ca*) by the grace of Viṣṇu all the Vedas together with the Pañcarātrasaṃhitās, summarizing the secret doctrines [of the Vedas], as well as the [fifth] Veda with Itihāsas and Purāṇas and also all other Vidyās in a very exact way.[110]

This book (= MBhTN) which comprises the definitive meaning of all canonical texts, which follows in a special way the path of Bhārata, was composed by none other than Ānandatīrtha who gratifies the Guru Hari, Creator of the world. Without him there is no final exposition [of the true doctrine].

Kṛṣṇa [dvaipāyaṇa] composed the Brahmasūtras based on the [true] statements in their entirety, which correspond exactly to those [put forward] by the sages. Other [= Advaita-]authors distorted [their meaning] as they commented savagely upon them, because the lord of the demons concealed the absolute sov-

---

108 Madhva appears everywhere as Pūrṇaprajña and the addition of *su* should be *metri causa.*

109 The Badarī-Āśrama is mentioned in the Epos as the place where the spiritual instruction takes place (cf. MBh XII 321,10; 14; XII 330,44; XII 331,15-16; 22).

110 According to this statement Madhva appears as the author of the Vedas in contradiction to a fictitious citation ascribed to BrāṇP (VTN p. 14,7f.; cf. below n 147, 252) that Viṣṇu alone proclaims the Vedas:

nitya vedāḥ samastāś ca śāsvatā viṣṇubuddhigāḥ |
sarge sarge 'munaivaita udgīryante tathaiva ca ||

cf. n 250f and MBhTN I 84:

vedāṃś ca pañcarātrāṇl setihāsapurāṇakān |
jñātvā viṣṇuparān eva mucyante nānyathā kvacit ||

cf. below n 335.

ereignty of God Viṣṇu, although it was taught in the Brahmasūtras, by proclaiming the identity of the individual soul with Īśvara. And on command of Vyāsa, [Ānandatīrtha], the third *avatāra*-form of Vāyu, explained the Brahmasūtras, and after composing [another] excellent commentary [upon them] and different other commentaries upon Upaniṣads, establishing that all [these texts] teach that Hari is the supreme Lord, he wrote this present work in order to illuminate the true meaning of Mahābhārata. The devotees of Hari with perfect knowledge rejoice at this. All this has been taught in the sentence of [Baḷitthāsūkta I 141,2-3] as well as in the Purāṇas and Pañcarātrasaṃhitās[111], namely: '[2]Wonderful, rich in nourishment, he dwells in food; next, in the seven auspicious Mothers in his home. Thirdly, that they might drain the treasures of the Bull, the maidens brought forth him for whom the ten provide. [3] What time from out the deep, from the Steer's wondrous form, the Chiefs who had the power produced him with their strength; When Mātariśvan rubbed forth him who lay concealed, for mixture of the sweet drink, in the days of old.'

All stories which have been told here has been explained as definitive doctrine of Vedas, Itihāsa etc. Therefore, this excellent work fulfils perfectly the four objects of human pursuit from Dharma to Mokṣa. Will these and other qualities proclaimed here find favour with Nārāyaṇa. Therefore, enough of consideration.“

A careful examination of this passage gives us plenty information which is very decisive for a judgement on the unknown sources. As we can see it is not a quotation but a self-statement of Madhva. Its contents are identical with the citations in disguise ascribed to 'Sadbhāva' and 'Bhaviṣyatparvan', which we analysed above. Of particular importance is not only the

[111] Cf. below n 112; Transl. GRIFFITH, cf. above n 96. For the interpretation of this passage in harmony with the faith of Madhva school cf. CHANDRA-VASU 1916 : 711; above n 97f.

mention of the prophecy in the Ṛgveda but also the refutation of Advaita school. Very significant is also the information that Madhva himself by the grace of Viṣṇu (*tatprasādāt*)[112] is the author of all canonical texts, beginning with the Vedas and ending with the fifth Veda and all Vidyās, in the same manner as he is the composer of the commentaries on Brahmasūtras, Upaniṣads and MBh. Equally expressive is also the statement that these commentaries are in perfect harmony with the meaning of canonical texts (*samastaśāstrārthavinirṇaya*). And Madhva emphasizes that there are no grounds for suspicion of a forgery, because the texts are proclaimed flawless according to their contents (*yathāvat*) and that he is the only one who is entitled to teach the true doctrine in the *kali* age (*vinirṇayo nāsty amunā vinā*). It is specially significant that Madhva puts side by side the canonical texts and the works composed by him with the clear intention to underline the identity of their authors in agreement with Mīmāṃsāsūtra I 3.2: *kartṛsāmānyāt pramāṇam anumānam syāt.* The identity of the authors implies also the identity of the contents. And the main purport of all canonical texts and Madhva's own works is Viṣṇu himself (*akhilān yaṃ puruṣottamaṃ ca hariṃ vadantīti samarthayitvā*).[113]

Behind these considerations we can see the play upon words: *vācyavaktṛsvarūpaka*, mentioned before, which renders the relation of identity between Nārāyaṇa as *vācya* and Vyāsa as *vaktṛ*.[114] For this reason, it is not incidental that Madhva speaks of himself, in the very context of this play upon words, as the third *avatāra*-Form of Vāyu, who proclaims the grandeur of Viṣṇu, when he declares:

sarvasya nirṇayasuvākyasamuddhṛtī tu
svadhyāyayor haripada smaraṇena kṛtvā /

---

[112] Cf. above n 94 (**B**): *yo veda vedavit sa syāt tattvavit tatprasadataḥ*.

[113] Cf. above n 59f.

[114] Cf. n 58f.

ānandatīrthavaranāmavatī tṛtīyā
bhaumī tanur maruta āha kathāḥ parasya ||[115]

„The third earthly form (= incarnation) of Vāyu, bearing the most excellent name Ānandatīrtha, narrates [now] the stories [of the grandeur] of the Supreme, after having exposed calling upon the name of Hari the true doctrine in [the foregoing] two bulky chapters [of this commentary] with the help of best sentences."

On further consideration, it follows that Madhva takes the place of Vyāsa as *vaktṛ*, since he is the proclaimer and author of all canonical texts, Vedas etc. in the *kali* age. And this fact fits well into the diagram drawn by Madhva explaining the intimate relation between *pūrṇāvatāras* and *aṃśāvatāras*. Consequently, in full agreement with this intimate relation Madhva attributes the authenticity of all texts proclaimed by him to Viṣṇu himself, the origin or source of all *avatāras*. Likewise, Madhva can ascribe the teaching of his own commentary on MBh to Hari: *artho 'yam . . . nirṇīyate sahṛdayaṃ hariṇā sadaiva*.[116] It is also recorded that

---

[115] MBhTN III 8: cf. also *ibid.* I 1; II,1; II 2:

uktaḥ pūrve 'dhyāye śāstrāṇāṃ nirṇayaḥ paro divyaḥ |
śrīmadbhāratavākyāny etair evādhyavasyante ||

This is in harmony with the statement of Madhva mentioning his year of birth (cf. above n 9), that he proclaims the truth about Hari hidden by the demons: . . . *daityair nirgūḍhaṃ haritattvam āha*; cf. also n 95 (**C**).

[116] Cf. MBhTN I 22:

artho 'yam eva nikhilair api vedavākyai
rāmāyaṇaiḥ sahitabhāratapañcarātraiḥ |
anyaiś ca śāstravacanaiḥ saha tattvasūtrair
nirṇīyate sahṛdayaṃ hariṇā sadaiva ||

Elsewhere (X 79-84) Vyāsa slips into this rôle; cf. BĀU IV 5,11 [ŚatapathaB XIV 5,4,10]: *asya mahato bhūtasya niśvasitam etad yad ṛgvedo yajurvedaḥ sāmavedo 'tharvāṅgirasa itihāsaḥ purāṇaṃ vidyā upaniṣadaḥ ślokāḥ sūtrāṇi anuvyākhyānāni vyākhyānāniṣṭam hutam āśitaṃ pāyitamayaṃ ca lokaḥ paraś ca lokaḥ sarvāṇi ca bhūtāni* | *asyaivaitāni sarvāṇi niśvasitāni*; *ibid.* VI 1 and MBh XII 13ff.

Madhva is acting on command of Viṣṇu (*viṣṇvājñayaiva*).[117] The fact that Madhva is a disciple of Viṣṇu, fits well in this context, since Viṣṇu gave him instruction at the holy place at Ganges, namely Badarī. In this connection, there is no mention of Vyāsa at first. His name appears only in relation with the commentaries of Madhva on BSū and Upaniṣads, which he composes on the command of Vyāsa (*vyāsājñayā*). Vyāsa as the author of BSū and other canonical texts is identical with Viṣṇu in human shape (*vyāsarūpin*). This means that Viṣṇu is ultimately the author (*vaktṛ*) of all texts and simultaneously also their content. Due to his inconceivable might Viṣṇu takes once possession of the human body of Vyāsa in the *dvāpara* age, some other time, in the *kali* age he seizes the body of Madhva through the intermediation of Vāyu, in order to proclaim the Sadāgamas. Here we can establish a connection with 'Bhaviṣyatparvan', which according to Madhva has been promulgated by Viṣṇu or Vyāsa (*ityādyuktaṃ bhagavatā bhaviṣyatparvaṇi sphuṭaṃ*; *bhaviṣyatparvagaṃ cāpi vaco vyāsasya sādaram*)[118] and which explains the purpose of BSū:

> *nirṇayāyaiva yat proktaṃ brahmasūtraṃ tu viṣṇunā /*
> *vyāsarūpeṇa tat grāhyaṃ tatroktāḥ sarvanirṇayāḥ //*
> *yathārthavacanānāṃ ca mohārthānāṃ ca saṃśayam /*
> *apanetuṃ hi bhagavān brahmasūtram acīkḷpat //*
> *tasmāt sūtrārtham āgṛhya kartavyaḥ sarvanirṇayaḥ /*
> . . .

---

[117] In the closing remark of the first Adhyāya of MBhTN (I 136f.) Madhva explains in a similar way, that he has composed his commentary on MBh on command of Viṣṇu with the help of spiritual elevation due to his grace and that the commentary contains the teaching of Sadāgamas:

> *viṣṇvājñayaiva viduṣā tatprasādabalonnateḥ /*
> *ānandatīrthamuninā pūrṇaprajñābhidhāyujā //*
> *tātparyaṃ śāstrāṇāṃ sarveṣām uttamaṃ mayā proktam /*
> *prāpyānujñāṃ viṣṇor etaj jñātvaiva viṣṇur āpyo 'sau //*

[118] Cf. I 47cd; II 112-118; below n 138.

„One should, however, accept the Brahmasūtra, which has been proclaimed by Viṣṇu in [human] form of Vyāsa only in order to explain the true meaning [of the Vedas]. In it all valid doctrines have been stated. Of course, the adorable Viṣṇu composed the BSū in order to remove the doubts not only about the true doctrines but also about the teaching to bewilder the demons. Therefore, one should proclaim [or understand] all true doctrines on the basis of BSū.“[119]

Another striking feature of the passage from MBhTN is that it gives a chronology of some of the works of Madhva. And it is somehow surprising that, so far, no scholar took notice of this important information. According to this statement, Madhva wrote his commentary on MBh after he had composed the commentaries on BSū and the Upaniṣads.[120] A further in-

---

[119] MBhTN I 42-47. Madhva lists in this connection his typical tenets (= *sarvanirṇayāḥ*; cf. also Anuv p. 152,21-153,28; below n 164); cf. an anonymous citation (ChUBh 445,10-11) from BrahVP:

> *brahmasūtrānusāreṇa vedādyaṃ sarvam eva ca |*
> *yojyaṃ na brahmasūtrāṇi dṛśyamānārthato 'nyathā |*

The first remark goes back to the fictitious Bhaviṣyatparvan and its closing statement is in harmony with the second remark. This fact shows that Madhva himself is behind this source, cf. below n 327. *Nirṇaya*/*vinirṇaya*, used very often by Madhva, is a part of a title, meaning proof or demonstration. It is synonym for true doctrine or *siddhānta*, cf. BSūBh p. 2,11:

> . . .
> *sūtreṣu yeṣu sarve 'pi nirṇayāḥ samuditāḥ |*
> *śabdajātasya sarvasya yatpramāṇaś ca nirṇayaḥ ||*

[120] On the basis of this information it is not possible to give a precise chronology of works mentioned here, in view of the fact that Madhva wrote four commentaries on BSū, namely Brahmasūtrabhāṣya, Anuvyākhyāna, Nyāyavivaraṇa and Anubhāṣya (= Sarvaśāstrārthasaṅgraha) and another ten on different upaniṣads. The description 'excellent commentary' (*bhāṣyavaram*), seems to fit to Anuvyākhyāna, since it gives an impression of well thought-out work (cf. SIAUVE 1971: 1f.). According to Sumadhvavijaya, however, it belongs to the later works of Madhva, and the BSūBh was composed by him after his very first work GīBh (SIAUVE 1968: 35). Madhva seems to hint at BSūBh with the wording: *vyākhyāya sūtrāṇi cakāra āviḥ*. It is very conspicious that Madhva never quotes from his own works or refers

formation from the above passage is that the commentaries on BSū had the purpose to combat the teaching of Advaita. This is in harmony with the other unknown sources cited by Madhva, as 'Sadbhāva' and 'Bhaviṣyatparvan'. And the reference made by Madhva that the prophecy about Madhva's arrival as the messenger of Viṣṇu in the *kali* age has been taught in the Purāṇa and Pañcarātra literature, should be an allusion to both these unknown sources.[121]

Another passage of MBhTN puts forward similar ideas, though in a modified form. Madhva is introduced here not as *aṃśāvatāra* and disciple of Viṣṇu but as his devotee and Marutsuta at Badarī, who proclaims the canonical texts and composes commentaries on BSū, Upaniṣads and MBh due to the grace of Viṣṇu (*viṣṇor eva prasādataḥ . . . mayeyam satkathoditā*).[122]

---

to them! The attempt of some scholars to give a relative chronology on basis of references to the unknown source 'Brahmatarka', which according to them Madhva came across after having composed GīBh, AiUBh and BSūBh on Adhyāyas I and II, (cf. RAO 1960:90; SIAUVE 1968: 30) proves to be unwarranted (see below n 161).

[121] Cf. above n 103. Appayadīkṣita introduces Bhaviṣyatparvan as a work belonging to *smṛti*, cf. below n 155.

[122] Vgl. MBhTN IX 116ff.:

svaṃ svaṃ ca sarve sadanaṃ surā yayuḥ
purandarādyāś ca viriñcapūrvakāḥ /
marutsuto (= Madhva!) *'tho badarīm avāpya*
nārāyaṇasyaiva padaṃ siṣeve //
. . .
itthaṃ sa gāyañ chatakoṭivistaraṃ
rāmāyaṇaṃ bhāratapañcarātram /
vedāṃś ca sarvān sahitabrahmasūtrān
vyacakṣāṇo nityasukhodbharo 'bhūt //
. . .
ity aśeṣapurāṇebhyaḥ pañcarātrebhya eva ca /
bhāratāc caiva vedebhyo mahārāmāyaṇād api //
parasparavirodhasya hānān nirṇīya tattvataḥ /
yuktyā buddhibalāc caiva viṣṇor eva prasādataḥ //
bahukalpānusāreṇa mayeyaṃ satkathoditā /

The question how Madhva justifies his claim to be the reliable proclaimer of all canonical texts, can now easily be answered on the basis of the afore-said considerations: As *aṃśāvatāra* Madhva feels, due to the inconceivable might (*acintya-śakti*) of Viṣṇu, authorized by him to act in his name (*bhagavat-kāryasādhaka*). From the several clear statements of Madhva we can also gather evidence for his sincere conviction that he, under Viṣṇu's guidance and witness, is entitled to announce the true doctrine (*vinirṇayo nāsty amunā vinā*). We may altogether miss the point, if we interpret this conviction of Madhva as a type of pathological fantasy. There is a clear indication that it stems from a supernatural inspiration, in the sense of a mystical experience. Madhva tried to conceptualize this experience, in the very depths of human being, as a spiritual phenomenon taking place through the mediation of Vāyu. Madhva appeals to an anonymous source (= *iti ca*), which describes this supernatural illumination (*jñānadīpana*) as the taking possession (*āveśa*) of Madhva through Viṣṇu and compares it with the 'demoniacal possession or frenzy', in allusion to the deep change in the human personality taking place in this state.[123] The source reference in question runs so:

> *pradhānaṃ dhāma viṣṇos tu prāṇa eva prakīrtitaḥ |*
> *upāyair yo vijānīyat prāṇasthaṃ parameśvaram |*
> *tasya prāṇe harir nityam āviṣṭo bhavati dhruvam |*
> *nityaṃ prāṇasthitasyaiva viṣṇor āveśa eva hi |*
> *prāṇadvāreṇa yajjñānadīpanaṃ jñāninaḥ sadā |*
> *sannidhānaṃ yathā prāptāḥ piśācāḥ puruṣeṣv api |*

---

[123] Madhva endorses here the popular belief referred to in the same context in the Śaiva literature and also in the Pañcarātrasaṃhitās (SCHRADER 1973: 55; cf. above n 86). In another connection (MBhTN I 124-125ab) Madhva remarks, following the opinion of Kauṇḍinya, that the spiritual instruction of a pupil takes place when Viṣṇu is present in the teacher (*haris tasminn āviṣṭaḥ*); cf. OBERHAMMER 1994: 67 n 177 and also M. HARA, Śraddhāviveśa, Indologica Taurinensia 7 (1979) specially p. 271.

tatra sthitvāpi bhuñjanta āviśeyuḥ punaś ca te |
mantrādibhis tathā viṣṇuḥ sadā prāṇasthito 'pi san |
jñānadīptyādikaṃ kuryāj jñāninaḥ punar eva tu |
iti ca.[124]

„The Prāṇa, however, is called the best abode of Viṣṇu. One who can know with the help of means (like *śravaṇa*, *manana*, etc.), that the almighty God is dwelling in the Prāṇa, Hari enters his Prāṇa by taking constantly [and] firmly possession of him, since it is a possession through Viṣṇu, who dwells always in this very Prāṇa. Due to knowledge of Viṣṇu an illumination of wise (*jñānin*) takes place without interruption through the mediation of Prāṇa, in a similar way as the demons too enter the human beings. They enjoy too dwelling in them, and again they take [complete] possession of them with the help of Mantras etc. In that manner, Viṣṇu also dwelling in the Prāṇa produces repeatedly illumination etc. of the wise men due to the knowledge [of Viṣṇu]."[125]

---

[124] MuUBh p. 497,22ff. ; cf. also BhāgTN p. 251,1-3:

prāpnoti vāyuḥ sarvaṃ tu svata eva hares tathā |
ataḥ prāptir iti prāhur vāyuṃ bhūtapatiṃ prabhum |
pradhānavāyur anyeṣu nityāviṣṭo yatas tataḥ |
tadguṇās teṣu cocyante nīcatā nāsya tatkṛtā |
iti brahmavaivarte.

[125] Cf. Translation SIAUVE 1971: 17n 2: „Mais Prāṇa est proclamé la demeure première de Viṣṇu. Celui qui peut connaître par les moyens (d'initiation?) le Suprême Seigneur se tenant en Prāṇa, en son propre *prāṇa* Hari se tient constamment le possédant fermement, car c'est une possession par Viṣṇu qui se tient constamment en Prāṇa. Par l'intermédiaire de Prāṇa se fait sans cesse l'embrasement de la connaissance de Viṣṇu, pour le *jñānin*, de même que les Piśaca entrent en contact avec les hommes et se tenant en eux se donnent leurs expériences, et peuvent les posséder davantage ensuite par l'effet de formules magiques, de mêmes Viṣṇu se tenant sans cesse en Prāṇa peut faire pour le *jñānin* un nouvel embrasement de sa connaissance.„In contrast to SIAUVE, who opines that 'initiation à une secte pāñcarātra' (*l. c.*) are means for the knowledge of God, Madhva understands by *upāya* the traditional means of Vedānta in the sense of BĀU (II 4,5) as *śravaṇa*, *manana*

Our special attention is to be paid to the fact that Madhva does not at all idealize the state of illumination or mystical insight, since he knows out of his own experience, that the painful human existence and phenomenon like sleep etc. endure in spite of the illumination, showing in this way the limitations of human life.[126] It is remarkable, the way how Madhva brings the above statement in an intimate relation to the cardinal tenet of his teaching of *aṃśāvatāra*, namely that Madhva is the third incarnation of Vāyu: *tṛtīyā bhaumī tanur marutaḥ*. In conformity with this teaching, Madhva appropriates spiritually Viṣṇu, whose best abode is Vāyu/Prāṇa, with the help of meditation. The immediate consequence of this appropriation is that Viṣṇu enters the Prāṇa of the meditating Madhva and takes possession of him (*āveśa*) imparting (*kuryāt*) him the illumination (*jñānadīptyādi*!).

---

etc. (cf. *e.g.* Anuv 152,21f.; BSūBh p. 6,4-5: . . . iti nāradīye; p. 161,9-11: . . . iti brahmatarke). The assumption of SIAUVE (*ibid.* 17 n 3), that GīBh does not yet know the thesis of incarnation of Vāyu, and that it has been expressed by Madhva for the first time in his BSūBh, seems to be unjustified, since the closing *ślokas* of GīBh speak of the incarnation of Vāyu (cf. above n 92).

[126] Cf. Anuv p. 174,16-19, where Madhva anew quotes from an unknown source :

> *apriyaṃ vṛjinaṃ duḥkham akaṃ toda itīryate /*
> *tatkāraṇatvāt pāpaṃ vā vṛjinaṃ nāma kathyate //*
> *ity uktaḥ svayam īśena nāmārthaḥ śabdanirṇaye /*
> *apāpatvaṃ ca naivāsti yāvat saṃsāram asya hi //*
> *ārabdhapāpam asty eva duḥkhaṃ ca jñānino'pi hi /*

also SIAUVE 1971: 18 „. . . Cette dernière image rapelle ce qu'il dit de la présence de Vāyu, embrasant la connaissance de Dieu. Tout se passe comme si Madhva après avoir connu une illumination si intense qu'il l'a éprouvée comme une habitation permanente du dieu même de la lumière spirituelle, avait ressenti vivement et doulouresement les limites de la condition humaine qui interdit la prolongation continue de cet état: le sommeil par exemple empêche la méditation, mais il faut s'y remettre aussitôt aprés, dit-il.“ (= Anuv p.153,18). Elsewhere, Madhva quotes a fictitious Purāṇa passage (BhāgTN p. 51,10-11, see also GīBh p. 70,11f. on this subject):

> *jñānādivyaktir avyaktiḥ sukhaduḥkhādikaṃ tathā /*
> *sudṛṣṭabrahmatattvānāṃ bhavaty ārabdhakarmaṇā /*
> iti brahmavaivarte.

Based on this fact, we can attest that Madhva underlines twice the special role of Vāyu: first, in his appearance as the third *aṃśāvatāra* and secondly, in his confirmation as the authorized proclaimer of all canonical texts due to his illumination through the mediation of Vāyu (*prāṇadvāreṇa*). With that we have a whole lot. In the framework of *aṃśāvatāra*, as the third incarnation of Vāyu, Madhva was allotted the task of imparting the knowledge (*jñānakārya*),[127] and the illumination authorized him to fulfill that task in the name of Viṣṇu (*bhagavatkāryasādhaka*).[128] His name *pūrṇaprajña* is possibly meant to allude to this authorization. This seems also to be the reason why Madhva is known as the disciple of Viṣṇu carrying out his deeds in his name and on his command.[129] As a matter of fact, Madhva is sincerely convinced of his mission, for again and again he refers to his divine charisma (*viṣṇuprasādat*), which empowers him to proclaim all canonical works in the name of Viṣṇu in the *kali* age. That means, he feels in his innermost being that he is provided with the fullness of power, not only to proclaim new texts, but also to supplement or modify the transmitted ones.[130]

---

[127] Cf. above n 75ff.

[128] The seizure (*āveśa*) of Madhva by Viṣṇu, implies that he is personally present in Madhva (cf. MBhTN II 17cd:) *anyāveśanimittaṃ ced balam anyātmakaṃ hi tat* ; (*ibid.* II 118): *bhagavatkāryasādhakaḥ* (cf. above n 81). In this connection Madhva differentiates (*ibid.* II 32) between two forms of seizure *viśeṣāveśino hareḥ* and *kiṃcidāveśino hareḥ* ; cf. above n 86; below n 133.

[129] Even SIAUVE (1971:17f.) did acknowledge the special importance of this passage, without, however, bringing it up in connection with the unknown sources of Madhva; cf. above n 89.

[130] Since Madhva is not identical with almighty God and is subject to all human weaknesses and infirmities (cf. above n 86f.) his role can be compared with that of the Prophets in Old Testament, *e.g.* with Isaiah (VI 5f.): „And I said: 'Woe is me! For I am lost; for I am a man of unclean lips, and I dwell in the midst of a people of unclean lips; for my eyes have seen the King, the Lord of hosts!' . . . And he touched my mouth, and said: 'Behold, this has touched your lips; your guilt is taken away, and your sin forgiven.' And I heard the voice of the Lord saying, 'Whom shall I send, and who will go for us ?' Then I said, 'Here am I! Send me'. And he said, 'Go,

What has been elaborated here in detail, is not a mere working hypothesis but – as we have seen – it stands in perfect harmony with several statements of Madhva himself. Madhva takes up this matter again when he refers, at the beginning of his MBhTN, to the variant, sometimes faulty and deficient, readings, as well as to the adulteration itself of the text of MBh. The passage in consideration runs as follows:

kvacid granthān prakṣipanti kvacid antaritān api |
kuryuḥ kvacic ca vyatyāsaṃ pramādāt kvacid anyathā ||
anutsannā api granthā vyākulā iti sarvaśaḥ |
utsannāḥ prāyaśaḥ sarve koṭyaṃśo 'pi na vartate ||
grantho 'py evaṃ vilulitaḥ kimv artho devadurgamaḥ |
kalāv evaṃ vyākulite nirṇayāya pracoditaḥ ||
hariṇā nirṇayān vacmi vijānaṃs tatprasādataḥ |
śāstrāntarāṇi sañjānan vedāṃś cāsya prasādataḥ ||
deśe deśe tathā granthān dṛṣṭvā caiva pṛthagvidhān |
yathā sa bhagavān vyāsaḥ sākṣān nārāyaṇaḥ prabhuḥ ||
jagāda bhāratādyeṣu tathā vakṣye tadīkṣayā |
saṃkṣepāt sarvaśāstrārthaṃ bhāratārthānusārataḥ ||
nirṇayaḥ sarvaśāstrāṇāṃ bhārataṃ parikīrtitam |

„They interpolate the texts in some places, they even delete in other places, [again] in other places due to carelessness they barter one [passage for another], elsewhere, they falsify them. Although the texts are not totally lost, [but they are] altogether disarranged. Other texts got lost mostly, since the most important

---

and say to this people . . .'"; Jeremiah (I 4f.): „Now the word of the Lord came to me saying, 'Before I formed you in the womb I knew you, and before you were born I consecrated you; I appointed you prophet to the nations.' Then I said, 'Ah, Lord God! Behold, I do not know how to speak, for I am only a youth' But the Lord said to me: Do not say, 'I am only a youth'; for to all to whom I send you you shall go, and whatever I command you you shall speak. Be not afraid of them, for I am with you to deliver you', says the Lord. Then the Lord put forth his hand and touched my mouth; and the Lord said to me, 'Behold, I have put my words in your mouth. See, I have set you this day over nations and over kingdoms, to pluck up and to break down, to destroy and to overthrow, to build and to plant."

portion has not been handed down. This is also the state of the MBh-Text. How much more is [its] meaning confused, for it is difficult to be understood [even] by gods. In order to put forward the true doctrine in this confused kali age, I proclaim, impelled by Hari [and] with the help of his grace the tenets of true doctrine after learning other canonical texts and also after learning the Vedas with the help of his grace. And after having seen in many places the different text[-manuscripts of MBh], I shall, considering [these different manuscripts], deliver exactly as – the adorable Vyāsa, who is identical in bodily form with Nārāyaṇa, the Lord, proclaimed in the books like Mahābhārata – the meaning of all canonical works in short, in agreement with the purport of Mahābhārata. [For] it has been taught that Mahābhārata is the final purport of all canonical texts."[131]

This passage supplies a very important methodical clue helping us to discriminate between the true and false traditions. Madhva draws a clear line between traditional literary sources which have been wrongfully modified or where an unauthorized deliberate change has taken place and his own works or his other sources he quotes. Any traditional source which has been deliberately changed due to carelessness or due to any another reason, they are to be considered as falsified. The trustworthiness of Madhva's sources depends above all on the fact, that they, on the one hand, are firmly established in the untainted original literary tradition, acknowledged as such by Madhva under the guidance of Viṣṇu, and that they, on the other hand, have been proclaimed or composed by Madhva on command of Viṣṇu, in order to restore the original doctrine which sank into oblivion in course of the time. One can be sure that Madhva with the allusion to the huge loss of the original literary sources (*koṭyaṃśo 'pi na vartate*) has felt called upon to restore in a divine mission also the lost portions of the traditional texts. In this sense, Madhva

---

[131] MBhTN II 3 - 8; cf. *ibid.* II 11ab: *nirṇayaḥ sarvaśāstrāṇāṃ sadṛṣṭānto hi bhārate*; also VTN (p. 27,1-9), where Madhva referring to MBh (XII 261, 47cd-50) labels those who falsify the true meaning of the tradition as clumsy (*anaipuṇāḥ*) and robbers (*śāstradasyavaḥ* bzw. *brahmastenāḥ*).

appears as a self-confident literary author with divine warrant not only of his own original and other commented works but also of all other literary texts which in the tradition are known as works of Viṣṇu or of Vyāsa.[132] His model of truthfulness and realization of his divine task is Vyāsa (*yathā sa bhagavān vyāsaḥ sākṣān nārāyaṇaḥ prabhuḥ / jagāda bhāratādyeṣu tathā vakṣye . . .*). Madhva underscores in this fact the difference between himself and Vyāsa. Whereas Viṣṇu is identical with Vyāsa, he is only present in Madhva due to the illumination (*jñānadīpana*), i. e. due to the taking possession (*āveśa*) through Viṣṇu.[133] With the help of this double-track which allows to put Viṣṇu's presence in Madhva and Viṣṇu's identity with Vyāsa side by side, Madhva can show in an emphatic way that in both cases Viṣṇu alone is ultimately the proclaimer of all canonical texts.

On the background of this teaching which – as we have seen – displays an intimate relation between Viṣṇu and Vyāsa on the one hand and Viṣṇu and Madhva on the other, it is not surprising, that Madhva transfers the characteristic qualities of one member to other members. Their roles are within certain limits exchangeable.[134] It is therefore obvious from this fact that not only Vyāsa and Madhva are called authors of all canonical

---

[132] In the Vaiṣṇavite circles, for instance, according to the Purāṇa and Saṃhitā literature Viṣṇu descends due to his inconceivable might (*acintyaśakti*) to the earth under different names as teacher in order to proclaim the divine message, *cf.* PadP (VI 235,23f.; 236,1ff.; I 1,45f.); ViṣP (III 2, 56ff.; III 3,2ff.; III 4,1ff.); VāyP (I 60,1ff.); BrāṇP (I 2,34,8ff.); ParameśvaraS (I 74ff.); ĪśvaraS (I 18ff.; 34f.; 70cd). Jayantabhaṭṭa (NM I p. 245,30f.) has worked out this doctrine in a system; cf. OBERHAMMER 1974: 85ff.

[133] Madhva declares in a long passage, which he ascribes to the Paiṅgiśruti (BĀUBh p. 261,11-264,5), that this seizure does not mean identity with Viṣṇu (*āviṣṭo viṣṇur eteṣu na viṣṇus tatsvarūpakaḥ . . . sarve te viṣṇunāviṣṭā viṣṇor bhinnāḥ sadaiva tu* [cf. also p. 262,11; 263,1]); above n 128; also MBh III 195,12 = Harivaṃśa IX 65; MBh XII 59,130; LiṅgP I 70,125; I 24,128.

[134] This restriction is indicated on the basis that Viṣṇu appears as *vyāsarūpin* or *vyāsātmanā* (MBhTN II 13a), but never as *madhvarūpin*, and on the other hand neither Vyāsa nor Madhva appear as *viṣṇurūpin*.

texts but also Viṣṇu in his divine and not merely in a borrowed human form.[135] Consequently, Madhva can attribute to Viṣṇu and to Vyāsa his own genuine and other works in disguise. For instance, his commentary on MBh and Bhaviṣyatparvan. This is the key to solve the mystery of the unknown sources of Madhva. So, it is high time now to concretise in the following exposition what we have so far frequently alluded to and put forward arguments based on the real statements of Madhva himself to prove our thesis. For instance, the following passage of MBhTN:

---

[135] Cf. above n 57; 110; 122. Madhva draws up from the already existing patterns when he calls Viṣṇu the author of all texts, as of the Vedas, Pañcarātrasaṃhitās or of the MBh: *vedānāṃ prathamo vaktā harir eva . . .* (BhāgTN p. 395,3-6: unknown source 'Śabdanirṇaya'), cf. also MBh VI 63, 5cd; ViṣP III 3,31cd; II 11,7ab; Gī XV 15cd; *pañcarātrasya kṛtsnasya vaktā nārāyaṇaḥ svayam* (Anuv 88,22); part quotation of the unknown source 'Hayagrīvasaṃhitā' (BĀUBh p. 294,17-19) :

> . . .
> *sarvaṃ viṣṇau sthitaṃ viṣṇor jātaṃ viṣṇor vaśe sadā |*
> *śaṅkhaśabdo yathā śaṅkhadevatāvaśagaḥ sthitaḥ ||*
> *tasmād vedāḥ samutpannā vidyākhyā mūlikā śrutiḥ |*
> *sarvopaniṣadaś caiva pañcarātrākhyasaṃhitāḥ ||*
> *brahmasūtrāṇi vedānāṃ vyākhyās tāsāṃ ca vistaraḥ |*

= MBh XII 337,63 = MBhTN II 101; *ko hy anyaḥ puṇḍarīkākṣān mahābhāratakṛd bhavet* (GīBh p. 4,2-4 = PadP I 1,44ab; ViṣP III 4,5). In the ṚgBh he comments on the hymn to Ṛbhus in such a artificial way as to deduce from it the authorship of Viṣṇu:

> *saptasaṅkhyāni ratnāni trikāleṣv api dhattana |*
> *purāṇapañcarātretihāsavedān haris tathā ||*
> *mīmāṃsātarkasahitān pañcavedān athāpi vā |*
> *sapta cchandāṃsi vaikaikaṃ tadguṇair akhilaiḥ saha ||*

(ṚgBh p. 89,1-2). The use of imperative-form (2nd p. pl. = *dhattana*) as in the basis text should be interpretated as *pluralis majestatis.* Also in BhāgTN (p. 613,14f.) Madhva refers to an unidentified quotation from BrāṇP:

> *śraddhā bhāgavate tantre vede bhāratapañcame |*
> *viṣṇor avyavadhānena vaktṛtvāt sarvathā bhavet |*
> . . .

cf. below n 281f.

artho 'yam eva nikhilair api vedavākyai
rāmāyaṇaiḥ sahita bhāratapañcarātraiḥ |
anyaiś ca śāstravacanaiḥ saha tattvasūtrair
nirṇīyate sahṛdayaṃ hariṇā sadaiva ||[136]

It is a striking fact that Madhva ascribes his own commentary on MBhTN together with other well known texts like BSū,[137] positively to Viṣṇu. In similar way, another testimony of Madhva on his work in disguise: *ityādy uktaṃ bhagavatā bhaviṣyatparvaṇi sphuṭam* bzw. *bhaviṣyatparvagaṃ cāpi vaco vyāsasya sādaram*.[138] Elsewhere, we find again a reference to a passage in the BrāṇP, which, however, has not been handed down: *ityādi kathitaṃ sarvaṃ brahmāṇḍe hariṇā svayam*.[139] It is also noteworthy, that in all these cases the authorship of Viṣṇu is particularly underlined through the use of special adverbs. Whereas in the first passage above the authorship of Madhva is also asserted, for it is in fact a work composed by him, in the remaining two other references this authorship is apparently or fictitiously excluded. As a mat-

---

136 MBhTN I 22; cf. above n 135.

137 Cf. also ṚgBh p. 10, v. 84cd:

ādhikye 'dhikam ity eva hariṇā sūtram (BSū II 1,22) *īritam*.

MBhTN I 42:

nirṇayāyaiva yat proktaṃ brahmasūtraṃ tu viṣṇunā |
vyāsarūpeṇa tad grāhyaṃ tatroktāḥ sarvanirṇayāḥ ||

138 MBhTN I 47; II 112ff. :

bhaviṣyatparvagaṃ cāpi vaco vyāsasya sādaram |
vāsudevasya mahimā bhārate nirṇayoditaḥ ||
. . .
bhāṣās tu trividhās tatra mayā vai saṃpradarśitāḥ |
. . .
tasmād viṣṇor hi mahimā bhāratokto yathārthataḥ ||

cf. above n 103 and below n 324f.

139 MBhTN II 49ab.

ter of fact, Bhaviṣyatparvan – as already shown earlier – goes back to Madhva himself. Similarly, the long passage of forty *ślokas*, rendering the peculiar tenets of Madhva, ascribed to BrāṇP has not been transmitted,[140] and as such it should be a supplement added by Madhva himself, a kind of textual extension observed very often in the so-called anonymous literature, which builds the backbone of these texts.[141] Applying this literary devise found also in the MBh, in the Gī or in the Pañcarātrasaṃhitās,[142] Madhva attributes directly to Viṣṇu not only his unknown sources but even his peculiar doctrinal tenets (*satsiddhāntāḥ* = *sarvanirṇayāḥ* [143]):

---

140 MBhTN II 9-49; cf. also below n 304.

141 A quite recent example of this procedure is Saurapurāṇa containing an interpolation of three chapters criticizing the teaching of Madhva [cf. B.N.K. SHARMA, An attack on Śrī Madhvācārya in the Saura Purāṇa, ABORI 13 (1931-32), p. 59-76] and Bhaviṣyatpurāṇa [cf. L. ROCHER, The Purāṇas (History of Indian Literature, ed. J. GONDA, II,3). Wiesbaden 1986, p. 151ff.].

142 Madhva refers to this practice expressly, for instance in Anuv (p. 135, 22-23) :

> *arthaḥ svayaṃ vinirṇīto vāsudevena sādaram* /
> *iti guhyatamaṃ śāstram idam uktaṃ mayānagha* /
> (= Gī XV 15cd - 20)
> *etad buddhvā buddhimān syāt kṛtakṛtyaś ca bhārata* //
> (Anuv p. 175,31f.)
> *daivī sampad vimokṣāya nibandhāyāsurī matā* /
> (= Gī XVI 5ab)
> *iti mokṣaviśeṣaś ca svayaṃ bhagavatoditaḥ* //

cf. below n 337; also MVD p. 53,12f.; KhN p. 247,8f.; BhāgP II 8; ĪśvaraS I 53cd-54ab:

> *prathamaṃ sātvataṃ śāstraṃ samyag ādhyāpitā mayā* //
> *vāsudevena yat proktaṃ śāstraṃ bhagavatā svayam* / . . .

cf. Śaṅkara (GīBh [upodghāta]): . . . *tam dharmaṃ bhagavatā yathopadiṣṭaṃ vedavyāsaḥ sarvajño bhagavān gītākhyaiḥ saptabhiḥ ślokaśatair upanibabandha; tathā imam eva gītārthaṃ dharmam uddiśya bhagavataivoktam.*

143 Cf. above n 135 and below n 269.

1. *manuṣyagandharvapitṛgaṇakārmikatāttvikāḥ |*
devāḥ śakraḥ śivo brahmā muktau saukhyādibhir guṇaiḥ ||
śatāyutottarā nityam anyonyaprītisaṃyutāḥ |
iti siddhāntagaṃ vākyaṃ svayaṃ bhagavateritam |[144]

2. *aśeṣaguṇapūrṇatvaṃ sarvadoṣasamujjñitiḥ |*
viṣṇor anyac ca tattantram iti samyag vinirṇayaḥ ||
svatantratvaṃ sadā tasya tasya bhedaś ca sarvataḥ |
adoṣatvasya siddhyarthaṃ yadabhede tadanvayaḥ ||
tattantratvaṃ ca muktānām api tadguṇapūrtaye |
muktānām api bhedaś ca na hi bhinnam abhinnatām ||
gacchad dṛṣṭaṃ kvacit tasyāpy abhāvo 'nubhavopagaḥ |
pūrvābhede doṣavattvam īśasyety atibhinnatā ||
nārāyaṇena muktānām api samyag iti sthitiḥ |
bhedābhede 'py abhedena doṣāṇām api saṃbhavaḥ ||
nirdoṣatvaṃ ramāyāś ca tadanantaratā tathā |
brahmā sarasvatī vīndraśeṣarudrāś ca tatstriyaḥ ||
śakrakāmau tadanye ca kramān muktāv apīti ca |
satsiddhānta iti jñeyo nirṇīto hariṇā svayam |
etadvirodhi yat sarvaṃ tamase 'ndhāya kevalam ||
andhaṃ tamo viśantīti prāha śrutir [145]*atisphuṭam |* [146]

---

[144] Ṛgbh p.11,6-8, v. 89-90; cf. the description of the state of release according to an unknown reference of Paiṅgiśruti (BĀUBh 264,4-5) :

> *na kadācid viyogaś ca na vidveśo na cāratiḥ |*
> *modante sahitāḥ sarve sadā viṣṇuparāyaṇāḥ ||*
> ityādi paiṅgiśruti

cf. also Anuv p. 166,19-22.

[145] BĀU IV 4,10; ĪśU IX.

[146] Anuv 153, 21f. Transl. SIAUVE 1971: 34-35: „La plénitude de toutes perfections, l'exemption totale de toute imperfection appartiennent à Viṣṇu, et les autres réalités dépendent de lui, telle est l'interprétation correcte. Dire qu'il ne dépend éternellement que de lui-même, et qu'il y a différence entre lui et l'univers, permet de poser qu'il est sans imperfections car celles-ci s'ensuivraient d'une doctrine de non-différence. De lui dépendent également les délivrés eux-mêmes, pour atteindre la plénitude de leurs qualités, et entre

3. *sarvottamo harir idaṃ tu tadājñayaiva*
cettuṃ kṣamaṃ sa tu hariḥ paramaḥ svatantraḥ /
pūrṇāvyayāgaṇitanityaguṇārṇavo 'sāv
ity eva vedavacanāni paroktayaś *ca* //
(MBhTN I 29).

4. *viṣṇoḥ paramotkarṣe hi sarvapramāṇānāṃ*
mahātātparyaṃ bhagavatābhihitam /
(ChUBh 441,16).

5. *bhāratārthas tridhā proktaḥ* svayaṃ bhagavataiva *hi* /
(MBhTN II 129cd).

6. *bhāṣās tu trividhās tatra* mayā *vai saṃpradarśitāḥ* /
(ibid. II 114ab).

7. After refuting the thesis of Śūnyavādins und Māyāvādins (= *māyāvādirāddhāntaḥ*) Madhva puts forward his own teaching as *bhagavadrāddhāntaḥ*)
(TU III 685,6-7).

8. Even his logical argumentation Madhva ascribes to Viṣṇu: *yuktayo nirṇayasyaiva* svayaṃ bhagavatoditāḥ /
(Anuv p. 108,23).

---

les délivrés aussi existe la différence, car on ne voit jamais ce qui a été différent atteindre l'état de non-différence: on peut affirmer que ceci n'arrive pas car c'est témoignage d'expérience. Si la non-différence existait antérieurement (au salut), le Seigneur possèderait les imperfections (des *jīva*): aussi la position correcte est-elle qu'une differénce absolue existe entre Nārāyaṇa et les délivrés eux-mêmes; s'il y avait seulement différence et non-différence entre eux, la même possibilité d'imperfections subsisterait du fait de la non-différence. 'Ramā est sans imperfections, tout en dépendant elle aussi immédiatement de lui, Brahmā, Sarasvatī, Vīndra, Śeṣa, Rudra et leurs épouses, Śakra avec Kāma, et tous les autres demeurent dans le même ordre jusque dans le salut' est-il dit encore. Voilà ce qu'il faut connaître comme vraie doctrine, expliquée par Hari lui-même. Tout ce qui lui est contraire ne peut conduire qu'aux ténèbres aveugles: la Śruti le dit très clairement: 'Ils entrent dans les ténèbres aveugles'."

It is obvious that Madhva with this thought pattern makes evident that his teaching ultimately has been revealed by Viṣṇu. In harmony with this position, he declares that Viṣṇu is the author of many of his unknown sources regarding to different subjects,[147] which in fact has been designed *ad hoc* by Madhva himself:

---

[147] It is remarkable, that this kind of statements is to be found mainly in the Anuv and twice in BhāgTN and ṚgBh respectively, but never in the BSūBh which is one of his earlier works. Similar observation has been made also by SIAUVE (1971: 77n 2). It did not escape her attention that Madhva attributes these works to Viṣṇu with an exceptional emphasis. SIAUVE is of the opinion that these works, known exclusively to Madhva (*ibid.* 1971: 14; 45n 4), belong to Pañcarātra, although she confesses that this fact does not suit well with the system of Madhva: „Il est certain que les textes pāñcarātra se donnent pour parole de Viṣṇu appelé Bhagavān, comme les āgama se donnent pour parole de Śiva. Mais il est assez difficile d'intégrer cette conception dans le système de Madhva, pour qui les textes ne peuvent être que deux sortes: la Śruti qui est sans auteur personnel, fût-il divin, (*apauruṣeya*) et les autres textes qui sont révélés par le Seigneur, sous sa forme de Vyāsa. Il es bien certain que Vyāsa et Viṣṇu ne font qu'un, mais si Madhva voulait dire que les textes pāñcarātra sont eux aussi attribués à Vyāsa, l'auteur des *Brahma-Sūtra*, il emploierait d'autres expressions . . ." (*ibid.* 77 n 2). These statements are, however, in clear disagreement with the fact that in the MBhTN (X 80cd-84; XXXII 157-158) Vyāsa and Madhva himself appear as authors of all canonical texts, including also the Pañcarātrasaṃhitās, cf. above n 57f. Madhva solves the apparent contradiction between *apauruṣeya* and *pauruṣeya*-works by appealing to the teaching of BrāṇP (quotation not located) that the eternal Vedas are always present in the mind of Viṣṇu and that he reveals them again and again at the beginning of each creation:

> *nityā vedāḥ samastāś ca śāśvatā viṣṇubuddhigāḥ |*
> *sarge sarge 'munaivaita udgīryante tathaiva ca ||*
> *tatkrameṇa ca tair varṇais taiḥ svarair eva nānyathā |* . . .

(VTN p. 14,7f.; cf. below n 248f.).

Madhva attributes also this teaching to an unknown source named Hayagrīvasaṃhitā (BĀUBh p. 294,17f.; cf. above n 135). The teaching in question is widespread, perhaps based on BĀU (IV 5,11); ŚatapathaB (XIV 5. 4,10) and it has been propounded also in the ViṣP II 11,8 and Kullūkabhaṭṭa *ad* Manu I 21-2; cf. above n 116.

1. *tatsamo nāsti paramo harir eva na cāparaḥ* I
saṃhitāyāṃ bṛhatyāṃ tu svayaṃ bhagavatoditam I
(Anuv p. 167,25).

2. *apāpatvam aduḥkhatvaṃ cāvṛjinatvam ihoditam* I
apriyaṃ vṛjinaṃ duḥkham akaṃ toda itīryate II
tatkāraṇatvāt pāpaṃ vā vṛjinaṃ nāma kathyate I
ity uktaḥ svayam īśena nāmārthaḥ śabdanirṇaye I
(*ibid.* p. 174,16f.).

3. *dravyasvātantryavijñānaprayatnair adhikaṃ phalam* I
devānām anyagaṃ cāpi teṣu yad brahmaṇo hi tat II
bṛhattantroditaṃ vākyaṃ hariṇā phalanirṇaye I
(*ibid.* p.189,26f.).

4. *śubhāśubhaphalaṃ devā asurāś ca samāpnuyuḥ* I
krameṇaiva yathāśakti yathā ye ye prayojakāḥ I
prerakā api pāpānāṃ na devāḥ pāpam āpnuyuḥ I
iti prakāśikāyāṃ hi provāca harir añjasā I
(*ibid.* p. 190,27f.).

5. *asurās tu vinā muktiṃ tamo 'ndham api cāpnuyuḥ* I
iti tattvavivekoktaṃ svayaṃ bhagavatā vacaḥ I
(*ibid.* 191,21-22).

6. *jñānadā api cācaryā viśeṣāt phalam āpnuyuḥ* I
muktāv aṣṭaguṇaṃ śiṣyād gurur āpnoti śobhanam II
tad gurur dviguṇaṃ tasmāt sārdhaṃ tāvat tato 'pare I
devāḥ sahasraguṇitaṃ kramāt tasmād yathottaram II
brahmā mahaughaguṇitam evaṃ phalavinirṇayaḥ I
ity āha bhagavāñ chāstre guruvṛttābhide svayam I
(*ibid.* 191,23f.).

7. *tataḥ proktās tu te sarve bhaktyogratapādayaḥ* I
apaśyan paramaṃ viṣṇuṃ tatprasādedhitāḥ sadā I
ity uktaṃ viṣṇunā sākṣād granthe sattattvasañjñite I
(*ibid.* 193,25-26).

8. *brahmadvid brahmadarśī ca tamomokṣāv avāpnutaḥ* I
brahmaṇāṃ śatakālāt tu pūrvam ārabdhasaṅkṣayaḥ II

brahmaṇas tv eva pañcāśād brahmaṇas tathā I
rudrasya viṃśad eva syād indrasyārkādike daśa II
anyeṣāṃ brahmamātrasya tv anta ārabdhasaṅkṣayaḥ I
brahmaṇaiva sahātaś ca paraṃ nārāyaṇaṃ vrajet I
iti sattattvavacanaṃ svayaṃ bhagavatoditam I
(*ibid.* p. 200,4f.).

9. *kālato balataś caiva jñānānandādikair api* I
sarvair guṇair viṣṇur eva śreṣṭhas tadavamā ramā I
anantāṃśena kālāt tu samā tasyāś caturmukhaḥ I
avaro bahulāṃśena tatsamo vāyur ucyate I
niyamād vāyur evaiko brahmatvaṃ yāti nāparaḥ I
tasmāt samānatā muktau vāyutve kiṃcid ūnatā I
daśavarṣaṃ tu tatpaścāj jananaṃ tatstriyor api I
ānandādis taddaśāṃśaḥ kālaḥ saṃvatsarāt paraḥ I
yāvat paścāj janis tāvat pūrvaṃ dehakṣayo bhavet I
brahmavāyvos tu ye devyau taddaśāṃśaḥ sukhādikaḥ I
śeṣasya garuḍasyāpi kālo divyasahasrakaḥ I
śeṣarudrau brahmavāyū yathā tadvat parasparam I
taddevyas taddaśāṃśāḥ syus tatas tv indrādayo matāḥ I
evaṃ muktau ca pūrvaṃ ca nānyathā kvacid iṣyate I
anyathoktir yatra ca syāt tanmohārthaṃ bhaviṣyati I
pūrvāparaviparyāso bahurūpatvahetutaḥ I
iti viṣṇukṛte tattvaviveke I
(BhāgTN 198,8f.).

10. *indrādyāḥ sanakādyāś ca dakṣādyā ye 'pi cāpare* I
ṛṣayo manavo devās tadvaṃśyā ye ca kecana I
umāyā avarāḥ sarve guṇaiḥ sarvair na saṃśayaḥ I
tatsamo bhaviṣyo vā na bhūto 'dyatano 'pi vā I
ṛte haribrahmavāyuśeṣavīndrān sabhāryakān I
śaṅkaraṃ ceti vettavyam anyanmohārtham iṣyate I
iti viṣṇukṛte tattvanirṇaye I
(*ibid.* 199,4f.).

11. pravṛtte *caitad akhilam* uktaṃ hi prabhuṇā svayam I
(ṚgBh p. 8,12-13).

12. *rūḍhim eva samāśritya vibhajyārthān yathākramam* I
vidoṣaguṇapūrtyarthaṃ viṣṇau yogārtham ānayet I

paścād eva yathāyogam itareṣv api san nayet I
ṛgvedasaṃhitāyāṃ ca prabhuṇaivaṃ samīritam I
(*ibid.* p.10 v 81f.).

13. *tasmān nityaṃ hariṃ dhyāyet kuryāt svādhyāyam añjasā* I
aihikāmuṣmikā bhogā raktasyānyas tu mucyate I
iti svādhyāyavacanaṃ svayaṃ bhagavatoditam I
(*ibid.* p.11 v. 95).

If we compare these special statements with the other similar expressions on Vyāsa as the author of the BSū, where Viṣṇu appears once with the human face of Vyāsa (*proktaṃ brahmasūtraṃ tu viṣṇunā vyāsarūpeṇa*) and some other time as Viṣṇu himself ([BSū III 1,7] *kathitaṃ svayaṃ bhagavatā*; *viṣṇunoktāni sūtreṣu*; *ityādibhagavadvacanena*),[148] we are then justified to apply them as a paradigm also for Madhva, exactly as the wordplay *vācyavaktṛsvarūpaka*, which in the first place implies the identity between Viṣṇu and Vyāsa, has been adapted to explain the intimate relation between Viṣṇu and Madhva.[149] *Mutatis mutandis* this interpretation is in clear agreement with the self-statement of Madhva in the sense of the supernatural influence on him due to the divine illumination (*jñānadīpana*): *pūrṇaprajñas tṛtīyas tu bhagavatkāryasādhakaḥ*. The use of special adverbs in this connection as *svayam* [*bhagavatoditam*], *añjasā*, *sākṣāt sahṛdayam*, *sādaram* or *eva* has the purpose to underscore the fact that Madhva speaks in the name of Viṣṇu.

---

148 MBhTN I 42f.; GīBh p. 3,2; GīT p.141,26; KN p. 101,13-14; KhN p. 247,23f.; ṚgBh p. 11, v. 84; Vāda p. 47,14-15; TU III p. 639, 23-24; MBh-TN II 112: *bhaviṣyatparvagaṃ cāpi vāco vyāsasya sādaram.*

149 Cf. above n 57f.

REDACTIONAL CRITERIA FOR THE AUTHORSHIP OF MADHVA

In corroboration of the point of view, exposed here so far, we find in BĀUBh a passage from an unknown source called Pratisāṅkhyāna:

sūtraṃ tu brahmasūtrākhyaṃ mahāmīmāṃsikā tathā /
tathā sāṅkarṣaṇaṃ sūtraṃ brahmatarkādayas tathā //
prakāśikā nirṇayaś ca tattvanirṇaya eva ca /
vyākhyeti kathitāḥ sarvāḥ svayaṃ bhagavatā kṛtāḥ //
bṛhattarkādayaḥ sarvā anuvyākhyāḥ prakīrtitāḥ /
iti pratisaṅkhyāne.[150]

It is clear from this reference that this source specifies Viṣṇu as the author of some well known works like Brahmasūtras, Mīmāṃsāsūtras, Saṅkarṣaṇakāṇḍa and also of some completely unknown sources. Three of them are identified as commentaries, namely Prakāśikā, Nirṇaya and Tattvanirṇaya. In case Nirṇaya is identical with Śabdanirṇaya,[151] we would have three commentaries quoted by Madhva also in his other works. Madhva refers here to subcommentaries like Bṛhattarka,[152] as well as to other independent works. Apart from Brahmatarka many other texts are implied here (°*ādayaḥ*). There seems to be a purpose, why Madhva mentions completely unknown sources together with the well known works. The implied message in this context is that the unknown works are not merely fabricated texts but that

150 BĀUBh p. 323, 20-23; cf. above n 66.

151 'Nirnaya' as a second member of a work title appears in several unknown sources of Madhva, as Upāsanā, Jīva, Tantra, Bhoga, Liṅga, Vākya, Vidyā, Śruti, Sūra. Śabdanirṇaya seems to be an etymological text according to the intention of Madhva (cf. Anuv p. 174,18).

152 Nowhere in the works of Madhva did I find a source with this name, but only Bṛhatśruti; Bṛhatsaṃhitā; Bṛhattantra.

they are as real as the well known sources.[153] This assumption is endorsed further by the fact that this information is garbed under a reference to a new and independent source, namely Pratisaṅkhyāna. And the mention of a foreign source in this connection lends a special weight to it. Since the contents of this source are in complete harmony with the ideas of Madhva elsewhere we may conclude that he himself is behind this source.[154] This intention becomes visible also in GīT, where Madhva introduces an unidentified passage of a known source, namely NārP mentioning Brahmatarka along with the orthodox and unorthodox philosophical systems. Brahmartarka is specified as a textbook of logic (*tarkaśāstra*)[155] proclaimed by Viṣṇu in the same way as all other texts named before.

---

[153] Cf. above n 113 and below n 187, 219. It should be mentioned in this connection that Madhva ascribes to Viṣṇu even the famous text of BhāgP (BhāgTN p. 4,7f.; elsewhere it is called *śruti*! cf. n above n 16; below n 258). As reference point he gives a passage from a Purāṇa:

> uktaṃ ca gāruḍe –
> *artho 'yaṃ brahmasūtrāṇāṃ bhāratārthavinirṇayaḥ |*
> *gāyatrībhāṣyarūpo 'sau vedārthaparibṛṃhitaḥ ||*
> *purāṇānām sārarūpaḥ sākṣād bhagavatoditaḥ |*
> *dvādaśaskandhayukto 'yam śatavicchedasaṃyutaḥ ||*
> *grantho 'ṣṭādaśasāhasraḥ śrīmadbhāgavatābhidhaḥ |*
> iti.

It is very strange that an earlier text GarP (circ. 10th cent.) renders precise information about a later text (circ. 11th cent.) not only about its size and divisions, but also about a long existing tradition, that BhāgP is called *gāyatrībhāṣya*. This tradition is based on the fact that the first verse of this Purāṇa ends with *dhīmahi* as *gāyatrī*. No wonder that the quoted passage is not found in the GarP!

[154] Cf. the part-quotation from Hayagrīvasaṃhitā (BĀUBh p. 294, 17ff.) ; above n 135.

[155] Cf. also Anuv p. 6,29f.:

> *etat sarvaṃ tarkaśāstre brahmatarke hi vistarāt |*
> *uktaṃ vidyāpṛthaktvāt tu saṅkṣepeṇātra sūcitam ||*
> *pramāṇanyāyasacchikṣā kriyate tarkaśāstrataḥ |*
> *mānanyāyais tu tatsiddhā mīmāṃsā meyaśodhanam ||*

brahmatarkas tarkaśāstraṃ viṣṇunā yat samīritaṃ /
akṣapādakaṇādau ca sāṃkhyayogau ca haitukāḥ //
bauddhapāśupatādyās tu pāṣaṇḍā iti kīrtitāḥ /
mīmāṃsā trividhā proktā brāhmī daivī[156] *ca kārmikī* //
brahmatarkaṃ ca mīmāṃsā seveta jñānasiddhaye /
vaidikajñānavairūpyān nānyat seveta paṇḍitaḥ //
ity . . . nāradīye.[157]

As a matter of fact, Brahmatarka stands clearly out from all other unknown sources of Madhva not only on account of its special title meaning inquiry of Brahman and therefore often mentioned together with *mīmāṃsā* in the sense of *brahmaniścayā*,[158] but specially because Madhva considers it as a key-work of his system, for he quotes from it more frequently than from any other of his sources. There are 148 references attributed to this text in the different works of Madhva and in BhāgTN alone 74! Several citations in contrast to his other quotations are

---

To judge from different citations from Brahmatarka, it is not primarly a textbook of logic, for only a few *ślokas* deal with the valid means of knowledge and with Vāda. It is, however, striking that in Brahmatarka there is no hint at *avatāra* doctrine, although it discusses all other peculiar teachings of Madhva. Brahmatarka does not quote from other sources. In the list of Appayadīkṣita (cf. above n 33; below n 345) it appears as a *smṛti* text together with Bhaviṣyatparvan.

156 This triple division could point out to Brahmamīmāṃsā, Saṅkarṣaṇakāṇḍa, known also as Devatākāṇḍa or Upāsanākāṇḍa, and Karmamīmāṃsā. It is strange, that Madhva (ChUBh p. 452,3f.) in connection with *upāsana* (*tasmād acetanopāsām na kuryāt kvāpi kaścana*) cites first BSū (II 1,5 and II 2,3), Devamīmāṃsā and immediately after Saṅkarṣaṇasutra. This might be a hint that they are not identical. Both quotations are not handed down in the Saṅkarṣaṇakāṇḍa.

157 GīT p. 23,24-28.

158 KeUBh p. 474,6f.; Anuv p. 153,31: *brahmatarkaś ca mīmāṃseti*; cf. *ibid.* p. 7,16; GīT p. 23,27; KāvM II p. 3, 22-23: *nigamavākyānāṃ nyāyaiḥ sahasreṇa vivektrī mīmāṃsā* / *sā ca dvidhā vidhivivecanī brahmanidarśanī ca.*

conspiciously very long.[159] Beyond that, Madhva remarks that his two other works are based on Brahmatarka.[160] Not to mention that it is the only unknown source comprising almost all the peculiar doctrines (*satsiddhāntāḥ*) of Madhva.[161] Another reason

---

[159] Cf. RAO 1960: 92. A. NARAYANA TANTRY has collected all quotations ascribed to Brahmatarka arranging them in groups according to their subject, in: RAO 1960: 11-55.

[160] Cf. The closing verse of PL and VL :

> *ānandatīrthamuninā brahmatarkoktimārgataḥ I*
> *mānalakṣaṇam ity uktaṃ saṅkṣepād brahmasiddhaye II*
> *ānandatīrthamuninā brahmatarkānusārataḥ I*
> *kathālakṣaṇam ity uktaṃ prītyarthaṃ śārṅgadhanvanaḥ II*

The title VL should be a slip of the pen for Kathālakṣaṇa, for Kathālakṣaṇa appears in the Maṅgala and in the closing verse.

[161] Cf. RAO 1960: 86ff.; SIAUVE 1968: 26ff.; 75n 5; above n 155; below n 164. The exceptional importance of this source has been underscored not only by the followers of Madhva, but also by some Indologists like SIAUVE (1968: 31), who remarks: „Faut-il faire résider l'originalité de la pensée de Madhva dans la seule force de synthèse avec laquelle elle met en oeuvre de notion déjà existantes? Faut-il pour sauver son génie créateur faire de lui l'auteur clandestin du *Brahmatarka* ? Il ne nous semble pas.“ The reason indicated by SIAUVE for her thesis, namely that Brahmatarka does not mention the teaching of Madhva regarding *sākṣin* is flawed. In fact, the expression used by Madhva, in a quotation from the Brahmatarka, while elaborating his teaching on the valid means of knowledge, namely *svadṛg anubhavaḥ*, is in contrast to the opinion of SIAUVE, synonymous: with *sākṣin*, and therefore interchangeable with *anubhava*: Brahmatarka (GīT p. 105,22f.): *viśeṣo 'nubhavād eva jñāyate sarvavastuṣu* = Anuv p. 101,19-20: *viśeṣāḥ sarva evaite sākṣipratyayagocarāḥ*. Elsewhere, (1968: 187n 2; cf. also p. 74ff.) SIAUVE herself accepted this fact! SIAUVE is in a very difficult position, for she cannot explain how a very recent work as Brahmatarka, initiating a new philosophical tradition, could disappear suddenly without leaving any traces, so that not even Madhva's immediate pupils had any knowledge of the same. Besides, Madhva would have been a plagiarist in the eyes of his contemporaries if he were to borrow the ideas from a recent book composed by someone else, as SIAUVE holds. In the same way, another contention of SIAUVE (*ibid.* p. 30; 1971:15), which she puts forward adopting the opinion of RAO (1960: 89f.) and SHARMA (1960: 115) has no foundation, that Madhva did not have Brahmatarka at his disposal at the time he composed GīBh and when he commented on first and second Adhyāyas of BSūBh as well,

strongly supporting our assumption is that the different quotations attributed to Brahmatarka show the same literary structure as the real works of Madhva. It is strange, that not even the immediate disciples of Madhva were ever aware of such an important source of the Madhva school, for they never quote from it.[162] And Jayatīrtha, whose *paramaguru* was Madhva, speaks about Brahmatarka in a very general and not binding way in his Ṭīkā on VTN. He speaks once of it as an old work: *prāktena granthena* and at another place as a lost work: *evam atītena prabandhenoktam.*[163] In case we are successful in proving positively that the author of Brahmatarka is Madhva himself,

---

since he found this work at a later date during his journey to the northern India. As a matter of fact, Madhva mentions the Brahmatarka in GīBh in an unidentified passage of NārP (cf. above n 157). In GīBh he quotes from this Purāṇa 19 times and in BSūBh (first Adhyāya) three times! This would imply that Madhva should have had knowledge of Brahmatarka while composing GīBh and BSūBh.

162 RAO (1960: 96) was of the opinion that he was in possession of a very strong argument for the authenticity of Brahmatarka, as he remarked: „ . . . but one quotation of three verses beginning *sarvābhimānino devās tatrāpi* is not found anywhere in Madhva's works. It must be a quotation taken by Trivikrama direct from the Brahma Tarka. If this view is correct, at once it concludes the matter.“ In fact, Madhva ascribes these three *śloka*s to an anonymous source (= *iti ca*) in his GīT (p. 49,15-18)! Also SIAUVE, who is convinced of the authenticity of Brahmatarka as a work composed at the time of Madhva or shortly before him (cf. above n 161; 176), rejects the said argumentation of RAO, as well as his conclusion, that Padmanābhatīrtha, who was an immediate pupil of Madhva exactly as Trivikrama (RAO 1960: 80f.), had a direct knowledge of the said source for – according to him – he could identify a quotation comprising five *śloka*s in Anuv (p. 55,2-7), which are not precisely marked off and introduced merely with *uktaṃ bhāllaviśākhāyāṃ brahmatarke ca sādaram.* SIAUVE (1968: 28) expressed her critical observation in the following remark: „Aucun des faits n'est décisif. Le premier commentateur peut avoir divisé les deux textes pour de simples raisons de vraisemblance, et l'un et l'autre pouvaient se souvenir d'un passage auquel Madhva s'était référé au cours de son enseignement.“ Some MSS (BhāgTN p. 85,9f.) ascribe one *śloka* associated with PadP to Brahmatarka. I was unable to locate it in the said Purāṇa.

163 Cf. VTNṬ p. 432,7-8; 360,16.

then it would be a decisive proof for the authorship of Madhva, which we could apply as paradigma for all other unknown sources of Madhva, which he as in the case of Brahmatarka attributes to Viṣṇu. In fact, Brahmatarka shows traces of a recent work, which was composed in the 12th cent., hence in the life time of Madhva, as will be argued below.

Although the different quotations attributed to Brahmatarka do not allow us to pass judgement on the particular form of the same, it nonetheless raises a query as to whether it was a book as a whole or a mere collection of single passages which Madhva *ad hoc* composed according to his spiritual needs in support of his peculiar teachings. In this case, Madhva would have created a completely new literary device allowing him to put forward his new ideas without giving the impression that they are not established in an existing tradition. As a matter of fact, there are many statements of Madhva giving strength to this interpretation, for instance, the following passage, which is very similar to the above quotation from NārP:

> *satsiddhānta iti jñeyo nirṃīto hariṇā svayam |*
> *etadvirodhi yat sarvaṃ tamase 'ndhāya kevalam ||*
> *andhaṃ tamo viśantīti prāha śrutir atisphuṭam |*
> *ity eva śrutayo 'śeṣāḥ pañcarātram athākhilam ||*
> *mūlarāmāyaṇaṃ caiva bhārataṃ smṛtayo 'khilāḥ |*
> *vaiṣṇavāni purāṇāni sāṅkhyayogau parāv api ||*
> *brahmatarkaś ca mīmāṃsety anantaḥ śabdasāgaraḥ |*
> *anantā yuktayaś caiva pratyakṣāgamamūlakāḥ ||*

„It should be known that the true Siddhānta has been established by Hari himself. All other [doctrines] which are in contradiction to it lead to intense darkness. In this sense, the *śruti* (BĀU IV 4) declares very clearly:'They enter intense darkness'. This is also taught by all [other] *śrutis*, by the whole [corpus] of the Pañcarātrasaṃhitās, as well as by the original Rāmāyaṇa, the Mahābhārata, all *smṛtis*, by the Vaiṣṇana Purāṇas, by the best [philosophical systems] Sāṃkhya and Yoga and [finally] by the Brahmatarka, an inquiry [about Brahman]. This is a huge sea of words. Besides, the endless [number of] logical arguments [supporting it] are based on the perception and on the Āgamas."[164]

Our special attention should in this connection be turned to the fact that Brahmatarka is mentioned at the end of this enumeration. It is the only 'single work' specified by name and in contrast to other texts, its contents are also marked off (*brahmamīmāṃsā*). Its doctrine comprises all the peculiar teachings of Madhva, proclaimed by Viṣṇu himself leading to the deliverance of the human beings. Consequently, Brahmatarka stands in the same line as the traditions handed down by wise teachers (*śiṣṭāḥ*), as *śruti*, *smṛti* and Sāṃkhya-Yoga.[165] As already remarked and supported also by other statements of Madhva, its contents are an inquiry about Brahman.[166] As a textbook of logic (*tarkaśāstra*)[167] it contains several logical arguments (*yuktayaḥ*) based on the perception and Āgamas. It is very extensive (*śabdasāgara*). In fact, this description suits collectively with the traditions mentioned here, but in a special way with Brahmatarka, as a single work. Madhva expounds this elsewhere in very clear terms:

> *brahmatarkaṃ ca bhagavān sa eva kṛtavān prabhuḥ /*
> *pañcaśātkoṭivistārān nārāyaṇatanau kṛtāt //*
> *uddhṛtya pañcasāhasraṃ kṛtavān bādarāyaṇaḥ /*
> *atas tadarthaṃ saṅkṣepād ata ity abhyasūcayat //* [168]

---

164 Anuv p. 153, 28 + 154,24; *ibid.* p. 60,17-19.

165 Cf. Baudhāyanadharmasūtra I 1,1,6:

> *dharmoṇādhigato yeṣāṃ vedaḥ saparibṛṃhaṇaḥ /*
> *śiṣṭās tadanumānajñāḥ śrutipratyakṣahetavaḥ //*

Manusmṛti XII 109; Vāsiṣṭhadharmaśāstra VI 43; NM 248,7ff. and OBERHAMMER 1974: 60ff.

166 Cf. above n 158.

167 Cf. above n 155.

168 Anuv p. 7, 16-18.

„And Viṣṇu, the adorable Lord, is truly the author of Brahmatarka, [i.e.] Bādarāyaṇa (=Vyāsa), in the [human] form of Nārāyaṇa, having drawn out 5.000 [*śloka*s] from the large mass of existing 500.000.000 *śloka*s] composed it. Therefore, [Bādarāyaṇa = Vyāsa] proclaimed concisely its meaning, when he said [in the BSū I 1.1. *atha*] *atas* [*brahmajijñāsā*].“

It is striking, that both these self-statements of Madhva are in agreement with the teaching of the unknown sources quoted above, namely Pratisaṅkhyāna and NārP, not only regarding the author of Brahmatarka but also with regard to the peculiar teachings and its intimate relation to Brahmajijñāsā and consequently to the Brahmasūtras. This fact gives the impression that Madhva himself is behind both these sources.[169]

Evidently, Madhva, appealing to his divine illumination, wants to line up the Brahmatarka with the well known texts as Mahābhārata and Brahmasūtras, which are ascribed by him to Viṣṇu:

---

[169] I have noticed that Madhva proceeds similary with the well known sources. For instance, he ascribes almost *verbatim* his opinion put forward in TS (p. 61,3-5; Anuv p. 8,19-20) to SkaP:

> *sṛṣṭiḥ sthitiḥ saṃhṛtiś ca niyamo 'jñānabodhane |*
> *bandho mokṣaḥ sukhaṃ duḥkhaṃ āvṛttir jyotir eva ca ||*
> *viṣṇunāsya samastasya samāsavyāsayogataḥ |*

(= BSūBh p. 8,11-12 and VTN p. 20,6-8):

> *utpattisthitisaṃhārā niyatir jñānam āvṛttiḥ |*
> *bandhamokṣau ca puruṣād yasmāt sa harir ekarāṭ ||*
> iti ca skānde (not located !)
> *sṛṣṭiḥ sthitiś ca saṃhāro niyatir jñānam āvṛtiḥ |*
> *bandhamokṣau ca kathyante yasyotkarṣaprasiddhaye |*
> *yasyotkarṣaprasiddhyarthaṃ sarvavedāś ca yuktayaḥ |*
> *jñātvaiva ca yadutkarṣaṃ mucyante sa hariḥ paraḥ |*

(anonymous citation= ChUBh p. 442,21-23); cf. below n 348.

In BĀUBh (p. 268, 20-270) in support to his teaching on *svataḥprāmāṇya* (cf. also Anuv p. 6, 20 f.) he adduces a fictitious quotation from Bhaviṣyatparvan and Brahmatarka; cf. above n 154 and below n 213f.

kṛṣṇadvaipāyanaṃ vyāsaṃ viddhi nārayaṇaṃ prabhum /
ko hy anyaḥ puṇḍarīkākṣān mahābhāratakṛd bhavet //
. . . proktaṃ brahmasūtraṃ tu viṣṇunā vyāsarūpeṇa / [170]

With the help of this procedure Madhva can raise the Brahmatarka, which he attributes also to Vyāsa, to the category of classical works, though it is clearly a modern composition, for it criticizes the famous dictum of Vimuktātman (10th cent.) in defence of Māyāvāda: *durghaṭatvam avidyāyā bhūṣaṇaṃ na tu dūṣaṇam.*[171] It is also target of sharp critic in the other works of Madhva.[172] In addition, the Pramāna-doctrine of Brahmatarka, which is also set forth by Madhva in his Pramāṇalakṣaṇa,[173] is based on the teaching of Pramāprameya of Bhāvasena, a Jaina contemporary of Madhva.[174] The fact that Madhva was under the

170 MBhTN II 51; II 7; I 42; cf. above n 56; 64; 116; 119.

171 Iṣṭasiddhi [crit. ed. M. HIRIYANNA, Baroda 1933] I 140; ChUBh p. 392,28-29 = RAO 1960: 17, No. 5.

172 Cf. MVUD v.16; UKh p. 336,21; 373,10f.: Anuv 174,15f.; GīT p.128,20f.; TU IV p. 8, 5-6; VTN p. 38,1f.

173 Cf. above n 160. Our credit is due to ZYDENBOS (1991: 248-271) who for the first time draw our attention to the fact that Madhva was following Bhāvasena in his Pramānavāda. ZYDENBOS was also able to show, that the doctrine of Brahmatarka on *yogyatā* of the individual souls justifying the doctrine of gradation (*tāratamya*) among them (RAO: 1960, Nos 107, 108,111,121,151.; cf. SIAUVE 1968: 27; 339f.), was most probably influenced by the Jaina teacher Bhāskaranandin, also a contemporary of Madhva (*ibid.* p. 252f.), and that the Viśeṣavāda in the Brahmatarka presupposes *anekāntavāda* of Jaina authors (p. 261f.). In my forthcoming publication in German [MESQUITA 2000: St. n 4ff., 41, 58, 277, 292, 351f.] I also have argued that Madhva is heavily drawing on Bhāvasena.

174 Cf. above n 173. Brahmatarka (RAO *o. c.* 14,8); PL p. 65,4-5: *yathārthaṃ pramāṇam* [= Anuv p. 60,19f.; PL p. 67,12: *yathārthyaṃ pramāṇam*] *tad dvividhaṃ kevalam anupramāṇaṃ ca / yathārthajñānaṃ kevalam / tatsādhanam anupramāṇam / kevalaṃ caturvidham.* Madhva closely follows Bhāvasenas 'Pramāprameya' (p. 1,11f.) not only when he gives the definition of *pramāṇa* but also when he accepts its dichotomy: *atha kiṃ pramāṇam / padārthayāthātmyaniścayaḥ pramāṇam / tac ca bhāvapramāṇaṃ karaṇapramāṇaṃ iti dvividham / pramitiḥ pramāṇam iti bhāvavyutpattyā samyag jñānam eva pramāṇam / prakarṣeṇa saṃśayaviparyāsānadhyavasāyavyavacchedena*

heavy influence of Jaina teachers rest on the particular situation that he was born in a country governed by Jaina rulers.[175] Taking into consideration all the above mentioned facts, we could maintain definitely that the Brahmatarka or the passages attributed to it, were composed during the life time of Madhva. This view is supported by the typical teachings of Brahmatarka, which are identical with those of Madhva, and also by the mythical garb used to introduce this work.[176]

As a matter of fact, Madhva uses here a traditional and mythical frame, which allows him to prove the unbroken orthodoxy of his philosophical system, for he traces back this

---

mīyate niścīyate vastutattvaṃ yena 'tat pramāṇam iti karaṇavyutpattyā samyagjñānasādhanaṃ pramāṇam. This applies also to the definition of *smṛti* as a valid knowledge (PL p. 66,5-6; Anuv p. 62,18f.): *mānasapratyakṣajā smṛtiḥ / smṛty anuvādayor nāprāmāṇyam / yathārthatvānubhāvāt / ahāneś ca*; (cf. PP p. 9,1f.:) *tathā smṛtiḥ pramāṇaṃ samyagjñānatvād jñātārthāvyabhicāritvād bādhakena vihīnatvād nirduṣṭapratyakṣatvat.*

175 Cf. ZYDENBOS 1991: 253: „This parallelism of views in Dvaita and Jainism acquires still greater significance when we consider the historical circumstances in which Dvaita originated. Madhva was born in a village very near the modern town of Udupi in southwestern Karnataka state,. and at that time that region was ruled by a staunch Jaina dynasty which has its capital at Barkur, only a few miles away from Madhva's birthplace."

176 In the opinion of SIAUVE, too, Brahmatarka was a modern work ('un texte récent, peut-être contemporain de Madhva') and she was astonished at the fact, that Madhva ascribed it to Vyāsa (1968:28). Nevertheless, she remarked that Madhva accepted it by *bona fide* as being an old text: „Même si ses références proviennent d'oeuvres récentes, il a recu celles-ci en toute bonne foi pour traditionnelles" (*o. c.* p. 32). She refers in this connection to the opinion of Madhva that all doctrines, consequently also the teaching of Vimuktātman, existed from the eternity (*anādikālato vṛttāḥ samayā hi pravāhataḥ / na cocchedo 'sti kasyāpi samayasya* Anuv p. 71,24). However, this is in a contradiction to the fact that Madhva shows historical conscience in his works, for instance when he gives details of his birth (cf. oben n 9; unten n 107), or when he identifies an advaita-opinion as being the teaching of *māyāvādī* (= Sarvajñātman), quoting the Maṅgala-Verse of Saṃkṣepaśarīraka (TU Bd. III p. 667,5; Vāda p. 48, 2-3), or when he speaks about his attempt, to secure the right readings among different variants of MBh (cf. above n 131).

system to Vyāsa, a renowned Teacher, accepted by all Vedānta schools. This is manifested – according to Madhva – in the fact that the Brahmatarka is a summary of an old voluminous text.[177]

If such an important work like Brahmatarka is unequivocally a literary composition or a deliberate literary invention of Madhva, then it is justified to bring forward the thesis that also other unknown sources or unknown quoted passages – which, on the one hand, are cited only by Madhva and, on the other hand, deal with his peculiar teachings – should equally have Madhva as their author, unconcerned about the fact whether they belong to the *śruti*, to the Pañcarātrasaṃhitās or to the Purāṇas. As we have explained before, these unknown texts or sources are by no means treatises or books as a whole but mere fictitious work-titles which Madhva uses as a rack for text-passages composed by him *ad hoc*. Sometimes, he attributes such passages in form of a secondary textual extension of the literary works transmitted in the tradition, as Purāṇas, or in many other cases they appear merely as anonymous citations under *iti* or *iti ca*.

On the basis of our several aforesaid observations we can name provisionally some criteria for the thesis that Madhva himself is speaking through his unknown sources, as follows: All unknown sources or passages ascribed to known sources or to other anonymous quotations have Madhva as their author,

1. when they are quoted only by him and when they deal with his peculiar teachings, or

2. when Madhva attributes them directly to Viṣṇu himself, or

---

[177] This thought pattern was used by Rāmānuja at the beginning of his Śrībhāṣya: *bhagavadbodhāyanakṛtāṃ vistīrṇāṃ brahmasūtravṛttiṃ pūrvācāryāḥ saṃcikṣipuḥ / tanmatānusāreṇa sūtrākṣarāṇi vyākhyāsyante*; cf. R. MESQUITA, Rāmānujas Quellen im Mahāpūrvapakṣa und Mahāsiddhānta des Śrībhāṣya; WZKS 28 (1984) p. 179f. This archetype is found also in the Pañcarātra literature, cf. *e. g.* Ahirbudhnyasaṃhitā I 70-73; Jayākhyasaṃhitā I 75; Pādmasaṃhitā I 1,32f.; Pārameśvarasaṃhitā I 90-93.

3. when they quote from or refer to the other texts, which should be unequivocally considered as literary productions of Madhva.

The first two criteria should be applied to the following work-titles: Bṛhatsaṃhitā,[178] Śabdanirṇaya, Bṛhattantra, Prakāśi-

---

[178] According to SIAUVE this literary source is very appropriate to prove decisively (= preuve décisive) that at least the Bṛhatsaṃhitā is a genuine and not a mere fictitious work of Madhva. In consequence, she extends this judgement to all other unknown sources of Madhva (cf. above n 26). The line of SIAUVE's argument is the hierarchical list, based on the gradation of gods (*tāratamya*), put forward in the unknown source 'Bṛhatsaṃhitā' and in the ChU (VII 1). Both these lists are not uniform with regard to the names and to the number of the gods. The first list mentions fourteen members with Vāyu/Prāṇa as the last and the second list contain fifteen gods with Vāyu, also in the last place. The attempts to harmonize these both lists in the ChUBh become difficult and intricate (cf. SIAUVE 1971: 46-51). Had Madhva himself invented his sources – argues SIAUVE – he would have been more skilful and had simplified the whole procedure (cf. 1968: 25: 'S'il avait forgé ses sources il aurait été plus habile'). In this sense she argues further (1971: 14): „Mais il est certain que cette exégèse n'est guère satisfaisante: il aurait été infiniment plus simple pour Madhva de se faire à lui-même une liste des divinités qui ne l'obligeât pas à de telles acrobaties." While arguing so, SIAUVE did not take notice of the fact, that in the exposition of the ChUBh analysed by her, it is not Madhva who tries to bring into harmony both these lists (*ibid.* p. 46n 1), but another unknown source ascribed to Viṣṇu, namely Tattvaviveka (ChUBh p. 446,20 + 450,29). But a mere and wilful levelling of the different sources on demand would have been clumsy and in sheer contradiction to the ingenious mind of Madhva. Therefore, Madhva does not choose – as postulated by SIAUVE – a skilful and plain course, but rather an intricated path through another unknown source, which is nothing more than an invention of Madhva himself. Our observation is supported by the fact that Madhva adopts in his later work Anuv (p. 167,26) – as SIAUVE had also indicated (*ibid.* p. 14) – without, however, quoting a foreign source (Anuv p. 209,20) the very same solution proposed by him in the ChUBh. This fits very well in the general picture of the unknown sources of Madhva, for the different literary sources, adduced as a proof for a particular teaching contain apart from some common features, some other complementary features, also contrary or even contradictory elements, so that they necessarily give the impression that they should go back to different traditions. A clear evidence for this kind of procedure are the literary sources on Vāyu (cf. above n 71 also n 21). We could say that the observation made

kā, Tattvaviveka,[179] Guruvṛtta, Sattattva,[180] Tattvanirṇaya, Ṛgvedasaṃhitā, Svādyāya and Bhaviṣyatparvan. Sadbhāva is the source complying only with the first criterion. The third criterion is fulfilled only by Pratisaṅkhyāna and NārP.[181] We could apply these criteria without difficulties also to similar work-titles, such as Prabhañjana, Pradhyāna, Prajāpatisaṃhitā and Sattattva, all dealing with Vāyu,[182] or to Sāmasaṃhita, which is adduced only in ChUBh sixteen times (in VIth Adhyāya alone five times). The Madhva's authorship for all the passages attributed to this source can be concluded specially due to the fact that these passages use

---

by SIAUVE proves just the opposite, for – as SIAUVE rightly remarked (1971: 10f., 48) – there is an intimate relation between Bṛhatsaṃhitā und Brahmatarka, which – as we have already seen – is a literary composition of Madhva. From this very fact we can draw the conclusion that Bṛhatsaṃhitā und Tattvaviveka, which according to Madhva go directly back to Viṣṇu, are also fictitious texts of Madhva. In addition, we have a new evidence for our thesis based on the fact that Madhva is the only person who attributes one *śloka* with regard to six exegetical principles (*ṣaḍvidhatātparyaliṅga*) referred to already by Sudarśanasūri (MESQUITA 1990:231f.) to Bṛhatsaṃhitā (BSūBh p.10,17-18). Sāyana Mādhava, the author of SDS was aware of this assignment of Madhva (cf. SDS p. 293,11-14), but he declines to accept it, for he ascribes it (SDS p. 770,8-11) merely to old teachers: *liṅgaṣaṭkaṃ ca pūrvācāryair darśitam* –

> *upakramopasaṃhārāv abhyāso 'pūrvatā phalam /*
> *arthavādopapattī ca liṅgaṃ tātparyanirṇaye //*
> iti.

179 Cf. above n 178. Under this very title a short work of Madhva, comprising eleven *śloka*s, has been handed down, cf. below n 226.

180 Cf. below n 182.

181 Cf. above n 150; 157.

182 Prabhañjana (= god of wind!) is quoted seven times in the ChUBh (p. 415, 22f.; 423,22f.), BhāgTN (p. 681,6f.; 708,10f., 721,4f.; 725,4f.) and PraśUBh (p. 504,22f.), Pradhyāna five times in the ChUBh (375,17f.), BĀUBh (244, 11f.; 252,23f.) and BhāgTN(725,11f.; 735,7f.), Prajāpatisaṃhitā is quoted only once (MuUBh p. 501,17 + 502,25), while the Sattattva, which is ascribed to Viṣṇu, is quoted thirteen times in six different works of Madhva. This source contains also passages with regard to other subjects.

a text-reading, which is against all the existing traditions, namely *atat tvam asi* [183] instead of *tat tvam asi*. This reading is made possible by using ChU-text without Daṇḍas![184] It is remarkable, that Madhva uses also this reading often in BĀUBh, however, without appealing to a source. This fact gives further support to the thesis that Madhva is behind the Sāmasaṃhitā.[185]

It is noteworthy that the inner structure of these passages lays open Madhva's mind to give Sāmasaṃhitā an appearance of a commentary on the Upaniṣads, for it comments on a primary text.[186] In addition, Madhva's commentary on ChU is very informative regarding the different sources quoted therein. In order to substantiate his thesis that the individual soul is not identical with Viṣṇu, he draws not only on passages from *śruti*, Gī and Mokṣadharma, which can be located, but also on completely unknown sources, for instance Vākyanirṇaya and Śabda-

183 Cf. ChUBh p. 437, 18f. ; 445, 13-17: . . .

atat tvam asi putreti ya ukto gautamena tu /
navakṛtvaḥ sadṛṣṭāntaṃ sarvabhedena keśavaḥ /
tasmai namo bhagavate cidacitpramāya te /
puruṣottamāya devāya pūrṇānandaikarūpiṇe /
iti sāmasaṃhitāyām.

184 The Vedānta schools committed to realism, e.g. Viśiṣṭādvaita deny as categorically as Madhva the relation of identity between *tat* and *tvam* keeping the traditional reading *tat tvam asi* (cf. MESQUITA 1990: 226). Strange is the fact that Madhva elsewhere sticks to the traditional reading too, cf. below n 185.

185 BĀUBh p. 258, 18f.: *tat satyaṃ sa ātmā atat tvam asīti bhedasya navakṛtvo 'bhyāsāt* . . . also in the ChUBh p. 442, 28-29; GīT p. 16,12-13; VTN p. 22,13f. It is surprising that Madhva in GīT (p. 14,27) and also in the fictitious work Brahmatarka (BĀUBh p. 244,18f.) brings into play also the traditional reading *tat tvam asi*! Similar inconsistencies we find elsewhere, e.g. in his commentary upon MāṇU (I 18d) (cf. above n 21 and below n 204).

186 One of the passages comments upon *ekam evādvitīyam* (VI 2,1) preceded by a similar interpretation ascribed to a source called Pravṛtta (cf. ChUBh p. 432, 11-15).

nirṇaya,[187] which has the appearance of etymological works, or on other commentaries, like Pravṛtta and Tattvaviveka.[188] We could identify two work-titles among them, namely Śabdanirṇaya and Tattvaviveka as not genuine, *i.e.* devised *ad hoc* by Madhva.[189] Since the inner structure of Vākyanirṇaya and Pravṛtta is very similar to the two other titles named above, we should assume that they too are not genuine works, although Madhva puts the last one into the class of the Pañcarātra texts.[190] Our attention is to be paid to the fact, that Madhva adduces in this connection quotations from the Purāṇas, namely three times from BrāṇP and once from PadP, BrahVP respectively.[191] All these quotations are not recorded and should be considered as secondary textual extensions done by Madhva himself.[192]

---

187 Cf. ChUBh p. 431,14-15; 431,20-21, 440,25-26.

188 *Ibid.* p. 432,11-12; 435,26-27; 444,19-20; ṚgBh p. 8,12-13.

189 Cf. above n 178-179.

190 Cf. Anuv p. 188,22-23:

> *iti pravṛttavacanaṃ sādhanasya vinirṇaye |*
> *pravṛtte pañcarātre hi sādhanasyātiniścayaḥ ||*

191 ChUBh p. 436,25-26, 442,25-26, 443,20-23; 445,8-9 (cf. above n 51); 445,10-11.

192 It is conspicuous that there are similarities between these different quotations in disguise, for instance (BSūBh p. 153,9-11[Brahmatarka]):

> *sarvān vedān setihāsān sapurāṇān sayuktikān |*
> *sapañcarātrān vijñāya viṣṇur jñeyo na cānyathā ||*

and BrāṇP (ChUBh 442,25-26):

> *mahātatparatā viṣṇor utkarṣe 'vāntarā tataḥ |*
> *anyatra sarvavākyānāṃ yuktīnāṃ ca viśeṣataḥ ||*
> iti brahmāṇḍe.

(cf. n 59; 110; also Caturvedaśikhā and Bhāllaveyaśruti BSūBh p. 153,8-9 + 154,5-6; below n 266; Paiṅgiśruti and VarP (VTN p. 19,13-16; cf. below n 337); see also Bhaviṣyatparvan (MBhTN I 44f.):

> *tasmāt sūtrārtham āgṛhya kartavyaḥ sarvanirṇayaḥ | . . .*
> *viṣṇor uktāni sūtreṣu sarvavedeḍyatā tathā |*

After having shown the ingenuineness of Madhva's literary passages, on the basis of known and unknown sources attributed to the *smṛti*, we can turn our attention to a text from the *śruti*, namely Paramaśruti. This *śruti* has nothing to do with the ChU, although Madhva sometimes calls this Upaniṣad as *paramā śrutiḥ*.[193] Sixteen entries from this source are to be found in five different works of Madhva.[194] The Paramaśruti has an exemplary character not only because it supports the peculiar teaching of Madhva of 'five-fold difference' (*pañcabheda*),[195] but also because it allows us to gain an insight into the method of working or into the literary form of the unknown sources of Madhva. The passage quoted by Madhva in the VTN elaborates the aforesaid teaching as follows:

jīveśvarabhidā caiva jaḍeśvarabhidā tathā /
jīvabhedo mithaś caiva jaḍajīvabhidā tathā // [1]

---

see also BrahVP (ChUBh p. 441,10-11):

brahmasūtrānusāreṇa vedādyaṃ sarvam eva ca /
yojyaṃ na brahmasūtrāṇi dṛśyamānārthato 'nyathā /

(cf. above n 119). In the same way, Madhva's ideas on the faults and deficiencies of *avatāras* in Bhaviṣyatparvan and BrāṇP (cf. above n 51) or his peculiar arguments for the reality of the world in BrāṇP, BrahVP and in the other unknown sources (cf. below n 201) are also similar. This list could be easily expanded.

193 Cf. ChUBh p. 432,15. The advaitin Anubhūtisvarūpa records in his Prakaṭārthavivaraṇa (on Śaṅkarabhāṣya: BSū IV 4,8) the passage in BĀU (IV 3,32) as a citation from the Paramaśruti: „*eṣo 'sya parama ānanda' iti paramaśruteś ca na duḥkhābhāvamātram ānanda iti.*

194 Cf. VTN (p. 32,13; 33,12, 17; 35,10; 40,8; 42,8; 43,16); GīT (p. 13, 25; 14,7; 17,27; 21,12; 38,29; 118,32) ; ChUBh (p. 467,5); BĀUBh (p. 300,26) and Anuv (p. 194,14).

195 As a matter of fact, this teaching corresponds to the doctrine of *tattvatrayaḥ*, (i. e. *cit, acit* und *īśvaraḥ*) in the Viśiṣṭādvaita, which Yāmuna seems to attribute to the founder of the School, Nāthamuni in the closing verse of Āgamaprāmaṇya: . . . *jīyān nāthamuniḥ svayogamahimapratyakṣa-tattvatrayaḥ*; cf. R. MESQUITA, Zur Vedānta- und Pāñcarātra-Tradition Nāthamunis, WZKS 23 (1979) p. 188.

mithaś ca jaḍabhedo yaḥ prapañco bhedapañcakaḥ /
so 'yaṃ satyo hy anādiś ca sāditve nāśam āpnuyāt // [2]
na ca nāśaṃ prayāty eṣa na cāsau bhrāntikalpitaḥ /
kalpitaś cen nivarteta na cāsau vinivartate // [3]
dvaitaṃ na vidyata iti tasmād ajñāninām matam /
mataṃ hi jñāninām etan mitaṃ trātaṃ ca viṣṇunā // [4]
tasmāt satyam iti proktaṃ paramo harir eva tu / [5ab]
iti hi paramaśrutiḥ.

„The universe consists of a five-fold difference: the difference between God and individual soul, that between insentient objects and Īśvara, and also that among individual souls themselves, that between insentient objects and individual soul, and [lastly] that among the insentient objects themselves. This [universe] is real and without beginning. If it had a beginning, it would perish. But it does not perish, nor is it a product of an illusion. If it were so, it would have disappeared. But it does not disappear. Therefore, the opinion: 'The duality/ plurality does not exist', is the view of the ignorant people. The view of the wise, on the contrary, is that this [duality/ plurality] is known and protected by Viṣṇu. Therefore, it is proclaimed by him that it is real. And Hari alone is supreme. [This] is namely the teaching of Paramaśruti.“[196]

Alone the fact that this *śruti* puts forward a special teaching of five-fold difference, which appears to be a derivation based on a popular etymology of *prapañca*,[197] seems to confirm

---

[196] VTN p. 35, 6-10.

[197] The formations *prapañca-* and *prapañcana-* in the sense of diffuseness in style or in the sense of manifoldness are referred to not until MBh and in the younger Upaniṣads. A recent formation based on it is *prapañcayati* (Dhp. 6,14 also *pañcate*), a derivation from *pañca* and it seems to convey its original meaning of 'counting on five fingers' (cf. A. DEBRUNNER/ J. WACKERNAGEL, Altindische Grammatik. Göttingen 1930, Bd. III, 354). Cf. also the explanation of Prakṛti by Madhva (BSūBh p. 51,21f.): *prakarṣeṇa karotīti prakṛtir iti yogāc*. In support of this interpretation Madhva quotes also from unknown sources. The prefix *pra-* (= excessively) in the sense of native

the authorship of Madhva. However, we have another much more weighty argument in this regard. In order to explain it accurately it is advisable to go into details. The starting point of our argumentation are the preliminary remarks of Madhva introducing the quotation of Paramaśruti. Madhva puts forward in these introductory remarks almost in the same wording the teaching of the Paramaśruti, which follows closely the interpretation of MāṇU (= *śruti*).[198] It deals with MāṇU I 17-18:

> *prapañco yadi vidyeta nivarteta na saṃśayaḥ I*
> *māyāmātram idaṃ dvaitam advaitaṃ paramārthataḥ II* 17
> *vikalpo vinivarteta kalpito yadi kenacit I*
> *upadeśād ayaṃ vādo jñāte dvaitaṃ na vidyate II* 18

„If the universe were to exist, it would undoubtedly disappear. This duality/plurality is only an illusion. In fact, there exists [only] a non-duality [= the absolute]. The manifold [world] would disappear, if someone would create it as a phantom existence. This doctrine [is communicated] through the instruction. If [the non-duality] is known, then there is no duality/plurality."

The thesis of monism expressed in these verses[199] is twisted by Madhva so that it means just the opposite.[200] Firstly, he treats

---

lexicographers (*utkarṣa*) is also referred to elsewhere, e.g. Śrīdhara (Nyāyakandalī. Varanasi 1963: 3,5-6): *praṇamyeti I prakarṣavācinā praśabdena bhaktiśraddhātiśayapūrvakaṃ namaskāram ācaṣṭe.*

198 Madhva considers MāṇU together with the first part of Gauḍapādīyakārikās (= Āgamaprakaraṇa) as an unified *śruti* text (ChUBh p. 393,2-4). His MāṇUBh is limited only to this part. The other three Adhikaraṇas are ascribed by him to Gauḍapāda. Śaṅkara und Sureśvara, on the contrary, are of the opinion that both these texts in their full extent are one unified work. However, in opposition to Śaṅkara, Sureśvara regards them as Śruti, cf. T. VETTER, Studien zur Lehre und Entwicklung Śaṅkaras. [Publications of the De Nobili Research Library 6]. Wien 1979: 27; 35f.

199 Cf. T. VETTER, Die Gauḍapādīya-Kārikās: Zur Entstehung und zur Bedeutung von (A)dvaita, WZKS 22 (1978), p. 95-131.

200 VTN p. 34,12- 35,5.

vidyeta as equivalent to *bhaveta/utpadyeta*: Were the duality come into existence, it would undoubtedly disappear. But it cannot come into existence, for the duality/ universe is without beginning (*anādir evāyam*). Secondly, Madhva identifies *māyā* with the intelligence/consciousness of Viṣṇu (*māyeti bhagavat-prajñā*). For this reason, the duality with the eminent five-fold difference (*prakṛṣṭaḥ pañcavidho bhedaḥ prapañca*) is absolutely real (*na cāvidyamāno 'yam*), and in consequence it cannot be a product of illusion (*na dvaitaṃ bhrāntikalpitam*), for the duality/ universe exists in the intelligence of Viṣṇu and is protected by him (*parameśvareṇa jñātatvād rakṣitatvāc ca*). And Madhva excludes the possibility that Viṣṇu is subject to illusion or error (*na hīśvarasya bhrāntiḥ*).[201] This would have been the case, had the

---

[201] Madhva takes up this matter again in BĀUBh (p. 334,12-21) quoting from the unknown sources (*iti ca*) : *yat kiṃcid vastu bhagavatā na dṛṣṭaṃ nāsty eva / vidyamānaṃ sarvaṃ paśyaty eva / na hi dvitīyo draṣṭā yo vibhaktvena jagat paśyati / tadvirodhena paśyaty abhrāntaḥ / taddṛṣṭād anyad vā / nānyo 'to 'si draṣṭetyādiśruteḥ* / = BĀU II 7,23

> *yat tad dṛṣṭaṃ bhagavatā tad evāsti na cāparam /*
> *na hy anyo vidyate draṣṭā yaḥ paśyet tadadarśitam //*
> *brahmādir api yo draṣṭā paśyet tasya prasādataḥ /*
> *tadadṛṣṭaṃ kutaḥ paśyed ataḥ ko vā virodhataḥ //*
> iti ca.

yad avatārādikaṃ dvaitatvena na paśyati na tu tato dvitīyam / nityajñānatvād bhramābhāvāt / yad vibhaktatvena viṣṇuḥ paśyati tat tato 'nyad asti ceti ca / yasmād viṣṇur viśvaṃ vibhaktatvenaiva paśyati tasmāt tadanyad asty eva / na ca jagadabhāvo 'rocyate / anyad vibhaktam iti viśeṣeṇavaiyarthyāt / na ca bhrāntikalpitaṃ jagad ity atra kiṃcin mānam.

In TU (III p. 617,1+623,18-19) he ascribes this view to BrāṇP:

> *na ca māyāvinā māyā dṛśyate viśvam īśvaraḥ /*
> *sadā paśyati tenedaṃ na māyety avadhāryatām //*
> *aparokṣadṛśo mithyādarśanaṃ na kvacid bhavet /*
> *sarvāparokṣavid viṣṇur viśvadṛk tan na tan mṛṣā //*
> iti brahmāṇḍe.

(not located; in VTN divided in two different *iti ca*-citations!). In TU III (p. 266,8f. and VTN (p. 36, 19 - 37, 3), on the contrary, this opinion (in VTN

universe been essentially an illusion. In support of this elaboration he adduces again a *śloka* from MāṇU (I 10)[202]: Viṣṇu is immutable, the all-pervading, non-dual among all entities, powerful, Lord of all things (*advaitaḥ sarvabhāvānām ity tasya vyapadeśaḥ*). In this way, he applies *advaitam* in (I 17d) to Viṣṇu (*paramārthāpekṣayādvaitatvam | sarvasmād uttamo 'rthaḥ sa eka evety arthaḥ | anyathā advaitaḥ sarvabhāvānām iti vyartham syāt*). Madhva summarizes the results of his interpretation in the following sentence: *ataḥ prapañcasyānādisatyatvaparam idaṃ vākyam*.

It is amazing, that Madhva immediately after this explanation brings in another conclusion, which was made possible only due to an unauthorized alteration of the original text.[203] Madhva replaces in (I 18d) *jñāte* by *ajñāte* :

> *ataḥ – upadeśād ayaṃ vādo 'jñāte dvaitaṃ na vidyate - ity āha | ajñāta eva dvaitaṃ na vidyate | ajñāninām pakṣa eva dvaitaṃ na vidyata ity arthaḥ.*

„Therefore, the MāṇU says: 'This doctrine is [communicated] through the instruction. If the [non-duality = the absolute] is not known, then [a wrong view arises that] the duality/plurality does not exist'. That means: 'Only the ignorant people are of the opinion, that the duality does not exist'."[204]

---

together with the doctrine of error) is assigned to Vyāsasmṛti and BrahVP respectively.

202 GK I 10:

> *nivṛtteḥ sarvaduḥkhānām īśānaḥ prabhur avyayaḥ |*
> *advaitaḥ sarvabhāvānāṃ devas turyo vibhuḥ smṛtaḥ ||*

203 Other authors, too, make use of such kind of a tricky change in the text-reading in order to come to a new interpretation, which is contrary to the original meaning, *e. g.* Śaṅkara (also in his MāṇUBh), cf. W. SLAJE, BĀU 4.3.14 (M 16) und die Entwicklung des subjektiven Illusionismus im älteren Vedānta (Studien zur Indologie und Iranistik 18 [1993] p. 238ff.)

204 One is utterly puzzled to see that Madhva interprets this very *śloka* in his MāṇUBh without changing the text-reading *jñāte* (p. 518,9f.). And this

Considering the results of our investigation, it is clear that Madhva with the help of a text-manipulation declares that the original monistic teaching of MāṇU is a view of the ignorant people, whereas his own interpretation is á common property of the wise people. It is also manifest that the doctrine of five-fold difference (*pañcabheda*), which is intimately connected with the afore-said text-manipulation, is in fact a creation of Madhva, although he introduces it as the teaching of MāṇU. As additional

---

makes the new interpretation above very strange. Similar contradiction can be seen also at his explanation of *tat tvam asi* (cf. above n 185). In MāṇUBh (p. 518,9f.) Madhva differentiates between the right and wrong knowledge of the duality. Both arise on account of Viṣṇu's desire. It is interesting, that Madhva does not identify *māyā*, in the original text of MāṇU, with *bhagavatprajñā*, as he does in VTN, but with *bhagavadicchā* : *dvaitaṃ dvidhā jñātam anyathā jñātam ajñaiḥ / paramārthataḥ parameśvarāt / tasyaiva māyāmātraṃ tadicchayā nirmitam / tadanyathājñānaṃ tasmāt tadicchayaiva nivartate.* Elsewhere in VTN (p. 30,1-5) Madhva quotes from an anonymous text (*iti ca*), which combines both these identifications. In BhāgTN (p. 47,3f.; 86,3; 125,3f.; 652,5f.), on the contrary, *māyā* is identified with Viṣṇuśakti basing on the authority of the unknown sources, as Nāmamahodadhi, Tantranirukta and Māyāvaibhava. In support of *māyā* as *bhagavadicchā* again an unknown passage is quoted (MāṇUBh p. 518,11-14):

> *pareṇa brahmaṇā yat tu dvidhā na jñātam añjasā /*
> *tad advaitaṃ paraṃ brahma tad eva jñātam anyathā //*
> *jīvena dvaitam uddiṣṭaṃ mithyājñānaṃ tad eva ca /*
> *paramārthāt parād viṣṇor jātam icchāvaśād anu //*
> *māyetīcchā samuddiṣṭā māyāmātraṃ tadudbhavam /*
> *uttamatvāt paramārtho 'sau bhagavān viṣṇur avyayaḥ //*
> iti ca.

In equidistance to it, Madhva supports also the view (*ibid.* p. 518,15f.), basing on an unknown source, that some people correct their wrong opinion with the help of the instruction of a teacher (*guruvākyāt*): . . . *kenacid ajñānādinā kāraṇena kalpito 'py upadeśān nivartate / ayaṃ satāṃ vādaḥ / jñāte sati brahmaṇi dvaitam anyathājñānaṃ nivartata iti –*

> *vikalpo dehabandhādiḥ kenacit kāraṇena tu /*
> *kalpito 'pi nivarteta guruvākyād asaṃśayam //*
> *eṣa eva satāṃ vādo jñāte brahmaṇi tattvataḥ /*
> *nivartate 'nyathājñānaṃ tata anandam ity asau //*
> iti ca.

corroboration of this teaching, he quotes from the Paramaśruti (unknown source) and Maitraśākhā (= Maitrāyaṇyupaniṣad VII 8-9). And it is significant that Madhva again adduces a citation from an unknown source side by side with a classical text, which has been handed down. As we have observed in many places, here also Madhva pursues the goal, namely to raise his own unknown sources in rank category of the classical texts accepted by all *śiṣṭāḥ*. The contrast between both these citations is also clear. While the Maitrāyaṇyupaniṣad speaks in general terms that one should avoid dealings with people who are unable to tell the difference between true and wrong knowledge of Veda and try to trouble the true followers of Veda through their deceitful argumentation.[205] The Paramaśruti, on the contrary, puts forward almost *verbatim* the teaching of Madhva, which he elaborated in the preliminary remarks and that is based on the text-manipulation of MāṇU.

The intimate link between the quotation from MāṇU (I 17-18) and Madhva's own teaching based on it, on the one hand, and the Paramaśruti, on the other, is indicated also in Anuv, although in an abridged form. For instance, the passage from the Paramaśruti is quoted here merely as *śruti* and not in full lenght (two *śloka*s [3,4cd,5ab] are missing). The fact that two principal statements of this *śruti*, namely that the universe is known and protected by Viṣṇu and that Viṣṇu is the Supreme, appears outside of the quotation of Paramaśruti, strengthens again my thesis that Madhva himself is the author of this unknown source.[206]

---

205 VTN p. 35,11-14: (= MaiU VII 8-9) *maitraśākhāyāṃ ca – atha jñānopasargā ity uktvātha ye cānye mithyātarkair dṛṣṭāntaiḥ kuhakendrajālair* (= text: *vṛthātarkadṛṣṭāntakuhakendrajālair*) *vaidikeṣu paristhātum icchanti taiḥ saha na saṃvaset prākāśyā hy ete* (= *prakāśabhūtā vai te*) *taskarā asvargyā ity hy āha* (= *ity evam āha*) / *nairātmyavādakuhakair mithyādṛṣṭāntahetubhiḥ* / *bhrāmyaṃl loko na jānāti vedavidyāntaraṃ tu yad iti* /

206 Cf. Anuv p. 56, 20-28 :

Another instance of this teaching of *pañcabheda*, is found in the ChUBh, which will be discussed below for the purpose of comparison with Paramaśruti. Here also the introductory remarks of Madhva serve as frame for a quotation of an unknown source, in this case, Brahmatarka. It is noteworthy, that this introduction deals with a detailed interpretation of the two *śloka*s of MāṇU (I 17-18), which are called *śruti*. The interpretation is interrupted by the inclusion of a citation from Brahmatarka. For our present investigation, above all, the preliminary remarks of Madhva together with the passage of Brahmatarka, are of special interest, since a parallelism with the quotation of Paramaśruti becomes visible here. The similarities between both these passages are manifest with only difference that Madhva replaces Paramaśruti with Brahmatarka, which – as we already have seen – is also a creation of Madhva. The wording of the passage in consideration without the initial part (MāṇU I 17-18) is as follows:

> *prapañco bhedo yadi vidyeta bhavetotpadyeta tarhi nivarteta / ato na jīveśvarādibheda utpadyate / kiṃtu nitya eva / ato māyayā bhagavajjñānena mātaṃ rataṃ ca mātram /*

---

prapañco yadi vidyeta nivarteta na saṃśayaḥ /
māyāmātram idaṃ dvaitam advaitaṃ paramārthataḥ //
vikalpo vinivarteta kalpito yadi kenacit /
upadeśād ayaṃ vādo 'jñāte dvaitaṃ na vidyeta //
ity atra yadiśabdau ca nivarteteti ca dvayam /

[cf. ChUBh p. 393,20f.; VTN p. 35,2f.]

viśvasya satyatām āhur vidyetotpattim eva ca //
vidotpattav iti hy asmād dhātor utpattir eva hi /
nivṛttivyāptiyuk prāyaḥ prapañco bhedapañcakaḥ //
jīveśvarabhidā caiva jaḍeśvarabhidā tathā /
jīvabhedo mithaś caiva jaḍajīvabhidā tathā //
mithaś ca jaḍabhedo yaḥ prapañco bhedapañcakaḥ /
so 'yaṃ satyo hy anādiś ca sādiś cen nāśam āpnuyāt //
dvaitaṃ na vidyata iti tasmād ajñāninām matam /
iti śruter mitaṃ trātaṃ māyākhyaharividyayā //
uttamo 'rtho haris tv ekas tadanyan madhyamādhamam //

bhagavāñ jānāti ramate cāsmin bheda iti / tac ca bhagavadrūpam advaitam / paramārtho bhagavān / tad-rūpeṇādvaitam / yad advaitaṃ nāmocyate tat paramārtha-bhagavadapekṣayety arthaḥ / svagatabhedo bhagavati nāstīty uktam / na ca kalpanāmātro bhedaḥ / yadi kenacit kalpito vikalpas tathāpi vinivarteta / tasmād upadeśād ayam eva vādaḥ / kenāpi tatprasādaṃ vināvijñātatvād ajñāto bhagavāṃs tadgato bhedo na vidyata iti / jīveśvaragato jīveṣv atha jīvajaḍātmanoḥ /

jaḍeśayor jaḍeṣv evaṃ pañcabhedaḥ prapañcakaḥ //
prakṛṣṭamokṣahetutvāt tajjñāne preti kathyate /
prakṛṣṭapañcakatvād vā prapañco 'yaṃ prakīrtitaḥ //
yady ayaṃ sādir eva syān nivarteta kadācana /
na nivartate yatas tena nāyaṃ sādir bhavet kvacit //
māyeti viṣṇuvijñānaṃ tanmitatvāc ca na kvacit /
bhrāntatvam asya yad viṣṇor naiva bhrāntiḥ kadācana //
ramate cātra yad viṣṇur na hi bhrāntau ramed dhariḥ /
paramārthe harau naiva bhedo 'sti jaḍajīvavat //
yady ayaṃ kalpito bhedaḥ kasmān naiva nivartate /
tasmād bhūtabhaviṣyākhyabhavadākhyaparābhidhāḥ //
tadanye caika evāsminn oṃkārākhye janārdane /
ajñātanāmake tasmin na bhedo 'sti kathañcana //
iti brahmatarke.

„If the universe with [five-fold] difference existed, [i. e.] if it was brought into existence or if it was produced, then it would disappear. Therefore, [the universe with five-fold difference], as the difference between the individual soul and Īśvara etc. is not produced, but it is always eternal. For this reason, it is fully cognized and delighted in by the Lord through [his] *māyā* [, that means,] through his consciousness. The Lord cognizes it and has great pleasure in this [five-fold] difference. Besides, the Lord's form is non-dual. The Lord is absolutely real [and] in this form one without second. That non-dual form, which is verily taught in (MāṇU I 17d), results from the connection with the Lord, who is absolutely real. This is the meaning. It has been already said that there is no internal division (= difference) in the Lord. And the [five-fold] difference is not a product of an imagination/ illusion. If someone has imagined this difference, then it would disappear. Therefore, this view [is communicated] only through the instruction. If the Lord is not known, then no one cognises the [five-fold] difference in the universe, since no one can be aware of [this difference] without his grace.[207] [In support of this interpretation] the Brahmatarka says: 'The five-fold difference [, namely] between the individual souls and Īśvara, between the individual souls themselves, between the individual souls and insentient objects, between the insentient objects and Īśvara [and finally] also between the insentient objects themselves, is identical with the universe. This [five-fold difference] is called *prapañca* either because the prefix *pra-* refers [to the difference], since it denotes the excellence of five-fold [difference], or because [the prefix] refers to its knowledge, since it is an excellent means of the release. If it had a beginning, it would certainly disappear at some time. Because it does not disappear, [it implies] therefore, that it never had any beginning. *Māyā* [means] the intelligence/consciousness of Viṣṇu. Since the universe is known by him, it can never be an illusion, for no illusion can ever exist in the Lord and because he has great pleasure in it. Viṣṇu would never take delight in [mere] illusion. In the absolute real Hari there is never an [internal] division/difference, as in the case of insentient objects and individual souls. If the difference is [merely] an imagination, why does it not disappear completely [like a dream]? Therefore, [all the time-divisions] called past, future, present [and] beyond, they exist in one and the same Janārdana, called Oṃkāra. In the [Lord], called 'unknown' there is not any [internal] division/difference'."[208]

---

[207] Cf. VTN p. 35,5: *ajñāta eva dvaitaṃ na vidyata / ajñāninām pakṣa eva dvaitam na vidyata ity arthaḥ*; above n 204.

[208] ChUBh p. 393,5-18.

Comparing both these quotations, namely from the Paramaśruti and Brahmatarka as well as the preliminary remarks on them by Madhva, we can ascertain that their contents are almost identical, with slight redactional changes. Both quotations follow the interpretation of MāṇU I 17-18 by Madhva and are intimately connected with the contents of the preliminary remarks. Their aim is to prove the reality and the beginninglessness of the universe (*prapañcasyānādisatyatva*). Under this generic term, a popular etymology of *prapañca* is attempted, as five-fold excellent difference. And as such, it cannot be a product of an illusion, which in this case would disappear like dream. Similarly, because Viṣṇu cognizes it and has great pleasure in it, the universe cannot be a mere illusion. Viṣṇu has never delight in mere illusion. The universe is, therefore, beginningless and eternal (*anādi/nitya*).[209] It is remarkable that Madhva attributes the above mentioned arguments for the reality and beginninglessness of the universe either to the unknown sources or to the known sources, where the quotations cannot be located.[210]

---

[209] The notion of the beginninglessness or eternal universe has been expounded by Madhva in a fictitious quotation ascribed to VarP (cf. below n 278). This notion is not identical with the similar conception of the Jainas and the Mīmāṃsakas, insofar as they maintain that the *hic et nunc* existing universe is factually eternal (*ārhatānāṃ mīmāṃsakānāṃ ca naivāsti vināśa eṣām* [= *div, pṛthivī, ākāśam*], cf. Bhartṛhari, Mahābhāṣyadīpikā, crit. ed. K. V. ABHYANKAR and V.P. LIMAYE. Poona 1970: 22,23; Helārāja, Prakīrṇaprakāśa on Vākyapadīya (ed. IYER 1963: 49,1-4): *tathā hi na kadācid anīdṛśaṃ jagad iti vadantaḥ . . .*; (*ibid.* p. 51,21f.): *na kadācid anīdṛśaṃ jagad iti jaiminīyaḥ*; R. MESQUITA, Das Problem der Gotteserkenntnis bei Yāmunamuni, Diss. Wien 1971:63ff.). For Madhva, on the contrary, the universe is eternal and imperishable only as a whole. It is subject to a permanent change (*nityam eva pravāhata* / *pravāhaikaprakāra*) between creation and destruction, followed by a longer pause. This whole process is completely dependent on the wish of Viṣṇu (*anādyanantakālīnaṃ sasarjātmecchayā prabhuḥ*). Madhva describes the universe, therefore, as *nityānitya* (cf. below n 250). For a detailed elaboration of this notion cf. R. MESQUITA 2000: St. n 598ff.

[210] Cf. above n 201 and 204. The argument of the protection by Viṣṇu is also recorded in the Viśiṣṭādvaita, cf. ĀP (p. 114,7-8): *sa eva bhagavān līlāviracitacaturbhedaḥ sakalam api jagat saṃrakṣati*; MESQUITA 1990: 211f.

Māyā is identified according to the teaching of *śruti* with *bhagavatprajñā/jñāna*. It is also noteworthy, that Paramaśruti and Brahmatarka base their argumentation on the textual manipulation of MāṇU (I 18d) as *ajñāte* instead of *jñāte* and emphasize the essential opposition between *prapañca* and Viṣṇu: The universe is five-fold, while Viṣṇu is non-dual (*advaita*), *i. e.* there is no other being which is equal or superior to him (*sarvabhāvānāṃ madhye tasyaikasyādvaitatvam ity ukte samādhikarāhityam evoktaṃ syāt / anyeṣāṃ sarvabhāvānāṃ ca samādhikabhāvaḥ*). Besides, his nature is without internal division/difference.[211] In case, one does not cognize Viṣṇu in this opposition, then he is not able to grasp the duality/plurality (*ajñāte dvaita na vidyate*).[212] In the Brahmatarka the soteriological aspect of the etymology of *prapañca* is put forward, for *prapañca* does not only mean the excellent five-fold difference, but also the excellent means of the deliverance (*prakṛṣṭamokṣahetu*), for the knowledge of the five-fold difference is an essential precondition for Mokṣa. And Madhva makes a very important addition at the end of his preliminary remarks to Brahmatarka that the five-fold difference cannot be grasped without the grace of Viṣṇu (*tatprasādaṃ vināvijñātatvād*).[213] With this statement Madhva repeats his expression of censure against Advaitins, which he reiterates in his different works, that the Māyāvādins are excluded from the divine grace, since they are unable or unwilling to accept the five-fold difference. For this reason, he calls them *mahāsurendrāḥ*.[214]

---

211 Cf. ChUBh p. 432,11-12:

> *ekam evādvitīyaṃ tat samādhikavivarjanāt /*
> *svagatānāṃ ca bhedānāṃ abhāvād brahma śāśvatam //*
> iti pravṛtte.

below n 228f.; see also BĀUBh p. 264,18-19.

212 Cf. above n 204.

213 Cf. also AiUBh 243,1-2, above n 94 [B]): *yo veda vedavit sa syāt tattvavit tatprasādataḥ*.

214 This rebuke is also recorded in Sāyana Mādhava's SDS (p. 262,13-18): *evaṃ ca parameśvarābhedatṛṣṇayā viṣṇor guṇotkarṣasya mṛgatṛṣṇikāsamatvābhidhānam vipulakadalīphalalipsayā jihvāc chedanam anuharati / etādṛśa-*

In the Paramaśruti the soteriological aspect remains rather in the background, since it speaks in this connection only about the view of wise (*matam hi jñāninām*). There are also other minor differences between these sources. While in the Paramaśruti Viṣṇu cognizes and protects the universe, in the Brahmatarka he cognises and has great pleasure in it (*ramate*). Besides, the motive of illusion and the etymological definition of *prapañca*, clearly formulated in the Brahmatarka, are present in the other source by the way of suggestion only. From all these observations together, connected with the fact that these sources put forward a peculiar doctrine of Madhva and that the Brahmatarka – as proved above – is a literary creation of Madhva, we can surely conclude that Madhva himself is behind the Paramaśruti, for text and context in both sources are identical.

On the background of this comparison we can declare that the slight variations in the contents and in the literary form of both sources are intended by Madhva. He uses this pattern very often to introduce his different unknown sources substantiating one and the same peculiar doctrine. Its purpose is to give the impression that these sources go back to different traditions and can by no means be a creation of the one and same person. This is clearly attested by other three quotations on the very same subject, which Madhva adduces in GīT and MBhTN. The first citation is inserted by Madhva at the end of series of passages in connection with the opinion that the individual soul does not loose its individuality in the state of liberation (*na ca jīveśvaraikyaṃ muktāv api*)[215]:

---

viṣṇuvidveṣaṇād andhatamasapraveśaprasaṅgāt | tad etat pratipāditaṃ madhyamandireṇa mahābhāratatātparyanirṇaye (I 109) –

> *anādidveṣiṇo daityā viṣṇau dveṣo vivardhitaḥ |*
> *tamasy andhe pātayati daityān ante viniścayāt ||*

Cf. MBhTN XXXII 160cd; above n 107f.

[215] GīT p. 14,8f.

jīveśvarabhidā caiva jaḍeśvarabhidā tathā /
jīvabhedo mithaś caiva jaḍajīvabhidā tathā //
jaḍabhedo mithaś ceti prapañco bhedapañcakaḥ /
sa nitya eva notpādya utpādyaś cen naśed api //
tasmād anādimān eva prakṛṣṭo bhedapañcakaḥ /
viṣṇoḥ prajñāmitaṃ yasmād dvaitaṃ na bhrāntikalpitam //
advaitaḥ paramārtho 'sau bhagavān viṣṇur avyayaḥ /
paramatvaṃ svatantratvaṃ sarvaśaktitvam eva ca //
sarvajñatvaṃ parānandaḥ sarvasya tadadhīnatā /
ityādayo guṇā viṣṇor naivānyasya kathañcana //
abhāvaḥ paramadvaite santy eva hy aparāṇi tu /
vikalpo vinivarteta kalpito yadi kenacit //
advaitaṃ jñāninām pakṣe na tasmād vidyate kvacit /
ityādiśrutibhyo 'rthāntarasyaivāvagatatvāt /[216]

This quotation, too, follows closely the MāṇU (I 17-18) as well as the similar ideas in the Brahmatarka and the Paramaśruti. But on one important point it differs from both other sources, when it emphasizes the transcendence of Viṣṇu with the help of several attributes, pointing out at the same time that the transcendence of Viṣṇu does not abolish the reality of the universe (*naivānyasya kathañcana abhāvaḥ*). In its last remark that non-duality can never be the view of wise men, this source refers to the text manipulation by Madhva (MāṇU I 18d): *ajñāte na dvaitam vidyate.* Elsewhere, Madhva comments on the same verse without, however, making any change in the text and giving another interpretation, which is not in conformity with the afore-said explanation. This deviating interpretation is also supported by unknown sources.[217]

Two other citations in this regard appearing in the MBhTN show another textual structure, not only because they are part of

[216] GīT p. 15,31 + 16,10.

[217] Cf. above n 204.

another longer quoted passage, but also because they do not refer to MāṇU (I 17-18) at all. The first part is ascribed to Veda in a general way (*vedavākya*)[218] and runs as follows:

satyā viṣṇor guṇāḥ sarve satyā jīveśayor bhidā /
satyo mitho jīvabhedaḥ satyaṃ ca jagad īdṛśam //
asatyaḥ svagato bhedo viṣṇor nānyad asatyakam /
jagatpravāhaḥ satyo 'yaṃ pañcabhedasamanvitaḥ //
jīveśayor bhidā caiva jīvabhedaḥ parasparaṃ /
jaḍeśayor jaḍānaṃ ca jaḍajīvabhidā tathā //
pañcabhedā ime nityāḥ sarvāvasthāsu sarvaśaḥ / [219]

A mere rough glance at this passage reveals that it is in clear agreement with all the former quotations on the subject, since it teaches first, the reality of the universe and secondly, the five-fold difference in the universe, in absolute opposition to the non-duality of Viṣṇu.[220] Both the following quotations are slightly different from the fictitious Bhaviṣyatparvan due to their

---

[218] Cf. MBhTN I 75a.

[219] MBhTN I 68-71ab. The immediate context, where these *śloka*s are embedded, consists of several quotations which has been handed down by the tradition (Ṛg VII 40,5; II 33,11ab; X 125,5cd; MahaU I 1; CaturvedaU I; MuU III 1,3; TaiU II 1; Ṛg II 15,1ab; IV 17,5cd; X 55,5cd; VII 3,4cd) and which are cited as evidence for the absolute sovereignty of Viṣṇu (MBhTN I 60cd- 67): *vedeṣu ca paro viṣṇuḥ sarvasmād ucyate sadā* . . . The verses on *pañcabheda* are attached to them, followed by another four *śloka*s in regard to the gradation among gods and as such also a proof for the sovereignty of Viṣṇu (*ibid.* I 71cd-74): *tato 'nantaguṇo viṣṇur na kaścit tatsamaḥ sadā.* It is interesting that Madhva attributes all these eight *śloka*s, referring to his peculiar teaching, to Veda (*ibid.* I 75ab: *ityādi vedavākyaṃ viṣṇor utkarṣam eva vakty uccaiḥ*). Immediately after he adduces again real citations on the same subject (*ibid.* I 75cd-77: *tātparyaṃ mahad atrety uktam . . . svayaṃ tena* . . . (Gī XV 19; BSū III 3,59; KathU II 23). We can also make here the same observation as above (cf. n 151f.), that Madhva puts side by side the well known classical sources with the absolutely unknown sources for the purpose of raising the latter to the rank category of the former.

[220] Cf. below n 153.

clear association with the notion of release, like the citation from Brahmatarka:

> *pañcabhedāṃś ca vijñāya viṣṇoḥ svābhedam eva ca |*
> *nirdoṣatvaṃ guṇodrekaṃ jñātvā muktir na cānyathā ||*[221]
> *jīveśvarabhidā caiva jīvabhedaḥ parasparam |*
> *jaḍeśvarabhidā caiva jaḍabhedas tathaiva ca ||*
> *jaḍajīvabhidā caiva satyo 'yaṃ bhedapañcakaḥ |*
> *na kadācin nivartyo 'yaṃ muktau saṃsāra eva vā ||*
> *ya etad anyathā brūyus te hi yānty adharaṃ tamaḥ |*
> iti bhaviṣyatparvaṇi.[222]

Since the fact that all the quotations analysed above have the very same literary style, we can conclude that not only Bhaviṣyatparvan and Brahmatarka, as already shown, are literary creations of Madhva, but also all other citations teaching the five-fold difference in the universe, are to be considered as Madhva's *ipsissima vox*!

We come to the same conclusion after analysing the passages ascribed to Paiṅgiśruti and Bhāllaveyaśruti[223] or to Mahopaniṣad which also are in close connection with the doctrine of five-fold difference and the absolute non-duality of Viṣṇu (*viṣṇoḥ svābheda*).

Strange is also the way how, for instance, the Paiṅgiśruti is quoted by Madhva, once in short form in BSūBh, once again in enlarged form and under the title of Śruti in VTN or some other time in the form of quotation in another inserted into completely different passage, namely in the Bhāllaveya śruti[224]:

---

221 *Ibid.* I 81; cf. below n 346f.

222 AiUBh p. 184,33-185,2.

223 These titles have nothing to do with the *śruti* texts transmitted under similar names, as *e. g.* Śaṅkara mentions in his commentary on BSū (I 2,12; I 3, 7; III 3,26) like Paiṅgirahasyabrāhmaṇa or Paiṅgyupaniṣad or Bhallavin, since their subject are not the peculiar teachings of Madhva; cf. n 227.

224 BSūBh p. 28,2-3; VTN p. 31,5-8; BhāgTN. 11,6-9.

satya ātmā satyo jīvaḥ satyaṃ bhidā satyaṃ bhidā satyaṃ bhidā maivāruvaṇyo maivāruvaṇyo maivāruvaṇya iti paiṅgiśruteḥ [225]; *satya ātmā satyo jīvaḥ satyaṃ bhidā satyaṃ bhidā satyaṃ bhidā maivāruvaṇya maivāruvaṇyo maivāruvaṇya ātmā hi svatantraḥ sarvavit sarvaśaktiḥ paramasukhaḥ paramo jīvas tu tadvaśo 'lpajño 'lpaśaktir ārto 'lpakaḥ* ityādiśruti; *satyatvaṃ ca bhedasyoktaṃ* bhāllaveyaśrutau – *sthānur hoccakrāma sa prajāpatim uvāca / ko 'si ke sma kaḥ sa iti / sa hovāca yo 'smi ye stha yaḥ sa iti / atha hainam upākrośat / satyaṃ bhidā satyaṃ bhidā satyaṃ bhideti / maivāruvaṇyo maivāruvaṇyo maivāruvaṇya itīti.*

These quotations deal with the five-fold difference despite some slight deviations. The enlargement in the VTN refers to the absolute transcendence of Viṣṇu, mentioned in the Paramaśruti and the Brahmatarka. The technical word *svatantra* used here points out to the typical teaching of the supremacy of Viṣṇu elaborated by Madhva specially in his short works Tattvasaṅkhyāna and Tattvaviveka:[226]

svatantram asvatantraṃ ca dvividhaṃ tattvam iṣyate /
svatantro bhagavān viṣṇur bhāvo 'bhāvo dvidhetarat //

---

[225] The fact that this passage deals with the teaching of five-fold difference implies that it should be fictitious. It is surely not casual that *satyam* is repeated five times! The only association with a *śruti*, alluded here, consists in the use of a rare subjunctive form (second pers. sing.) *ruvaṇyaḥ* of verbal root *ru*, which appears only once in the Ṛg (VIII 96,12c ; cf. CH. WERBA, Verba Indoarica. Die primären und sekundären Wurzeln der Sanskrit-Sprache, Vienna 1997: 371): *upa bhūṣa jaritar mā ruvaṇyaḥ śrāvaya vācam . . .* Madhva replaces it by *maivāruvaṇyaḥ*!

[226] TV 1:

svatantram asvatantraṃ ca prameyaṃ dvividhaṃ matam /
svatantro bhagavān viṣṇur nirdoṣākhilasadguṇaḥ //

This is a work of Madhva consisting of eleven *ślokas*, which should not be mixed up with the fictitious text of the same name (cf. above n 178-179).

We can surely take these passages as literary compositions of Madhva.[227] This very judgement can be applied also to Mahopaniṣad, which according to Madhva teaches that the nature of Viṣṇu is without any internal division or difference (*viṣṇoḥ svābheda*). As a matter of fact, it is in agreement with a self-statement of Madhva:

abhinno bhagavān svena tadanyena vibhedavān /
nityā dharmās tadīyās tu sarve 'smān naiva bhedinaḥ //

„The Lord is in his nature without divisions [but] he is different from all other [beings]. All his attributes, however, are eternal. By no means, are they distinct from him."[228]

Obviously, this statement is aimed at the Advaitins, whose view of *nirguṇa/nirviśeṣabrahman* Madhva wants to reject in all strictness. This point is elaborated in the Mahopaniṣad and even in more details in Brahmatarka:

guṇakriyādayo viṣṇoḥ svarūpaṃ nānyad iṣyate /
ato mitho 'pi bhedo na teṣāṃ kaścit kadācana //
svarūpe 'pi viśeṣo 'sti svarūpatvavad eva tu /
bhedābhāve 'pi tenaiva vyavahāraś ca vartate //
iti mahopaniṣadi.

It has been said in the Mahopaniṣad: „The nature of Viṣṇu is identical with [his] attributes, actions. It is not regarded as something different. Therefore, there is no mutual difference whatever among them [and] between them and [his nature]. Surely, there is an essential attribute in the nature exactly as [his] nature itself. Though there is no difference [in his nature] the use

---

[227] Under the circumstances Madhva (BSūBh p. 51,18-24) adduces the authority of Bhāllaveyaśruti and of Paiṅgiśruti to prove his view, which is in contradiction to the whole Vedānta-Tradition, that the Brahman is not the material cause of the world, (cf. GHATE 1981: 30; 67ff.) speaks for their ingenuineness.

[228] Anuv p. 77, 29-30.

of conceptual and verbal language [in regard to the difference] is made possible only by virtue of this [essential property].“[229]

On close scrutiny of this passage, it is conspicuous that Madhva bases his doctrine of *abheda* of Viṣṇu's nature on a very important concept, namely on an essential attribute (*viśeṣa*), which Madhva developed in direct opposition to the teaching of Nyāya-Vaiśeṣika. In a passage from Brahmatarka this 'essential attribute' is introduced as a special category, which is identical with the nature of Viṣṇu and which carries itself (= self-subsisting): *viśeṣaḥ svarūpaṃ sa svanirvāhaka eva.*[230] That means: it does not need another attribute in order to come into existence, like *samavāya*: *viśeṣaś ca viśeṣī sa svenaiva samavāyavat / kalpanāgurutādoṣāt padārthāntaratā na hi.* This essential attribute is, therefore, the basis for the use of conceptual and verbal language of difference (*nānāvyavahṛter hetur anantatvaṃ viśeṣataḥ*). As such it is present in all beings without exception (*viśeṣo nāma kathitaḥ so 'sti vastuṣv aśeṣataḥ*),[231] since a being, without this essential attribute cannot be known, nor expressed, nor analysed.[232] For this reason, this attribute is grasped intuitively in all beings (*viśeṣo 'nubhavād eva jñāyate sarvavastuṣu / na cāviśeṣitaṃ kiṃcid vācyaṃ lakṣyaṃ tathā mitam*).[233] The passage attributed to Mahopaniṣad presupposes unequivocally this concept of *viśeṣa*. For the infinite number of different attributes etc. of Viṣṇu are, on the one hand, absolutely identical with his nature, since they are inseparable from it, and on the other hand, there is no internal division or difference among them (*svagatabhedavi-*

---

[229] VTN p. 43,3-5. There is a *varia lectio* replacing Mahopaniṣad by Paramopaniṣad; cf. SIAUVE 1968: 29n 4.

[230] Cf. GīT p. 104,28; VTN p. 43,5-9; below n 242 and Anuv. p. 9,21.

[231] Cf Anuv p. 77,17f.; 9,22.

[232] Cf. GīT p. 105,22-23; below n 243; Rāmānuja, Vedārthasaṅgraha (ed. J.A.B VAN BUITENEN. Poona 1956) p. 88,5f.: *ataḥ prāmāṇikānāṃ na kenāpi pramāṇena nirviśeṣavastusiddhiḥ . . .* ; MESQUITA 1990: 135f.

[233] GīT p. 105,22-23. It is possible that Madhva was influenced in his teaching of *viśeṣa* by the *anekāntavāda* of the Jainas, cf. ZYDENBOS 1991: 261ff. and above n 173.

varjita).[234] This implies that there is no real difference between the attributes of Viṣṇu (*bhedābhāva*),[235] and that there is also no relation of difference *cum* non-difference (*bhedābhedo na tu kvāpi viṣṇor asti kadācana*).[236] On the other side, this presupposes also that the nature of Viṣṇu is not *nirviśeṣa*, but *saviśeṣa.*[237] But the essential attribute (*viśeṣa*) as an ontological principle renders possible the conceptual and verbal language of the difference, *e. g.* that Viṣṇu is Being, Consciousness and pure Happiness.[238]

---

234 Cf. MBhTN I 11d; vgl. ChUBh p. 393,8: *svagatabhedo bhagavati nāsti*; 432,10: *ekam evādvitīyaṃ svagatabhedavarjitaṃ samānavarjitaṃ ca*; above n 211.

235 In clear contradiction to this teaching Madhva maintains that the nature of wordly beings is identical with *bheda* : *svarupaṃ vastuno bhedaḥ*, (Anuv p. 84,18; VTN p. 20,24f.): *bhedas tu svarūpadarśana eva siddhaḥ / prāyaḥ sarvato vilakṣaṇaṃ hi padārthasvarūpaṃ dṛśyate / asya bheda iti tu padārthasya svarūpam itivat / yadi na svarūpaṃ bhedas tadā padārthe dṛṣṭe prāyaḥ sarvato vailakṣaṇyaṃ tasya na jñāyeta / ajñāte ca vailakṣaṇya ātmani ghaṭa ity api saṃśayaḥ syāt* . . . This view stands in complete agreement with his doctrine, exposed above, (n 195f.) that the universe unlike Viṣṇu, whose nature is *abheda*, consists of five-fold difference (*bhedapañcakaḥ*) ; cf. above n 234. For details see MESQUITA 2000: St. n 503ff.

236 Cf. BĀUBh p. 269, 31; KathUBh p. 483,27+484,12; above n 42.

237 Cf. Anuv p. 143, 26-27:

> *ato 'nantaguṇātmaiko bhagavān eka eva tu /*
> *ucyate sarvavedaiś ca te cākhilavilakṣaṇāḥ //*
> *sarve sarvaguṇātmānaḥ sarvakartāra eva ca /*
> *tathāpi saviśeṣāś ca* . . .

238 Cf. ĪśUBh p. 511,14-15:

> *sajjñānānandaśīrṣo 'sau sajjñānānandabāhukaḥ /*
> *sajjñānānandadehaś ca sajjñānānandapādavān //*

A partial quotation attributed to VarP cf. above n 49. Similarly in MBhTN I 11; cf. above n 42. In his fictitious work Bhaviṣyatparvan Madhva declares that those striving for emancipation should meditate on the attributes of Viṣṇu (MBhTN I 92):

> *sarvair guṇair brahmaṇā tu samupāsyo hariḥ sadā /*
> *ānando jñaḥ sad ātmeti hy upāsyo mānuṣair hariḥ //*

Without going into details on Madhva's doctrine of *viśeṣa*,[239] a short note is to be made in connection with the un-

[239] A detailed exposition of this doctrine is not possible at the present stage of research, since the preparatory studies on the matter are lacking. The comments in this respect by B.N.K. SHARMA (Philosophy of Śri Madhvācārya. Delhi 1986: 73-105) and by SIAUVE (1968: 171-188; 249ff.) are not helpful, for they do not take into account all the statements on the matter made by Madhva (cf. below n 243). According to these passages there is a dichotomy in the teaching of *viśeṣa*. While Madhva accepts for the nature of Viṣṇu an *abheda* intimately connected with the essential attribute of *viśeṣa*, which he applies also to Śrī and the liberated individual souls, he interprets the individual souls in the *saṃsāra* and the worldly beings as *bhedābheda*, for they presuppose a real material development consisting in their coming into being and perishing. In order to describe this process Madhva employs dual concepts, which are in use also in Viśiṣṭādvaita (MESQUITA 1990: 221ff.). These concepts explain the dual character of the worldly beings, so far their properties and qualities are intimately connected with the bearer *dharmin*. This view has been exposed by Madhva in Anuv (p. 77,29f.) and in TV (v. 8-11) without quoting from the sources. In BĀUBh (p. 169,24f.), however, he ascribes this opinion to the Brahmatarka:

. . .
abhede 'pi viśeṣeṇa vyavahāraḥ pṛthag bhavet /
viṣṇor jaḍena jīvaiś ca bheda eva śriyā tathā /
viṣṇoḥ kriyāś ca yāḥ kāścid abhedas tair api dhruvaḥ /
kādācitkatvam apy āsāṃ viśeṣeṇaiva yujyate /
evaṃ vimuktajīvānāṃ svarūpaiḥ svaguṇair api /
svakriyābhis tathaivaikyaṃ nityaṃ svāvayavair api /
bhedābhedas tu baddhānāṃ guṇaiḥ svaiḥ karmabhis tathā /
aṃśāṃśinor guṇasyāpi guṇinaḥ karmatadvatoḥ /
kāryopādānayoś caiva vyaktisāmānyayor api /
bhedābhedaḥ samuddiṣṭo vināśo yatra dṛśyate /
ekasmin vidyamāne 'pi tayor ekasya kasyacit /
avinābhāvaniyamo yatrābhedas tu tatra ha /
abhedaś ca svabhinnena bhedābhedas tu tatra ca /
bhedābhedo na tu kvāpi viṣṇor asti kadācana /

Consequently, Madhva denies in a passage attributed also to the Brahmatarka (BhāgTN p. 269,1f.) the dual concepts implying *bhedābheda*-relation, in case of Viṣṇu, Śrī and also in case of the liberated individual souls, for their nature is devoid of internal division or difference (*svagatabhedavarjita*):

avayavyavayavānāṃ ca guṇāṇāṃ guṇinas tathā /
śaktiśaktimatoś caiva kriyāyās tadvatos tathā /

known source Mahopaniṣad. Madhva renders this very same doctrine in several fictitious passages of Brahmatarka.[240] Madhva tries to formulate here more accurately the intimate connection between *svarūpa* and the attributes, comparing this kind of relation with jewel and its shine.[241] It is remarkable, that Madhva appeals to the almight of Viṣṇu in order to prove this doctrine, which according to him is difficult to be reasoned about (*dustarkyabalato hareḥ*). In one quotation attributed to Brahmatarka he puts forward this reasoning in the following way: . . . *ityādiśrutimānāc paramaiśvaryatas tathā | sarvaṃ tu ghaṭate viṣṇau yat kalyāṇaguṇātmakam|* ityādi brahmatarke.[242] For illustration some few passages among many others will be given below:

> . . .
> *svarūpeṇāpi saṃyogaḥ svarūpasyaiva yujyate |*
> *yathā ratnasya saṃyogas tatprakāśena nityadā ||*
> *ratnasya ca prakāśasya na bhedaḥ kaścid iṣyate |*
> *viśeṣo nāma vijñeyo viśeṣād dṛṣṭigocaraḥ ||*
> *viṣṇor eva svarūpāṇāṃ tadguṇānāṃ tathaiva ca |*
> *tasyaiva śirādīnāṃ naiva bhedo 'sti kaścana ||*
> *abhede 'pi viśeṣeṇa vyavahāraḥ pṛthag bhavet |* . . .
> *viśeṣasya viśeṣo 'nyo na caivāsti kathañcana |*
> *svasyāpi tu viśeṣaḥ sa svayam eva bhaviṣyati ||*

> *svarūpāṃśāṃśinoś caiva nityābhedo janārdane |*
> *jīvasvarūpeṣu tathā tathaiva prakṛtāv api |*
> *cidrūpayām* (= śrī) *ato 'naṃśā aguṇā akriyā iti |*
> *hīnā avayavaiś ceti kathyante te hy abhedataḥ |*
> . . .

240 Cf. below n 243; above n 237.

241 This type of comparison has been drawn also by the followers of Viśiṣṭādvaita school, cf. MESQUITA 1990: 221ff. The position of both these schools implies a faint form of Bhedābhedavāda. They reject expressly its original form, cf. also R. MESQUITA, Yāmuna's Vedānta and Pañcarātra: A Review, WZKS 24 (1980) p. 213ff.; cf. above 239.

242 Cf. GīT p. 106, 30-31; below n 243; above n 52.

yathā janer janir nānyā tasyā vastujanir janiḥ I
tathāpi tu janitvāt sā sattvaṃ vastuna ānayet II
evam eva viśeṣo 'sau viśeṣāntaravarjitaḥ I
. . .
iti brahmatarke
abhinnatvam abhedaś ca yathā bhedavivarjitam I
vyavahāryaṃ pṛthak ca syād evaṃ sarve guṇā hareḥ II
abhedābhinnayor bhedo yad ivābhedabhinnayoḥ I
anavasthitir eva syān na viśeṣaṇatāmatiḥ II
mūlasaṃbandham ajñātvā tasmād ekam anantadhā I
vyavahāryaṃ viśeṣeṇa dustarkyabalato hareḥ II
viśeṣo 'pi svarūpaṃ sa svanirvāhakatāsya ca I
iti brahmatarke.[243]

We see here again the same procedure Madhva used to prove the doctrine of five-fold difference in the universe. Quoting from the fictitious Mahopaniṣad and Brahmatarka Madhva justifies his teaching on *abheda* of Viṣṇu's nature, which he himself developed in a very original way and gives the impression, that it is an old teaching supported by Vedānta sources.

The teaching of Sadāgamas and Durāgamas formulated by Madhva in the frame of the fifth Veda (*pañcamaveda*) offers us abundant materials for further important observations. This thought pattern mentioned for the first time in the ChU (VII 1,4), which then had a wide dissemination in the Paurāṇic literature and also in the MBh,[244] adds to the existing four Vedas the fifth Veda, consisting of Purāṇas and Itihāsas: *itihāsapurāṇaḥ pañcamo vedānāṃ vedaḥ*. The special feature in the interpretation of

---

[243] BĀUBh p. 269, 20ff.; GīT p. 104,25 + 106,31; VTN p. 43,5-9; also MāṇUBh p. 515,16-17; GīT p. 104,25 + 106, 31; BhāgTN p. 162,9-10; 510,5-511,2; 649,1-9; Anuv p. 77,13f.; TV v. 8-10; above n 42. For a detailed discussion of these passages see MESQUITA 2000: St. n 180f., 533ff.

[244] Cf. BrāṇP I 2,34,8ff.; VāyP I 60,2ff.; ViṣP III 4; BhāgP I 4,20; PadP I 2,50-51; MBh I 1,204; I 57,73-74; XII 327,18; Arthaśāstra (I 3,1-2): *sāmargyajurvedās trayas trayī I atharvavedetihāsavedau ca vedāḥ*; auch BĀU II 4,10; MaiU VI 32; Śaṅkarabhāṣya on ChU VII 1,2.

Madhva is the fact that Madhva takes the ordinal number 'fifth' not only in the sense adopted in the ChU, namely four Vedas plus its supplements: Purāṇas and Itihāsas, as the fifth Veda,[245] but also, beyond that, he understands the four Vedas, also as a 'collective unit' (= one) complemented by four other texts together, namely Mahābhārata, Mūlarāmāyaṇa (= Itihāsa)[246], Purāṇa and Pañcarātra, so that we have again the ordinal number 'fifth'. For the support of the last alternative Madhva claims the authority of an unknown source, (here in partial citation):

vedād api paraṃ cakre pañcamaṃ vedam uttamam |
bhārataṃ pañcarātraṃ ca mūlarāmāyaṇaṃ tathā ||
purāṇaṃ bhāgavataṃ ceti saṃbhinnaḥ śāstrapuṅgavaḥ |
iti nārāyaṇāṣṭākṣarakalpe. [247]

It is noteworthy, that between the four Vedas as a whole and the fifth Veda there is somehow a relation of discordance. For, the four Vedas are eternal (*nitya*) and authorless (*apauruṣeya*)[248], while the fifth Veda is not everlasting (*anitya*) and has an author (*pauruṣeya*). Madhva attempts to put both these views together in a very inventive form with the help of a disguised quotation, which he attributes to BrāṇP:

nityā vedāḥ samastāś ca śāśvatā viṣṇubuddhigāḥ |
sarge sarge 'munaivaita udgīryante tathaiva ca ||

---

245 Cf. VTN p. 12,3-4. This scheme has been interpreted otherwise, e. g. in the KāvM (p. 2, 24) an opinion of an old teacher of musical sciences has been handed down that the fifth Veda is the Veda of singing: *vedopavedātmā sārvavarṇikaḥ pañcamo geyaveda iti drauhiniḥ*; or the Veda of dramatic art (Nāṭyaśāstra I 15cd): *nāṭyākhyaṃ pañcamaṃ vedaṃ setihāsaṃ karomy aham*.

246 Cf. BĀU II 4,10; MBh XVII 5,30; KāvM (p. 3,11f.): *tatra vedākhyanopanibandhanaprāpyaṃ purāṇaṃ aṣṭādaśadhā . . . purāṇapravibheda evetihāsa ity eke | sa ca dvidhā parakriyāpurākalpābhyam . . . tatra rāmāyaṇaṃ bhārataṃ codaharaṇe.*

247 GīBh p. 2,5f.; cf. below n 271; ChUBh p. 397, 18-19.

248 Cf. VTN p. 12,9-13: . . . *apauruṣeyavākyāṅgīkāre na kiṃcit kalpyam | apauruṣeyatvaṃ ca svata eva siddham | vedakartur aprasiddheḥ | aprasiddhau ca kartus tatkalpane kalpanāgauravam| akalpane cākartṛkatvaṃ siddham eva ||*

tatkramena ca tair varnais taiḥ svarair eva nānyathā |
ataḥ śrutitvam etāsāṃ śrutā eva yato 'khilaiḥ ||
janmāntare śrutās tās tu vāsudevaprasādataḥ |
munīnāṃ pratibhāsyanti bhāgenaiva na sarvaśaḥ ||
yatas tā hariṇā dṛṣṭāḥ śrutā evāparair janaiḥ |
śrutayo dṛṣṭayaś ceti tenocyante purātanaiḥ ||
tadutpattivacaś caiva bhaved vyaktim apekṣya tu |
cetanasya janir yadvad ucyate sarvalaukikaiḥ ||
purāṇāni tadarthāni sarge sarge 'nyathaiva tu |
kriyante 'tas tv anityāni tadarthāḥ pūrvasargavat ||
vedānāṃ sṛṣṭivākyāni bhaveyur vyaktyapekṣayā |
avāntarābhimānānāṃ devānāṃ vā vyapekṣayā ||
nānityatvāt kutas teṣām anityatvaṃ sthirātmanāṃ |
iti brahmāṇḍe.

„It is recorded in the BrāṇP: 'The Vedas are eternal and they are in their entirety always in the mind/consciousness of Viṣṇu. In each creation they are uttered by him alone[249] in the same form [as they exist] and not otherwise, [namely] in the very same order, with the very same letters and with the very same accent. Therefore, they are *śruti* because they are only heard by all. And they were also heard in the previous lives. [In the present life] they manifest themselves to the wise through the grace of Vāsudeva only partially and not in its entirety. Because the Vedas are perceived by Hari and because they are only heard by other people, they are called by the ancient [sage s] 'that which is heard' and 'that which is perceived'. And the references to its origin is to be taken in terms of its manifestation, exactly as all people speak [metaphorically] of the origin of the individual soul [although it is eternal]. But the Purāṇas which correspond in their meaning to the Vedas are brought forth in each creation in a

[249] Elsewhere (cf. n 110) Madhva appears as the exclusive proclaimer of the Vedas!

different form.[250] Therefore, they are not everlasting. Their meaning corresponds [to the Vedas] as in the previous creations. Since the Vedas are eternal, the references to their origin should be interpreted in the sense of manifestation, or in the sense of [bringing forth] the intermediate presiding deities.[251] How can the Vedas with a stable nature not be eternal?"[252]

These clear statements allow us to pursue accurately the train of thoughts of Madhva. In the present context it is specially noteworthy, how Madhva justifies the authority of the fifth Veda. As a matter of fact, he grants it an authority, which is rooted in the Veda (*vedamūlatva*), for the texts belonging to the fifth Veda are in complete agreement with the import of the eternal and authorless Vedas, exactly in the same way as Viṣṇu perceives them from eternity. Another important aspect of argumentation emerges here, since the immediate perception of Viṣṇu is taken here as proof for the real existence of the eternal and authorless Vedas exactly in the same way as elsewhere the direct perception is considered as testimony for the real existence of the universe.[253]

---

[250] Cf. TS p. 60,10-61,1:

> *nityānityavibhāgena dvidhaivācetanaṃ matam /*
> *nityā vedāḥ purāṇādyāḥ kālaḥ prakṛtir eva ca //*
> *nityānityaṃ tridhā proktam anityaṃ dvividhaṃ matam /*

[251] VTN p. 15,11; cf. Śaṅkarabrahmasūtrabhāṣya (Delhi 1980) p. 260,6-7: *svatantrasya kartur asmaraṇādibhiḥ sthite vedasya nityatve devādivyaktiprabhavābhyupagamena tasya virodham āśaṅkhya – ataḥ prabhavād iti* (BSū I 3,28) *parihṛtyedānīṃ tad eva vedanityatvaṃ sthitaṃ draḍhayati*; Śrībhāṣya [Madras 1967] III 66,4-5: *ato vedanityatvavādinā devādīnāṃ vigrahavattvābhyupagame 'pi lokavyavahārasya pravāhānādināśrayaṇīyeti.*

[252] VTN p. 14,7-15,5. Madhva adduces immediately after another unidentified citation from VarP, which is in agreement with a fictitious passage from BrāṇP and therefore should be accounted for Madhva's authorship:

> *vedās te nityavinnatvāc chrutayaś cākhilaiḥ śruteḥ /*
> *āmnāyo 'nanyathāpāṭhād īśabuddhisthitāḥ sadā //*
> iti mahāvarāhe.

[253] Cf. above n 201ff.

It is a specially striking fact, that Madhva differentiates between a Veda, which is only partially perceived by the Ṛṣis (*bhāgenaiva na sarvaśaḥ*) and consequently is incomplete and the entire complete Veda, which is directly perceived by Viṣṇu from the eternity. The fifth Veda is rooted in the Veda perceived by Viṣṇu. The view of an 'incomplete Veda' is intimately connected with the current conception that the *kali* age, the worst of the four yugas, is marked by the decay of the Veda knowledge and moral behaviour. The authority of the fifth Veda is therefore not derived from the fact that is proclaimed by the omniscient Viṣṇu (*āptopadeśa*/*īśvarapraṇītatva*) but alone from the fact that it corresponds with the import of the 'entire Veda'. The omniscience of Viṣṇu functions merely as a guarantor that the fifth Veda renders the unadulterated original Vedas. And it cannot be purely coincidental that whenever Madhva speaks of the texts of the fifth Veda, he uses special expressions like *tadātmaka*, *tadanusara*, *tadanuyāyi*, *tadanukūla* etc., which imply that they are in full agreement with the eternal Vedas.[254] Consequently, this is the basis for the view of Madhva that the fifth Veda is self-evident (*svataḥprāmāṇya*) just as the eternal Veda.[255] The not everlasting

---

[254] Cf. above n 249f.; below n 268f.; 272 and n 326f.

[255] Cf. below n 327; 342. In order to prove the authenticity of the fifth Veda Madhva seems *mutatis mutandis* to make use of a conception, which Yāmunācarya put forward. Yāmunācārya based his proof for the credibility of Pañcarātrasaṃhitās on *īśvarapraṇītatva* as well as on *vedamūlatva* and on *apauruṣeyatva* of the eternal Veda. Like Madhva, he too sticks to the opinion that Viṣṇu perceives directly the Vedas in its entirety from eternity (*bhagavān amoghasahajasaṃvedanasākṣādbhavadakhilavedarāśiḥ*). For the explanation of the defectiveness of the Vedas handed down in the present *kali* age Yāmunācārya utilized, in opposition to Madhva, another thought pattern, developed in the Mīmāṃsā-School, namely that of the lost branches of the Veda (*pralīṇaśākhā*). According to Yāmunācārya, the Pañcarātrasaṃhitās proclaimed by the omniscient Viṣṇu are based in the eternal Veda as perceived by Viṣṇu in its entirety and the omniscience of Viṣṇu is only a guarantee for the complete agreement of the teaching of the Pañcarātrasaṃhitās with the eternal Vedas. It implies that the real basis for the credibility of Pañcarātra is not the omniscience of Viṣṇu but its agreement with the doctrine of the eternal Vedas. This is why Pañcarātra is selfevident (*svataḥprāmāṇya*) as the Veda;

character of the fifth Veda is explained also through the fact that it has a different literary shape in each creation (*sarge sarge anyathaiva tu*). And in the self-statement immediately after the quotation from BrāṇP Madhva adds: *purāṇānām apy anyathāśabdaracanam evānityatvam.*[256] The eternal Vedas, on the contrary, are proclaimed always as they are (*udgīryante tathaiva ca*). The discussion above shows clearly how Madhva used the fictitious frame of BrāṇP to put forward his original ideas on the *pañcamo vedaḥ*.

It is particulary significant for the present context that Madhva on one hand, widens the original frame of the fifth Veda in ChU, for he includes in its list Pañcarātrasaṃhitās, although they neither belong to Itihāsa, nor to Purāṇas.[257] And on the other

---

cf. ĀP p. 102,7ff.; OBERHAMMER 1971: 64ff. ; 99 and OBERHAMMER 1974: 81ff.

256 VTN p. 15,11; cf. also the fictitious quotation in BĀUBh (p. 294,24-27):

sarge sarge tu yo naiva śabdato 'py anyathā bhavet |
śrutyākhyaḥ sa tu vijñeya itihāsādir arthataḥ |
bhagavaddṛṣṭam evānyair brahmādyair dṛśyate yadi |
ṛṣibhedas tu tatra syād vedo nāviṣṇunirgataḥ |
veda ity eva viṣṇūktas tapasā dṛśyate paraiḥ ||
iti ca.

257 Madhva establishes the authenticity of Pañcarātra (cf. BSūBh p. 10,10-12; Anuv p. 88,22f.) exactly as in the Viśiṣṭādvaita (cf. ĀP p. 128,3f.) referring not only to MBh (XII 337, 59; 326,100), where it is declared that Pañcarātra is in complete agreement with the four Vedas, but also to MBh (XII 337,63), where Nārāyaṇa appears as the proclaimer of all Pañcarātrasaṃhitās (*pañcarātrasya kṛtsnasya vaktā nārāyaṇaḥ svayam*); cf. above n 135. In Anuv (p. 88,26-27) Madhva records also an opinion that Veda and Pañcarātra were originally one single text: *pañcarātraṃ ca vedaś ca vidyaikaiva dvidheyate*. In support of this view a longer passage from an unknown source, namely Nārāyaṇasaṃhitā is adduced (MuUBh p. 491,6-21). According to it both these texts were known in the *kṛta* age as original Veda and their division as four Vedas and Pañcarātra took place in the *dvāpara* age:

pañcarātrām ṛgādyāś ca sarvam ekaṃ purābhavat |
mūlaveda iti hy ākhyā kāle kṛtayuge tadā ||

hand, he describes BhāgP, which is for him the Purāṇa *par excellence* (*purāṇaṃ bhagavatparam*)[258] with the term of 'fifth Veda' (*purāṇaṃ bhāgavataṃ caiva pañcamo veda ucyate*).[259] In fact, according to the understanding of Madhva, every member in the list of the above mentioned four texts can be separately called as 'fifth Veda'. For instance MBh: *cakāra pañcamaṃ vedaṃ mahābhāratasañjñitam.*[260]

The name 'Mūlarāmāyaṇa' is uncommon. It seems to be in accordance with the opinion of Madhva that the original size of the epic texts, namely MBh[261] and Rāmāyaṇa got lost in the *kali* age and that it is up to Madhva to restore them on divine mission. The name 'Mūlarāmāyaṇa' refers to the original Rāmāyaṇa-text of Vālmīki, which is identified by him as *rāmasya caritam* or *rāmakathā.*[262] So, it is not a wonder that Madhva in the context

---

cf. also another unknown source called Hayagrīvasaṃhitā (BĀUBh 294,17-19; above n 135). Similar views are referred to also in BrāṇP I 2,34,1ff.; VāyP I 60,2ff.; ViṣṇP III 4,1ff.; PārameśvaraS I 74ff.; ĪśvaraS I 18ff.

258 Cf. KeUBh p. 474,8.; cf. below 260; 266. In (BĀUBh p. 268,13-14) he replaces BhāgP by BrahP:

> *pañcarātraṃ bhārataṃ ca mūlarāmāyaṇaṃ tathā |*
> *itihāsa iti prokto brāhmādyaṃ ca purāṇakam ||*
> iti prakāśikāyām.

Sometimes Madhva introduces BhāgP as *śruti*, cf. Anuv p. 54,15f. (= BhāgP III 26,10f.); *ibid.* 74,21-22 (= BhāgP II 10,12).

259 Cf. ChUBh p. 397,19-20.

260 Cf. GīT p. 1,16-17; GīBh p. 3,3-4 (perhaps following MBh I 57,73-74); MBhTN X 59: *samastaśāstrārthanidarśanātmakaṃ cakre mahābhāratanāmadheyam | vedottamam . . .* ; cf. also KeUBh p. 474,7-9:

> *ṛgyajuḥsāmātharvākhyāḥ pañcarātraṃ ca bhārataṃ |*
> *mūlarāmāyaṇaṃ caiva purāṇaṃ bhagavatparam ||*
> *vedā ity ucyate sadbhiḥ śikṣādyaṃ smṛtayas tathā |*
> *aṅgāni satyaṃ mīmāṃsā tad vidyāyatanaṃ trayam ||*
> iti vidyānirṇaye.

261 Cf. MBhTN II 3cd-8 : *utsannāḥ prāyaśaḥ sarve koṭyaṃśo 'pi na vartate* ...; above n 132.

262 Cf. BĀUBh p. 269,3; MBhTN II 48ab; below n 304; 343.

of the fifth Veda sometimes replaces 'Mūlarāmāyaṇa' by 'Mahārāmāyaṇa'.[263] In his MBhTN, where Madhva appears as Marutsuta to proclaim in divine mission all the classical texts, he refers to the size of the Rāmāyaṇa as one billion *śloka*s.[264] The investigation above surely allows us to draw the conclusion that Mūlarāmāyaṇa was a fixed part of the fifth Veda.

It is now interesting to observe how Madhva unites this interpretation of the fifth Veda with another teaching qualifying the Sadāgamas. For the essential characteristic of all Sadāgamas is that they are proclaimed by the omniscient Viṣṇu or by his *avatāras*, and that Viṣṇu is their main purport (*mahātātparya*). This corresponds to the teaching of the Gī[265] and specially of the BhāgP, which according to Madhva holds a distinct position among the Purāṇas, specially because the author of this text has at the culminating point enhanced the absolute transcendence of Viṣṇu, the Lord of the universe.[266]

---

263 Cf. MBhTN IX 122; X 79; II 8; cf. also the etymological interpretation of the name 'Mahābhārata' (MBh I 1,209ab): *mahattvād bhāravattvāc ca mahābhāratam ucyate* (GīT p. 1,15; GīBh p. 3,10-11; MBhTN II 10ab, below n 292f.).

264 Cf. *Ibid.* IX 119ab; above n 122. Madhva seems to base this information about the size of Rāmāyaṇa on a *śloka* in this text, which, however, is purged in the critical edition (Baroda 1960: I 29* 1 pr.). It runs as follows:

> *caritaṃ raghunāthasya śatakoṭipravistaram |*
> *ekaikam akṣaraṃ puṃsāṃ mahāpātakanāśanam ||*

265 Gī XV 15cd: *vedaiś ca sarvair aham eva vedyo vedāntakṛd vedavid eva cāham*; cf. above n 59.

266 Cf. P. HACKER. Purāṇen und Geschichte des Hinduismus. Methodologische, programmatische und geistesgeschichtliche Bemerkungen, Orientalistische Literaturzeitung 55 (1960), p. 345 (= Kl. Schr. 1978: 3). Most probably the present teaching of Madhva has been formulated under the influence of Harivaṃśa (III 132, 95, [in the crit. ed. has been eliminated], which was known also in the Śaṅkara and Viśiṣṭādvaita-Tradition (cf. above n 59). Madhva not only quotes this *śloka* very often (*e. g.* MuUBh p. 490,17-18; BSūBh p. 7,9-10), but he even makes changes in the transmitted version of the same, in order to fit it into his own teaching: *puṇye bhārate bharatarṣabha* is replaced by *caiva purāṇe bhārate tathā*:

In agreement with this view Madhva declares that the meaning of the Sadāgamas is the absolute sovereignty of Viṣṇu (*viṣṇor ādhikya/sarvottamatva*) and the true doctrine (*satsiddhānta*), since it has been revealed by Viṣṇu himself. Madhva introduces this tenet in his VL[267] by the way of a self-assertion, when he explains the doctrine of Bhakti:

naiṣā tarkeṇāpaneyā matir ity āha hi śrutiḥ /[268]
anyārtha evāgamasya vaktavyaḥ prativādinā //
ṛgyajuḥsāmātharvāḥ sapañcarātraṃ ca bhāratam /
mūlarāmāyaṇaṃ caiva saṃprocyante sadāgamāḥ //
anukūlā ya eteṣāṃ te ca proktāḥ sadāgamāḥ /
anye durāgamā nāma tair na sādhyaṃ hi sādhyate //

Although the Purāṇas are not mentioned in this list by name, still, the expression *anukūlā ya eteṣām* should include them as well as other texts, like Madhva's own original works, for they also fulfill the pre-condition of Sadāgamas in delivering the true doctrine (*satsiddhānta*). In this way, the original frame of the 'fifth Veda' with the addition of four other texts, referred to

---

vede rāmāyaṇe caiva purāṇe bhārate tathā /
ādāv ante ca madhye ca viṣṇuḥ sarvatra gīyate //

Pañcarātra is not referred to here, nevertheless it is very close to Madhva's wording elsewhere. For instance in the Brahmatarka (BSūBh p. 153,9-11):

sarvān vedān setihāsān sapurāṇān sayuktikān /
sapañcarātrān vijñāya viṣṇur jñeyo na cānyathā //

or in the NyāV (p. 147,11-12): *nānāvedair itihāsaiḥ purāṇaiḥ sujñeya eko bhagavān yuktibhiś ceti śruteḥ suṣṭhu jñeyatvād viṣṇoḥ*; cf. also *śruti* (BSūBh p.154,5-6):

upāsya ekaḥ parataḥ paro yo vedaiś ca sarvaiḥ saha cetihāsaiḥ /
sapañcarātraiḥ sapurāṇaiś ca devaḥ sarvair guṇais tatra tatra pratītaiḥ /
iti hi bhāllaveyaśrutiḥ.

cf. above n 192.

267 VL vv. 16-18

268 KathU II 9; cf. below n 275.

in ChU, is enlarged again with the inclusion of many other texts. In this sense Madhva makes a clear statement in Anuv that all traditions (*smṛtayo 'khilāḥ*), Sāṃkhya-Yoga and Brahmatarka are integral parts of the Sadāgamas (= *pañcamo vedaḥ*).[269]

In order to corroborate the view discussed above, Madhva quotes in his different commentaries and in VTN many passages, which he attributes to known and unknown sources, such as BrāṇP, SkaP, NārP, BhavişP, Bhaviṣyatparvan, Prakāśikā, Vyāsasmṛti, Nārāyaṇāṣṭakṣarakalpa, Vidyānirṇaya and Brahmatarka.[270] All these passages with textual, contextual and other mutual deviations cannot be located, not even in the Purāṇas, so that we are forced to assume that they are literary compositions of Madhva belonging to the frame of the fifth Veda.[271]

With the purpose of gaining an insight into the compositional style and structure, we shall analyse below some selected fictitious citations produced by Madhva. Most appropriate for such a scrutiny is a passage attributed to BrāṇP, which

---

269 Anuv p. 153,28-31:

satsiddhānta iti jñeyo nirṇīto hariṇā svayam |
etadvirodhi yat sarvaṃ tamase 'ndhāya kevalam ||
andhaṃ tamo viśantīti prāha śrutir atisphuṭam |
ity eva śrutayo 'śeṣāḥ pañcarātram athākhilam ||
mūlarāmāyaṇaṃ caiva bhārataṃ smṛtayo 'khilāḥ |
vaiṣṇavāni purāṇāni sāṅkhyayogau parāv api ||
brahmatarkaś ca mīmāṃsety anantaḥ śabdasāgaraḥ |

cf. above n 164f. and n 57. In contradiction to it, another unidentified citation from the PadP (BĀUBh p. 268,11-13; cf. below n 325) ascribes Sāṃkhya-Yoga together with other systems to the Durāgamas.

270 Cf. VTN p. 16,6 9; GīT p.1,12-17; BhāgTN p. 614,5-9; BSūBh p. 10,6-8; GīBh p. 3,-5; GīT p. 35,22-36,2; MBhTN I 30-47; BSūBh p. 60,3 8; BĀUBh p. 268,13-14, 15-17; GīBh p. 2,2 + 3,1; ChUBh p. 397,14-20 (anonymously with *iti ca*); KeUBh p. 474,7-10; BSūBh p. 153,8-11; BĀUBh p. 311,14-16.

271 Similar observations we could make regarding Madhva's other doctrinal tenets, cf. above n 192.

appears in five works of Madhva, each time in a different context and with some textual variations, namely:

> *ṛgādyā bhāratam̱ caiva pañcarātram athākhilam* /
> *mūlarāmāyaṇam̱ caiva purāṇam̱ caitadātmakam* //
> *ye cānuyāyinas tv eṣām̱ sarve te ca sadāgamāḥ* /
> *durāgamās tadanye ye tair na jñeyo janārdanaḥ* //
> *jñeya etaiḥ sadā yuktair bhaktimadbhiḥ suniṣṭhitaiḥ* /
> *na ca kevalatarkeṇa nākṣajena na kenacit* //
> *kevalāgamavijñeyo bhaktair eva na cānyathā* /
> iti brahmāṇḍe.

„It is said in the BrāṇP:'[The four Vedas, namely] Ṛg- etc. as well as the Mahābhārata and all the Pañcarātrasaṃhitās, and also the original Rāmāyaṇa and [finally] the Purāṇas have him [= Viṣṇu] as their [main] purport. And all [other texts], which follow them, are Sadāgamas. Texts differing from them are Durāgamas. Viṣṇu cannot be known through them. He can be perceived with the help of those [Sadāgamas] by people devoted to their study without interruption, who have a loving devotion to him and who are well established in it. No one can grasp him by mere reasoning or by perception. He can be perceived only by devotees [and] only through the canonical scriptures. There is no other way'."[272]

This passage at the very beginning of VTN, which is closely connected with the Maṅgala-verse, is not transmitted in BrāṇP, however, it shows amazing similarities with a passage of SkaP:

> *sa viṣṇur brahmasañjño 'sau kavīnāṃ saṃmato vibhuḥ* /
> . . . .
> *nānyeṣāṃ brahmatā kvāpi tacchaktyekāṃśabhāginām* //
> *tad etac chāstragamyaṃ hi janmādy asya* [273]*mahāvibhoḥ* /
> *śāstraṃ ca vedāḥ smṛtayaḥ purāṇaṃ vai tadātmakam* //
> *itihāsaḥ pañcarātraṃ bhārataṃ ca mahāmate* /

---

[272] VTN p. 11,6-9.

[273] Cf. BSū I 1,2: *janmādy asya yataḥ*, ib. I 1,3: *śāstrayonitvāt.*

etair eva mahāviṣṇur jñeyo nānyaiḥ kathaṃcana ||
nāvedavid amuṃ viṣṇuṃ manute [274] *ca naraḥ kvacit |*
nendriyair nānumānaiś ca na tarkaiḥ [275] *śakyate vibhum ||*
jñātuṃ nārāyaṇaṃ devaṃ vedavedyaṃ sanātanam | [276]

A close scrutiny of these passages makes it clear that both speak, in the first place, about the authentical and non-authentical scriptures. Following KathU they teach that Viṣṇu cannot be grasped by perception and logical reasoning but only with the help of canonical scriptures. Whereas SkaP includes Rāmāyaṇa in the Itihāsa, but mentions MBh by name, Madhva's citation from BrāṇP puts forward his typical doctrine of the fifth Veda, mentioning by name also Mūlarāmāyaṇa, being a special feature of this doctrine. We can see also here clear signs of a reshaping of the original SkaP in the sense of Sadāgamas and Bhakti[277] which corresponds by and large to Madhva's self-assertion in VL mentioned above.[278] It is significant that the above quoted

---

274 Cf. ŚaṭyāyanīU 4:

nāvedavin manute taṃ bṛhantaṃ
nābrahmavit paraṃ praiti dhāma |
viṣṇukrāntaṃ vāsudevaṃ vijānan
vipro vipratvaṃ gacchate tattvadarśī ||

275 Cf. KathU II 9, cf. above n 268.

276 Cf. SkaP II 7,19, 9cd-14.

277 Compare also the identical wording in BrāṇP and SkaP: *purāṇaṃ caitadātmakam = purāṇaṃ vai tadātmakam.* As a matter of fact, there is no immediate reference in BrāṇP for *tad°* within the quotation, in opposition to SkaP, namely Viṣṇu. In BrāṇP, this reference is outside of the quotation!

278 Another instance of such kind of rearrangement is found in ĪśUBh, where Madhva reshapes the text of this Upaniṣad (ĪśU 7-8):

yasmin sarvāṇi bhūtāny ātmaivābhūd vijānataḥ |
tatra ko mohaḥ kaḥ śoka ekatvam anupaśyataḥ ||
sa paryagāc chukram akāyam avraṇam
asnāviraṃ śuddham apāpaviddham |
kavir manīṣī paribhūḥ svayaṃbhūr yāthātathyato
'rthān vyadadhāc chāśvatībhyaḥ samābhyaḥ ||

The reshuffling of this passage is obvious since Madhva, committed to realism, replaces the original monistic intention of the text – that the whole passage from SkaP has a special relation to the Vedānta thought, not only because it refers to BSū (I 1,2/3) but also to the teaching of the Upaniṣads. For this reason one is not surprised that Madhva composes another similar passage based on the above mentioned citation from SkaP and having an intimate relation to BSū (I 1,3).[279] Interestingly enough he ascribes it also to SkaP:

---

plurality of the world lies in the depths of divine unity and that the illusion of the individual existence is destroyed by renouncing the pluralistic world – with the teaching that deliverance can be achieved only through knowledge of Viṣṇu's omnipresence in the universe and through knowledge of the reality of the universe. The universe is real because Viṣṇu has created it. Viṣṇu as Creator has no material body (*prākṛta/sthūladeha*) but a body out of Being, Knowledge and pure Happiness (cf. above n 48f.). In this connection Madhva explains how the universe is beginningless (*anādi* cf. above n 196ff.). In support for this interpretation he quotes from two fictitious sources, namely Pippalādaśākhā and VarP, where the rearrangement of ĪśU (7-8a) and ĪśU (8) respectively (ĪśUBh p. 410,21f.) takes place:

> *yasmin sarvāṇi bhūtāni sa ātmā sarvabhūtagaḥ |*
> *evaṃ sarvatra yo viṣṇuṃ paśyet tasya vijānataḥ ||*
> *ko mohaḥ ko 'thavā śokaḥ sa viṣṇuṃ paryagād ataḥ |*
> iti pippalādaśākhā
> *pūrvoktānuvādena śokamohābhāvo vijānataś cātrocyate |*
> *abhyāsaś ca sarvagatatvasya tātparyadyotanārthaḥ |*
> *śukraṃ tacchokarāhityād avraṇaṃ nityapūrṇataḥ |*
> *pāvanatvāt sadā śuddhaṃ akāyaṃ liṅgavarjanāt ||*
> *sthūladehasya rāhityād asnāviram udāhṛtam |*
> *evaṃbhūto 'pi sārvajñyāt kavir ity eva śabdyate ||*
> *brahmādisarvamanasāṃ prakṛtyā manaso 'pi ca |*
> *īśitṛtvān manīṣī sa paribhūḥ sarvato varaḥ ||*
> *sadānanyāśrayatvāc ca svayaṃbhūḥ parikīrtitaḥ |*
> *sa satyaṃ jagad etādṛṅ nityam eva pravāhataḥ ||*
> *anādyanantakāleṣu pravāhaikaprakārakam |*
> *niyamenaiva sasṛje bhagavān puruṣottamaḥ ||*
> *sajjñānānandaśīrṣo 'sau sajjñānānandabāhukaḥ |*
> *sajjñānānandadehaś ca sajjñānānandapādavān ||*
> *evaṃbhūto mahāviṣṇur yathārthaṃ jagadīdṛśam |*
> *anādyanantakālīnaṃ sasarjātmecchayā prabhuḥ ||*
> iti vārāhe.

279 Cf. BSūBh p. 10,8-10.

ṛgyajuḥsāmātharvāś ca bhārataṃ pañcarātrakam /
mūlarāmāyaṇaṃ caiva śāstram ity abhidhīyate //
yac cānukūlam etasya tac ca śāstraṃ prakīrtitam /
ato 'nyo granthavistāro naiva śāstraṃ kuvartma tat //
iti skānde.

It is remarkable that Madhva replaces here Sadāgama by Śāstra following the citation from SkaP (II 7,19,9cd-14) quoted above. And also Purāṇa is not mentioned by name, exactly as in the self-statement of Madhva in VL, quoted above. Likewise, two other fictitious quotations in BĀUBh in connection with the fifth Veda use the term Śāstra instead of Sadāgama:

viṣṇoḥ sarvottamatvasya jñānārthaṃ śāstram iṣyate /
atas tatsādhakaṃ śāstraṃ duḥśāstraṃ tadvirodhi yat //
iti brahmāṇḍe.
viṣṇoḥ sarvottamatvaṃ ca tadbhaktyā mokṣa eva ca /
śāstrārtha iti nirdiṣṭaḥ sarvaśāstrārthanirṇayāt //
iti pādme.[280]

Although the textual origin of the Purāṇa literature implies a manifold historical development, in which a single text took shape slowly over centuries through the redaction of several authors, so that one could theoretically assume that Madhva might have had knowledge of textual portions unknown to us. Nevertheless, we should accept, based on our many observations, that Madhva actually reshaped a particular passage of SkaP, quoted above, in such a way as to deliver his teaching of

---

280 BĀUBh p. 268,17-19; cf. also another self-statement of Madhva in Oṃ-tatsatpraṇavakalpa (see VTN) vv. 23-25:

anyāṃś ca vaiṣṇavān mantrān japethā bhaktipūrvakam /
śṛṇuṣva vaiṣṇavaṃ śāstraṃ sadā vedārthatatparaḥ //
vedān mantrān upaniṣatsahitān sarvadā śṛṇu /
itihāsapurāṇe ca pañcarātraṃ tathaiva ca //
tadarthān brahmasūtraiś ca samyaṅnirṇīya tattvataḥ /
viṣṇoḥ sarvottamatvaṃ tu sarvadā pratipādaya //

the the fifth Veda or Sadāgamas. This observation can be corroborated with the help of a statement by Madhva himself[281] that the *mohaśāstrāṇi* like Śaivāgamas (= SkaP) should be brought in harmony with the teaching of Sadāgamas (*yojyāni*) and this implies also the textual reshuffling.

Madhva uses this very procedure in BhāgTN, when he comments upon a *śloka* about *śraddhā* (BhāgP XI 3,26). In support of his interpretation he adduces a fictitious quotation from BrāṇP, which combines the idea of *śraddhā* with the thought pattern of the fifth Veda, as follows:

śraddhā bhāgavate tantre vede bhāratapañcame |
viṣṇor avyavadhānena vaktṛtvāt sarvathā bhavet ||
kalāvidyāsv anindā ca vyavadhānena keśave |
praveśād yatibhiḥ kāryā hy anyathā nirayaṃ vrajet ||
śraddhā tv āstikyabuddhiḥ syāt sā caiva dvividhā matā |
atroktam astīty ekā tu mamātrāsti prayojanam ||
ity anyā tatra pūrvā tu yateḥ kāryā kalāsv api |
dvitīyā tu na kartavyā pañcarātravirodhiṣu ||
sadaiva nindā sarvaiś ca brahmādisthāvarāntakaiḥ |
samyak kāryā tad vinā ca tamo yāti viniścayāt |
kurvanty eva surās tatra tadanyeṣāṃ tamo bhavet |
pañcarātraṃ ca vedāś ca mūlarāmāyaṇaṃ tathā |
purāṇaṃ bhāgavataṃ caiva bhārataṃ ca na bhidyate ||
eteṣv api yathā viṣṇor ādhikyapratipādanam |
tadbhaktānāṃ ca kramaśaḥ sa evārtho na cāparaḥ ||
anyathā dṛśyamānaṃ tu mohāyaiva vinirdiśet |
tasmāt sarveṣu śāstreṣu viṣṇor ādhikyam eva tu ||
krameṇa ca tadīyānāṃ pratipādyaṃ na cāparam |
iti brahmāṇḍe.

„One should trust [the Sadāgamas, like] BhāgP, Tantras, Vedas and MBh as the fifth [Veda], for Viṣṇu is in every sense

281 Cf. below n 340ff.

their immediate author. And the ascetics should not criticize the sciences of arts, since it indirectly affects Viṣṇu. Otherwise, they would go to hell. Now, the trust is a positive belief in God. And it has been handed down as twofold. The one form is: 'What has been taught there is true', the other form is: 'What has been taught there, is advantageous for me'. The ascetic should choose the first one out of both, also in regard to the sciences of arts and avoid the second one. All [beings] from Brahmā up to the immovable [belonging to the vegetable world] should always criticize in due form [the teaching], which is in contradiction to Pañcarātra. If [the ascetic does] not [behave like] that, he will surely enter darkness. The Suras behave in the same way with regard to that. To others [, namely the Asuras] darkness would be granted. And there is no difference between Pañcarātra, Vedas, Mūlarāmāyaṇa, BhāgP and MBh. Exactly in the way the [absolute] sovereignty of Viṣṇu is taught in these [Sadāgamas], in that way, and not otherwise, should the devotees of Viṣṇu appropriate this teaching. When someone proclaims that [there] another [teaching] is manifested, it brings about only the darkness of mind. Therefore, all Śāstras (= Sadāgamas) teach without exception the [absolute] sovereignty of Viṣṇu. And his [devotees] should learn [this teaching] and nothing else. This is taught in BrāṇP."

A close scrutiny of this quotation shows that Madhva is relating in his own words the traditional views on *śraddhā*, which are referred to in the Gī and its commentaries. In this sense, he understands *śraddhā* as a faithful acceptance of all canonical scriptures without adverse criticism (*anindālanasūyā*), for this would imply direct or indirect contempt of Viṣṇu, its ultimate author.[282] Also the definition of *śraddhā* as *āstikya*-

[282] In MBhTN (I 111-112) Madhva counts the criticism (*nindā*) of the canonical scriptures among the nine blasphemies against God (*dveṣa*); cf. also Manusmṛti II 10-11:

śrutis tu vedo vijñeyo dharmaśāstraṃ tu vai smṛtiḥ |
te sarvārtheṣv amīmāṃsye tābhyāṃ dharmo hi nirbabhau ||

buddhi, namely a positive belief in God is in full agreement with the conventional standpoint.[283] Accordingly, *āstikyabuddhi* means that the knowledge handed down in the canonical scriptures, which is to be appropriated intellectually by those striving for release, is true (*asti*). It includes not only the knowledge of the absolute sovereignty of Viṣṇu, and the knowledge of the fact that Madhva appears on the earth in divine form (*divyaṃ rūpam*) as exponent of the deeds of Viṣṇu (*bhagavatkārya-sādhaka*),[284] but also the worldly knowledge of the science of arts.[285]

With the twofold division of *śraddhā*, namely into a superior and into an inferior, latter characterized as striving for

---

yo 'vamanyeta te mūle hetuśāstrāśrayād dvijaḥ |
sa sādhubhir bahiṣkāryo nāstiko vedanindakaḥ ||

cf. Śaṅkara (GīBh on III 31): . . . *ye me madīyam idaṃ matam anutiṣṭhanty anuvartante mānavā manuṣyāḥ śraddhāvantaḥ śraddhānā anasūyanto 'sūyāṃ ca mayi gurau vāsudeve 'kurvanto mucyante te 'py evaṃbhūtāḥ karmabhir dharmādharmākhyaiḥ.*

283 Cf. Śaṅkaras commentary (on Gī XVII 1; KathU I 1,2). For detailed discussion cf. P. HACKER, *śraddhā*, WZKSO 7 (1963), p.151-189 and M. HARA, Śraddhā in the Sense of Desire. In: Asiatische Studien 46 (1992) [= FS Jacques May], p. 180-194.

284 Cf. above n 81f.; below n 371.

285 This corresponds more or less to the doctrine of Thomas Aquinas who interprets the faith (*fides*) mainly as an intellectual acceptance not only of the truths of the revelation but also as acceptance of the knowledge of human nature and other worldly things, cf. Summa Theologiae II-II 1-2: *Illud enim videtur esse obiectum fidei quod nobis proponitur ad credendum. Sed non solum proponuntur nobis ad credendum ea quae pertinent ad Divinitatem, quae est veritas prima; sed etiam ea quae pertinent ad humanitatem Christi et Ecclesiae sacramenta et creaturarum conditionem. Ergo non solum veritas prima est fidei obiectum. Praeterea, fides et infidelitas sund circa idem: cum sint opposita. Sed circa omnia quae in sacra Scriptura continentur potest esse infidelitas: quidquid enim horum homo negaverit, infidelis reputatur. Ergo etiam fides est circa omnia quae in sacra Scriptura continentur. Sed ibi multa continentur de hominibus et de aliis rebus creatis. Ergo obiectum fidei non solum est veritas prima, sed etiam veritas creata.*

personal advantage (*mamātrāsti prayojanam*), and therefore to be avoided, Madhva seems to polemize against the opinion of Rāmānuja (ca. 12th cent.) and his followers. Rāmānuja understands *śraddhā* not as *āstikyabuddhi*, but rather as a pleasure or as something loved by oneself: *yatra rucis tatra śraddhā jāyate / śraddhā hi svābhimataṃ sādhayaty etad iti viśvāsapūrvikā sādhane tvarā.*[286] Precisely this view is the focus of interest in Madhva's critical remarks. And he reinforces his criticism when he emphasizes that the position of Rāmānuja, who like Madhva, is committed to Pañcarātra, contradicts this tradition and therefore is to be rejected by everyone (*pañcarātravirodhiṣu sadaiva nindā sarvaiś ca*).

In case this is true, we have then another reason for assuming that Madhva himself composed all the above mentioned quotations in disguise and ascribed them to BrāṇP.

Madhva proceeds likewise also in GīT, GīBh and MBh-TN, only with a slight deviation that not a framework of a Purāṇa is used, but that of MBh.[287] Whereas the passages analysed so far, implied that all texts belonging to the fifth Veda are equal, since their main purport is the absolute sovereignty of Viṣṇu, the following quotations show a certain shift in favour of MBh. This could be related to the fact that the quotations appear only in the commentaries of MBh and the purpose of eulogizing becomes manifest. In this sense, MBh is praised as the best text (*na bhāratasamaṃ śāstram*) or that MBh contains doctrines, which are not taught by the Vedas since their sole origin is the omniscience of Viṣṇu (*kṛpāluḥ sarvavedādyarthopabṛṃhitāṃ tadanuk-*

---

286 Rāmānujas Bhāṣya on Gī XVII 2: „Faith is born in regard to something in that one takes pleasure. For faith is zeal in respect to the means with the conviction that [these means] can bring forth one's desired object." Veṅkaṭanātha explains in his sub-commentary (Gītābhāṣyatātparyacandrikā) that the interpretation of Rāmānuja has its origin in the etymological definition of old teachers: *śraddhā viśvāsakāṅkṣayor iti tvarāparyantaviśvāse 'pi hi śraddhāśabdaṃ naighanṭukāḥ paṭhanti.*

287 It is noteworthy to remark in this connection that Madhva ascribes fictitious *ślokas* on his *avatāra*-doctrine to MBh (cf. above n 47 and 51).

takevaleśvarajñānadṛṣṭārthayuktāṃ ca . . . mahābhāratasaṃhitām aciklpat).[288] Madhva explains now the thesis of the equality of all texts of the fifth Veda based on the principle of eulogy. For, the reason of their equality lies in the fact that they comprise the quintessence (*sāra*) of MBh. This very sense convey also the following sentences: *nirṇayaḥ sarvasāstrāṇāṃ bhārataṃ parikīrtitam* or *atroktaṃ sarvaśāstreṣu na hi samyag udāhṛtam.*[289] The identical text-portions in the following quotations are underlined for easy identification.

---

[288] Cf. GīT p. 1,13; GīBh p. 1,6f. In agreement with this view two other Purāṇa-citations are adduced in MBhTN (II 49cd - 51). Only the second *śloka* has been handed down in ViṣP und PadP (cf. above n 56) and also in MBh XII 334,8 (cf. App. I 2 and 3):

> mārkaṇḍeye *'pi kathitaṃ bhāratasya praśaṃsanam* /
> *devatānāṃ yathā vyāso dvipadāṃ brāhmaṇo varaḥ* //
> *āyudhānāṃ yathā vajraṃ oṣadhīnāṃ yathā yavāḥ* /
> *tathaiva sarvaśāstrāṇāṃ mahābhāratam uttamam* //
> vāyuprokte *'pi tat proktaṃ bhāratasya praśaṃsanam* /
> *kṛṣṇadvaipāyanaṃ vyāsaṃ viddhi nārāyaṇaṃ prabhum* //
> *ko hy anyaḥ puṇḍarīkākṣān mahābhāratakṛd bhavet* /

The passage from MārP is structurally very close to MBh (I 1, 201-202):

> *bhāratasya vāpur hy etat satyaṃ cāmṛtam eva ca* /
> *navanītaṃ yathā dadhno dvipadāṃ brāhmaṇo yathā* //
> *hradānām udadhiḥ śreṣṭho gaur variṣṭhā catuṣpadām* /
> *yathaitāni variṣṭhāṇi tathā bhāratam ucyate* //

In GīBh (p. 3,3-5) another fictitious citation from SkaP is put forward, which praises MBh as *sarvatra vedād apy uttamam* (cf. below n 306).

[289] MBhTN II 8cd; 48cd; cf. *ibid.* X 59:

> *samastaśāstrārthanidarśanātmakaṃ cakre mahābhāratanāmadheyam* /
> *vedottamam* . . .

cf. MBhTN II 129:

> *tasmād yo mahimā viṣṇoḥ sarvasāstroditaḥ sa hi* /
> *nānyad ity eṣa śāstrāṇāṃ nirṇayaḥ samudāhṛtaḥ* //
> *bhāratārthas tridhā proktaḥ svayaṃ bhagavataiva hi* /

cf. below n 297.

1)

śāstreṣu bhāratam sāram tatra nāmasahasrakam |
vaiṣṇavam kṛṣṇagītā ca tajjñānān mucyate 'ñjasā ||
na bhāratasamam śāstram kuta evānayoḥ samam |
bhāratam sarvavedāś ca tulām āropitāḥ purā ||[290]
devair brahmādibhiḥ sarvair ṛṣibhiś ca samanvitaiḥ ||
vyāsasyaivājñayā[291] *tatra tv atyaricyata bhāratam |*
mahattvād bhāravattvāc ca mahābhāratam ucyate ||
niruktam asya yo veda sarvapāpaiḥ pramucyate[292] *||*

---

[290] Cf. MBh I 1,208-209 :

catvāra ekato vedā bhāratam caikam ekataḥ |
samāgataiḥ surarṣibhis tulām āropitam purā |
mahattve ca gurutve ca dhriyamāṇam tato 'dhikam |
mahattvād bhāravattvāc ca mahābhāratam ucyate |
niruktam asya yo veda sarvapāpaiḥ pramucyate ||

cf. also Kumārila, Tantravārttika (on Sū I 3,11); ĀP p. 104,4-7. In the critical apparatus of the MBh the following *śloka* has been transmitted:

caturbhyaḥ sarahasyebhyo vedebhyo hy adhikam yadā |
tadā prabhṛti loke 'smin mahābhāratam ucyate ||

cf. below n 296.

[291] Vgl. MBh XVIII 5,30-31ab:

etat te sarvam ākhyātam vaiśampāyanakīrtitam |
vyāsājñayā samākhyātam sarpasattre nṛpasya ha ||
puṇyo 'yam itihāsākhyaḥ pavitram cedam uttamam /

cf. above n 246.

[292] MBhTN X 57-59. This quotation could not be located in BrāṇP with an exception of half *śloka* giving the etymology of Purāṇa (III 4,4,54cd-55ab; I 1,173):

yasmāt purā hy aṇamtīdam purāṇam tena cocyate |
niruktam asya yo veda sarvapāpaiḥ pramucyate ||

cf. PadP I 2,53:

purāparam parām vakti purāṇam tena vai smṛtam |
niruktam asya yo veda sarvapāpaiḥ pramucyate ||

Rāmāyaṇa I 1,77:

idam pavitram pāpaghnam puṇyam vedaiś ca sammitam |
yaḥ paṭhed rāmacaritam sarvapāpaiḥ pramucyate ||

svayaṃ nārāyaṇo devair brahmarudrendrapūrvakaiḥ |
arthito vyāsatāṃ prāpya kevalaṃ tattvanirṇayam ||
cakāra pañcamaṃ vedaṃ mahābhāratasañjñitam |
iti brahmāṇḍe.[293]

„The Śāstras (= Vedas) comprise the quintessence of MBh, the thousand names of Viṣṇu and the Song of Kṛṣṇa. Through their knowledge one is instantly released. There is no Śāstra, which is equal to MBh. How can there be a similarity between these both [, namely Veda and MBh]? In a previous existence, MBh and all Vedas have been weighed by all gods like Brahmā together with the Ṛṣis on the order of Vyāsa. And MBh was found to be heavier. Because it is voluminous and heavier [in its significance this text] is called Mahābhārata. One who knows this etymology, will be freed from all [his] sins.[294] Nārāyaṇa himself composed the fifth Veda, named MBh, which propounds the true doctrine at the request of gods like Brahmā, Rudra and Indra, after taking the [human] shape of Vyāsa."

2)
yadi vidyāc caturvedān sāṅgopaniṣadān dvijaḥ |
na cet purāṇaṃ saṃvidyān naiva sa syād vicakṣaṇaḥ ||[295]

---

[293] GiT p. 1,12-17. Strange is the fact that some copies of this very edition omit the text-portions referring to the order of Vyāsa and to Ṛṣis. This seems to be based on the remark in the appendix (*pariśiṣṭa*): *tatra pracalitāḥ pāṭhāḥ pūrvatra granthe mudritāḥ*.

[294] Other etymologies have been handed down, *e. g.* (MBh I 56,31f.):

bhāratānāṃ mahaj janma mahābhāratam ucyate |
niruktam asya yo veda sarvapāpaiḥ pramucyate || . . .
yad ihāsti tadanyatra yan nehāsti na tat kvacit ||

Some MSS have transmitted the following two *ślokas* (App. I 2):

kṛṣṇadvaipāyanaṃ vyāsaṃ viddhi nārāyaṇaṃ prabhum |
ko hy anyaḥ puṇḍarīkākṣān mahābhāratakṛd bhavet ||
bhāti sarveṣu vedeṣu ratiḥ sarveṣu jantuṣu |
taraṇaṃ sarvalokānāṃ tasmād bhāratam ucyate ||

[295] Cf. MBh I 2,235:

yo vidyāc caturo vedān sāṅgopaṇiṣadān dvijaḥ |
na cākhyānam idaṃ vidyān naiva sa syād vicakṣaṇaḥ ||

itihāsapurāṇābhyāṃ vedaṃ samupabṛṃhayet /
bibhety alpaśrutād vedo mām ayaṃ pracaliṣyati //[296]
manvādi kecid bruvate hy āstīkādi tathāpare /
tathoparicarādy anye bhārataṃ paricakṣate //[297]
bhārataṃ sarvavedās ca tulām āropitāḥ purā /
devair brahmādibhiḥ sarvair ṛṣibhiś ca samanvitaiḥ //
vyāsasyaivājñayā tatra tv atyaricyata bhāratam /
mahattvād bhāravattvāc ca mahābhāratam ucyate //
niruktam asya yo veda sarvapāpaiḥ pramucyate /
yad ihāsti tadanyatra yan nehāsti na kutracit //[298]
virāṭodyogasāravān[299] *ityāditadvākyaparyālocanayā*
ṛṣisaṃpradāyāt / *ko hy anyaḥ puṇḍarīkākṣān mahā-*

---

[296] Cf. MBh I 1,204:

itihāsapurāṇābhyāṃ vedaṃ samupabṛṃhayet /
bibhety alpaśrutād vedo mām ayaṃ pratariṣyati //

cf. also PadP I 2, 50-51:

yo vidyāc caturo vedān sāṅgopaniṣado dvijaḥ /
purāṇaṃ ca vijānāti yaḥ sa tasmād vicakṣaṇaḥ //
itihāsapurāṇābhyāṃ vedaṃ samupabṛṃhayet /
bibhety alpaśrutād vedo mām ayaṃ pratariṣyati //

BrāṇP I 1,170-171; NM 3,5-7; PadP VI 28,55:

itihāsapurāṇābhyāṃ puṇyaṃ pustakavācanam /
sarvān kāmān avāpnoti sūryalokaṃ bhinatti saḥ //

[297] Cf. MBh I 1,50:

manvādi bhārataṃ kecid āstīkādi tathāpare /
tathoparicarādy anye viprāḥ samyag adhīyate //

In (MBhTN II 129-133) Madhva does not take this threefold division as a hint at three different beginnings of the story of MBh, but he understands it as a hermeneutical principle, proclaimed by Viṣṇu himself, to interpret the contents of MBh in agreement to the absolute sovereignty of Viṣṇu, which he ascribes to Vyāsa (MBhTN II 141ab: *ityādi vyasavākyais tu viṣṇūtkarṣo 'vagamyate*); cf. also below n 336f.

[298] This half *śloka* is handed down in MBh I 56,33cd (= XVIII 5.38cd; App. 3,11pr.; 5,2pr.): *yad ihāsti tad anyatra yan nehāsti na tat kvacit.*

[299] Cf. MBh (App. I 1, 49d) where the different Adhyāyas of MBh are compared with a tree (*bhāratadrumaḥ*) (*ibid.* I 1,46cd-56).

bhāratakṛd bhaved[300] *ityādipurāṇa granthāntargatavākyānyathānupapattyā nāradādhyayanādiliṅgaiś*[301] *cāvasīyate | katham anyathā bhārataniruktijñānamātreṇa sarvapāpakṣayaḥ | prasiddhaś ca so 'rthaḥ |*[302]

„If a Brahmin knows [only] the four Vedas including other parts and Upaniṣads [but] does not know the Purāṇas, then by no means he can be considered a sage. [Therefore,] the Veda should be replenished with Itihāsas and Purāṇas. The Veda is afraid of people with defective knowledge (= ignorants). I will be perplexed by it. Some tell [the story of] Mahābharata beginning from Manu, but others beginning from [the Adhyāya on] Āstīka, and others beginning from Uparicara . . . What has been handed down in this [Itihāsa] is also found else where. What has not been handed down there, doesn't exist anywhere. [This follows] on

---

300 Cf. MBh XII 334, 9:

kṛṣṇadvaipāyanaṃ vyāsaṃ viddhi nārāyaṇaṃ prabhum |
ko hy anyaḥ puruṣavyāghra (v. l. *puṇḍarīkākṣān*) *mahābhāratakṛd bhavet ||*

cf. above n 56; 294 and below n 301.

301 The precise meaning of this remark is not known to me. Probably it refers to the revelation of Viṣṇu Nārāyaṇa (MBh XII 326, 1ff.) to Nārada, which Nārada hands down in literary form to the Brahmins (*ibid.* XII 326 100-101):

idaṃ mahopaniṣadaṃ caturvedasamanvitam |
sāṃkhyayogakṛtaṃ tena pañcarātrānuśabditam ||
nārāyaṇamukhodgītaṃ nārado 'śrāvayat punaḥ |
brahmaṇaḥ sadane tāta yathā dṛṣṭaṃ yathā śrutam ||

Perhaps it points out to MBh (XII 334,1- 17), where it is related that Nārada becomes a part of Viṣṇu (*ekāntitvam upeyivān*) through his unbroken meditation, after having heard the story about the Lord (*śrutvā bhagavad-ākhyāna*). Nārada reveals in this connection the mystery of the identity between Kṛṣṇa and Nārāyaṇa. It is also noteworthy that in this very Adhyāya the *śloka* has been handed down (cf. above n 300), in which the identity of Vyāsa and Viṣṇu is proclaimed; cf. above n 56; 298.

302 GīBh p. 3,5-4,3.

account of the tradition of the Ṛṣis [in Mahābhārata][303] after pondering over its sentence: '[its] quintessence are Virāṭa- and Udyoga [Parvans]'. Besides, it is established on account of the characteristics of the study etc. by Nārada. Otherwise the statement included in the text of the Purāṇas, namely 'Who else other than Viṣṇu could be the author of MBh?', would be impossible. How else could all the sins be deleted only by the knowledge of the etymology of MBh? And this meaning is clear."

> *bhārataṃ sarvavedāś ca tulām āropitaḥ purā /*
> *devair brahmādibhiḥ sarvair ṛṣibhiś ca samanvitaiḥ //*
> *vyāsasyaivājñayā tatra tv atyaricyata bhāratam /*
> *mahattvād bhāravattvāc ca mahābhāratam ucyate //*
> *niruktam asya yo veda sarvapāpaiḥ pramucyate /*
> *nirṇayaḥ sarvaśāstrāṇāṃ sadṛṣṭānto hi bhārate //*
> *kṛto viṣṇuvaśatvaṃ hi brahmādīnāṃ prakāśitam /*
> . . .
> *tasmād yad bhārate noktaṃ tad dhi naivāsti kutracit /*
> *atroktaṃ sarvaśāstreṣu na hi samyag udāhṛtam //*
> *ityādi kathitaṃ sarvaṃ* brahmāṇḍe *hariṇā svayam /* [304]

Drawing a comparison between these three passages we are able to make some very interesting observations. Whereas the first and the third citation is attributed to BrāṇP, the second one is anonymous. We can identify some word to word quotations from the MBh, which are put together with an *iti* at the end. It is conspicuous that all the three have two and half homonymous *śloka*s from MBh, which correspond only partially with the text of MBh, and which supply an etymology of the work-title MBh. The common characteristic of all the three passages is that they

---

303 This remark deals with the tradition, in which Vyāsa appears as *ṛṣiśreṣṭha* (MBh III 46,2c), or *maharṣi* (*ibid.* I 1,23), or as *brahmarṣisattama* leading the line of the Ṛṣis (*ibid.* XII 1,3-4; XIII 151,4); cf. SULLIVAN 1990: 29f.

304 MBhTN II 9-11; 48 49ab; cf. 8cd.

deal with the typical teaching of the fifth Veda. An important thought pattern referred to in this connection is that Viṣṇu in the *dvāpara* age, which is marked by a sudden decay of moral behaviour and of Veda-knowledge, descends to earth on request of Brahmā etc. taking the human shape of Vyāsa in order to proclaim the original Veda-knowledge by composing for this purpose the fifth Veda, namely MBh.[305] Besides, Madhva makes changes in the original text of MBh in such a way that the

---

[305] Madhva quotes as evidence an unknown source (GīBh p. 2,2-3,1) :

> *lokeśā brahmarudrādyāḥ saṃsāre kleśinaṃ janam /*
> *vedārthajñam adhikāravarjitaṃ ca striyādikam //*
> *avekṣya prārthayāmāsur deveśaṃ puruṣottamam /*
> *tataḥ prasanno bhagavān vyāso bhūtvā ca tena ca //*
> *anyāvatārarūpaiś ca vedānuktārthabhūṣitam /*
> *kevalenātmabodhena dṛṣṭaṃ vedārthasaṃyutam //*
> *vedād api paraṃ cakre pañcamaṃ vedam uttamam /*
> *bhārataṃ pañcarātraṃ ca mūlarāmāyaṇaṃ tathā //*
> *purāṇaṃ bhāgavataṃ ceti saṃbhinnaḥ śāstrapuṅgavaḥ /*
> iti nārāyaṇāṣṭākṣarakalpe.

Since our analysis above showed clearly that this doctrine has been put forward by Madhva (cf. GīBh p. 1,5-9; above n 56f.; 244ff.; 282f.), we should assume that he himself is behind this source. This judgement is valid for the following quotation, too (*ibid.* p. 3,2-3):

> *brahmādyaiḥ prārthito viṣṇur bhārataṃ sa cakāra ha /*
> *yasmin daśārthāḥ sarvatra na jñeyāḥ sarvajantubhiḥ //*
> iti nāradīye.

Likewise, Madhva formulates in the introduction to BSūBh (p. 1,5-2,15; Anuv p. 2,19f.) the reason for obscuration of the original Veda knowledge in the *dvāpara* age (cf.VāyP I 60,1ff.; BhāgP XII 6,48ff.), in order to explain why a new commentary to BSū has been composed. To substantiate this thesis again he adduces a fictitious quotation ascribed to SkaP, and which reproduces word to word a frequently cited *śloka* on the definition of a *sūtra* (Yuktidīpikā [crit. ed. by A. WEZLER and SH. MOTEGI. Stuttgart 1998], p. 4,1-3; Nyāyavārttikatātparyaṭīkā of Vācaspati [Kyoto 1982], p. 70,13-18; ViṣṇudharmottaraP III 5, 1; KāvM p. 5,1-3; cf. also N. BALBIR, The Perfect Sūtra as defined by the Jainas, Berliner Ind. Studien 3 [1987], p. 7):

> *alpākṣaram asandigdhaṃ sāravad viśvatomukham /*
> *astobham anavadyaṃ ca sūtraṃ sūtravido viduḥ //*

etymology of the work-title MBh can be drawn back directly to Vyāsa: The gods together with the Ṛṣis proof on command of Vyāsa the weight of the Vedas and of MBh and ascertain that MBh excells the Vedas by far.[306] This proves that Mahābhārata is not only a bulky text but also weighty in its significance.[307] It is remarkable that Madhva remains within the frame of MBh while reworking its original text. For, this reworking takes place with the help of the frame work used in MBh, however in a completely different connection, namely in the first Adhyāya of Ādiparvan. It is reported here that Vyāsa narrated MBh first, which was then retold by Ṛṣi Vaiśaṃpāyana, on his command (*dvaipāyanājñayā*) together with the four Vedas (*vedaiś caturbhiḥ samitām*) at the snake-sacrifice (*sattre*) to the king Janamejaya.[308] The reason, why Madhva makes some changes in the standard text of MBh becomes obvious from his comments thereafter. They supply the proof, why a mere knowledge of the etymology of the work-title MBh can destroy all the sins. Since the Itihāsa-work of MBh and its etymology go back to Vyāsa (= Viṣṇu), every person who knows this fact, is absolutely free from all his sins (*sarvapāpa-kṣaya*). Special attention should be paid to the fact that the two and half homonymous *ślokas* are placed differently within its re-

---

306 Cf. GīBh p. 19,4; 3, 3-5:

> *bhārataṃ cāpi kṛtavān pañcamaṃ vedam uttamam |*
> *daśāvarārthaṃ sarvatra kevalaṃ viṣṇubodhakam ||*
> *parokṣārthaṃ tu sarvatra vedād apy uttamaṃ tu yat |*
> iti skānde (not found!).

cf. *ibid.* p. 19,4.

307 Madhva bases this statement on a fictitious citation too (GīBh p. 3,1-2):

> *brahmāpi tan na jānāti īṣat sarvo 'pi jānati |*
> *bahvartham ṛṣayas tat tu bhārataṃ pravadanti hi ||*
> ity upanāradīye.

308 Cf. MBh I 1,15f.; XVIII 5,6ff. Madhva claims that he himself composed his commentaries on MBh, BSū and on the Upaniṣads based on the order of Vyāsa, cf. p. 110f.

spective context. In the third passage they are at the very beginning of about 45 *śloka*s, dealing not only with the fifth Veda but also with other peculiar teachings of Madhva. In the first and second passage they belong to their closing part.[309] Both these passages refer only to the teaching of the fifth Veda but not to other peculiar tenets of Madhva. The passage (1) mentions two other important portions of the MBh, namely Viṣṇusahasranāma and Bhagavadgītā. The passages (2) and (3) close with half a *śloka* from MBh, which proclaims again the pre-eminence of this text over all other classical works, for it is source of all-comprising knowledge.

In theory, it could be assumed that the afore-said changes in the original text of MBh are a work of a redactor, a well-known phenomenon within the so-called Sanskrit anonymous literature. Similar observation we made in PadP, too.[310] However, in our present case the textual changes have, on the one hand, an intimate relation with the typical teachings of Madhva, and on the other hand, the phrasing in these passages bears Madhva's mark[311]. This fact implies that Madhva himself introduced the changes. A convincing corroboration of our thesis is supplied by the longest passage (3), which Madhva together with the passage (1) ascribes to BrāṇP. Diverging from the passage (1) it presents, as already mentioned above, several typical doctrinal tenets of Madhva, *e.g.* the teaching on hierarchy among gods (*tāratamya*)

---

309 In connection with the second passage Madhva puts forward four other fictitious passages dealing with the fifth Veda, which bears Madhva's mark (cf. above n 305f.).

310 Cf. above n 296 and below n 324.

311 For instance the passage (3): *nirṇayaḥ sarvasāstrāṇāṃ sadṛṣṭānto hi bhārate* <> MBhTN II 135f.;8: *nirṇayaḥ sarvaśastrāṇāṃ bhāratam parikīrtitam* ; passage (1): *śāstreṣu bhāratam sāram* . . . <> *ibid.* II 8: . . . *vakṣye . . . saṃkṣepāt sarvaśāstrārthaṃ bhāratārthānusārataḥ* . . . ; cf. above n 278.

together with the absolute sovereignty of Viṣṇu,[312] or the doctrine of the *avatāras*, which is closely connected with the view that Madhva himself is an *avatāra* of Vāyu,[313] or the teaching on Bhakti.[314] The way how Madhva closes this passage it is specially interesting: *ityādi kathitaṃ sarvaṃ* brahmāṇḍe *hariṇā svayam.* A literary device used by Madhva, as we have already seen, to introduce his unknown sources, as well as his citations in disguise, he himself composed.[315]

On looking more carefully, it cannot escape our attention, that Madhva puts forward his doctrine of the fifth Veda mainly in the fictitious passages ascribed to BrāṇP. And he pursues this very line when he describes in details the Durāgamas, which so far have been introduced in the passages quoted above in a general form, namely as texts in opposition to the Sadāgamas. More information about them is supplied in the following citation in MBhTN:

> *eṣa mohaṃ sṛjāmy āśu yo janān mohayiṣyati /*
> *tvaṃ ca rudra mahābāho mohaśāstrāṇi kāraya //*
> *atatthyāni vitatthyāni darśayasva mahābhuja /*
> *prakāsaṃ kuru cātmanam aprakāśaṃ ca māṃ kuru //*
> iti vārāhavacanaṃ brahmāṇḍoktaṃ . . . /[316]

---

[312] Cf. MBhTN II 11cdff. and SIAUVE 1971: 3 „En atmosphère polythéiste, devant le foisonnement des écrits exaltant tel ou tel dieu, devant la multiplicité des dévotions populaires, ces problèmes se présentent dans toute leur acuité. C'est pourquoi la doctrine de la hiérarchie, *Tāratamya*, des *deva* est un des points essentiels de la théologie mādhva, et elle apparaît à diverses reprises et sous divers aspects dans ces derniers chapitres de l'*Anuvyākhyāna*, comme un des éléments de la 'vraie doctrine', longuement expliqué, justifié par les textes et le raisonnement. ... La connaissance de la hiérarchie est donc un des moyens indispensables au salut, parce qu'elle seule est capable de concilier la multiplicité des *deva* et l'unique souveraineté de Viṣṇu."

[313] Cf. MBhTN II 23ff.; above n 76ff.

[314] Cf MBhTN II 35ff.

[315] Cf. above n 136ff.

[316] MBhTN I 48-50ab; cf. GīBh p. 35,21f.

„I will create illusion, which will quickly deceive the people. And you, long armed Rudra, compose texts, which cause illusion. Proclaim, o long armed, [texts,] which do not ever exist, or which are false. And make yourself known, and conceal me. This is a statement of VarP handed down in BrāṇP . . . ."[317]

Indeed, this quotation from VarP is not only not to be located in BrāṇP, but also deviates from the wording in VarP, which is as follows:

antye yuge praviralā bhaviṣyanti madāśrayāḥ /
eṣa mohaṃ sṛjāmy āśu yo janaṃ mohayiṣyati // 35
tvaṃ ca rudra mahābāho mohaśāstrāṇi kāraya /
alpāyāsaṃ darśayitvā [phalaṃ dīrghaṃ pradarśaya // 36
kuhakaṃ cendrajālāni viruddhācaraṇāni ca /
darśayitvā janaṃ sarvaṃ] mohayāśu maheśvara // 37
evam uktvā tadā tena devena parameṣṭhinā /
ātmā tu gopitaḥ sadyaḥ prakāśyo 'haṃ [318] *kṛtas tadā //*38 [319]

The fact that the critical edition of this Purāṇa mentions several variant readings to the *śloka*s concerned and even puts one whole *śloka* in brackets, shows that the written records of this Purāṇa are not uniform, and therefore not safe. This is supported by some authors, who lived before and after Madhva, like Yāmunācārya and Veṅkaṭanātha, for their respective quotations contain also different readings.[320] In opposition to it, Sudar-

---

[317] For the doctrine of Sadāgamas cf. above n 244ff.

[318] Cf. VarP 70,34ab: *evam uktas tato devair mām uvāca janārdanaḥ.*

[319] VarP 70, 35-38.

[320] Cf. ĀP p. 97,14-98,4: tathā ca vārāhe –

tvaṃ ca rudra mahābāho mohaśāstrāṇi kāraya /
kuhakādīndrajālāni viruddhācaraṇāni ca //
darśayitvālpam āyāsam phalaṃ śīghraṃ pradarśaya /
darśayitvā janaṃ sarvaṃ mohayāśu maheśvara //
iti.

cf. also Veṅkaṭanātha, Pañcarātrarakṣā (ed. P.B. AṆṆAṄGARĀCĀRYA. Madras 1941), p. 103,11:

śanasūri transmits the reading of the critical edition although with some slight variations.[321]

It is remarkable that the 'quotation' from BrāṇP presented by Madhva differs not only in the wording but also in the contents. According to VarP (v. 38) Viṣṇu is the one who conceals himself and makes Rudra known. In Madhva's statement, on the contrary, Rudra is the one who, on order of Viṣṇu, makes himself known and conceals Viṣṇu. Besides, Madhva replaces the *śloka*-portion (37ab), which defines precisely *mohaśāstrāṇi* as: *kuhakaṃ cendrajālāni viruddhācaraṇāni ca* by a more general remark: *atathyāni vitathyāni darśayasva mahābhuja*. And Madhva

---

> *tvaṃ hi rudra mahābāho mohaśāstrāṇi kāraya /*
> *darsayitvālpam āyāsaṃ phalaṃ śīghraṃ pradarśaya /*

Veṅkaṭanātha, Nyāyapariśuddhi (ed. P.B. AṆṆAṄGARĀCĀRYA. Madras 1940), p. 167,9-11:

> *yathoktaṃ bhagavataiva –*
> *tvaṃ hi rudra mahābāho mohaśāstrāṇi kāraya /*
> *alpāyāsaṃ darśayitvā phalaṃ śīghraṃ pradarśaya //*
> (v. l.: *darśayitvā alpām āyāsaṃ*)
> *ahaṃ mohaṃ kariṣyāmi yo janaṃ mohayiṣyāmi /*
> iti.

The editor of the critical edition remarks in this regard (Introduction p. IX): „A number of the *ślokas* of the *Varāha Purāṇa* has been quoted by the scholars, such as Vedāntadeśika, in their works of the Rāmānuja sect, which are mentioned as quoted from the *Varāha Purāṇa*, but which are not actually traceable in the available editions of this Purāṇa. Such *ślokas*, in the opinion of this writer, either might have been lost from the Varāha Purāṇa or might be traced in some south Indian manuscripts of this Purāṇa."

[321] Sudarśanasūri quotes in his Śrutaprakāśikā (on Sū II 2,38) seven *ślokas* from VarP (33-39). For our present context the following are relevant:

> *antye yuge praviralā bhaviṣyanti madāśrayāḥ /*
> *eṣa mohaṃ sṛjāmy āśu yo janaṃ mohayiṣyati* // 35
> *tvaṃ ca rudra mahābāho mohaśāstrāṇi kāraya /*
> *alpāyāsaṃ darśayitvā phalaṃ dīrghaṃ pradarśaya* // 36
> *kuhakānīndrajālāni viruddhācaraṇāni ca /*
> *darśayitvā janaṃ sarvaṃ mohayāśu maheśvara* // 37
> *evam uktas* (*uktvā* ?) *tadā tena devena parameṣṭhinā /*
> *ātmā tu gopitaḥ sadyaḥ prakāśo 'haṃ kṛtas tataḥ* // 38

sticks to this textual change in BSūBh as well as in GīT.[322] So, it is surprising that Madhva in his KN (= KhN) quotes in the way, as it is handed down in VarP:

> *kuhakam cendrajālaṃ ca viruddhācaraṇāni ca /*
> *darśayitvā janaṃ sarvaṃ mohayāśu maheśvara //*
> ityādi vārāhe.

Madhva uses this quotation as a proof for the view that passages of the Purāṇas, which are in contradiction to the Vedas, have only a secondary or metaphorical meaning (*purāṇādīnāṃ tu śrutyādivirodhe gauṇo 'py artho yujyate*),[323] for the basis of the Purāṇas is illusion, cheat and forbidden practices. This implies that Madhva was really aware of the reading handed down in VarP. And the reason why he nevertheless makes use of a deviating reading, lies on the fact that Madhva contaminated it with the analogous text of PadP, where exactly the same wording used by Madhva is recorded.[324] He quotes in this connection two other *śloka*s from PadP:

> *uktaṃ pādmapurāṇe ca śaiva eva śivena tu /*
> *yad uktaṃ hariṇā pūrvam umāyai prāha tad haraḥ //*
> *tvām ārādhya tathā śambho grahīṣyāmi varaṃ sadā /*
> *dvāparādāu yuge bhūtvā kalayā mānuṣādiṣu /*
> *svāgamaiḥ kalpitais tvaṃ ca janān madvimukhān kuru /*
> *mām ca gopāya yena syāt sṛṣṭir eṣottarādhārā //* [325]

---

[322] Cf. BSūBh p. 7,12 + 8,1 and GīT p. 35,22-24.

[323] KN p. 101,14-16 = KhN p. 247, 24-25.

[324] Cf. MBhTN I 48- 49 = PadP VI 71,108-109.

[325] MBhTN I 56-58 (= PadP VI 71, 106-107). In the same context three other *ślokas* with slight changes are cited in MBhTN I 53-56ab = PadP [VI 71,114-116]); cf. also PadP (VI 235,23-25) :

> *śrī bhagavān uvāca –*
> *tvaṃ hi rudra mahābāho mohanārthe suradviṣām /*
> *pāṣaṇḍācaraṇaṃ dharmaṃ kuruṣva surasattama //*
> *tāmasāni purāṇāni kathayasva ca tān prati /*

On account of these observations we can ascertain that Madhva integrated the concept of *mohaśāstrāṇi*, taught in the Purāṇas, into his doctrine of the fifth Veda. Madhva makes use of the main elements of that view, as recorded in the Purāṇas, in a passage ascribed to Bhaviṣyatparvan with a very significant remark: *ityādy uktam bhagavatā bhaviṣyatparvaṇi sphuṭam*. As we have already proved above, this unknown work or work-title is a literary invention of Madhva.[326] The present passage com-

---

mohanāni ca śāstrāṇi kuruṣva ca mahāmate ||
mayi muktāś ca viprāś ca bhaviṣyanti maharṣayaḥ |

In BĀUBh (p. 268,11-13) Madhva quotes from PadP, however, the *śloka*s could not be identified:

akṣapādakaṇādau ca sāṅkhyayogārhatās tathā |
śivaśaktimahāyānalokāyatapuraḥsarāḥ ||
gāṇapatyāś ca saurāś ca sarve proktā durāgamāḥ |
ṛgyajuḥsāmātharvāś cetihāsapurāṇakau ||
svāgamā iti saṃproktā mīmāṃsā dharma eva ca |
iti pādme.

The original passage in PadP, which mentions the rise of several texts contradicting Veda and the appearance of misleading traditions (*tāmasāni śāstrāṇi*) brought forth under the command of Rudra by the founders of the philosophical schools like Vaiśeṣika and by other teachers, as well as texts, like eighteen Purāṇas (*sāttvikāni/rājasāni/tāmasāni* (VI 236,1-22), has a completely different wording (cf. ibid VI 106ff. = MBhTN I 48-58.). BhāgTN (p. 737,11-13; cf. also GīBh p. 35,17-18) quotes from an unknown source, where the founders of the different schools are called heretics:

yogasāṅkhyakaṇādākṣapādā vai hetuvādinaḥ|
paśvīśaśāktabuddhādyās pāṣaṇḍā iti kīrtitāḥ ||

This judgement corresponds to the definition of a Pāṣaṇḍa in PadP (*l. c.* 235, 2-11), cf. Manusmṛti IV 30; XII 95; J. ABS, Beiträge zur Kritik heterodoxer Philosophie-Systeme in der Purāṇa-Literatur. Beiträge zur Literaturwissenschaft und Geistesgeschichte Indiens. Festgabe Hermann Jacobi. Bonn 1926, p. 386-396; W.D.O' FLAHERTY, The Origin of Heresy in Hindu Mythology, History of Religions 10 (1971), p. 271-333.

326 Cf. above n 34f. Madhva brings under this work-title a long citation in BĀUBh (p. 268,24-269,13) dealing with *svataḥprāmāṇya* of Sadāgamas; cf. below n 343.

prises seventeen and half *śloka*s intimately associated with the peculiar teachings of Madhva. Only the beginning of this passage is of special interest for our purpose, which runs as follows:

ṛgādayaś ca catvāraḥ pañcarātraṃ ca bhāratam /
mūlarāmāyaṇaṃ brahmasūtraṃ mānaṃ svataḥ smṛtam //
aviruddhaṃ ca yat tv asya pramāṇaṃ tac ca nānyathā /
etadviruddhaṃ yat tu syān na tan mānaṃ kathañcana //
vaiṣṇavāni purāṇāni pañcarātrātmakatvataḥ /
pramāṇāny eva manvādyāḥ smṛtayo 'py anukūlataḥ /
eteṣu viṣṇor ādhikyam ucyate 'nyasya na kvacit /
atas tad eva mantavyaṃ nānyathā tu kathañcana //
mohārthāny anyaśāstrāṇi kṛtāny evājñayā hareḥ /
atas teṣūktam agrāhyam asurāṇāṃ tamogateḥ //
yasmāt kṛtāni tānīha viṣṇunoktaiḥ śivādibhiḥ
eṣāṃ yan na virodhi syāt tatroktaṃ tan na vāryate //
viṣṇvādhikyavirodhīni yāni vedavacāṃsy api /
tāni yojyāny ānukūlyād viṣṇvādhikyasya sarvaśaḥ //

„It has been handed down in the tradition, that the four Vedas, as well as Pañcarātra, [Mahā]Bhārata, the original Rāmāyaṇa and the Brahmasūtras [etc.] are self-evident means of knowledge. All [other means of knowledge], which do not contradict them, are too [in this way] valid [and] not otherwise. Whatever is in contradiction to them, is under no circumstances valid. The Vaiṣṇavite-Purāṇas are also valid means of knowledge, as their teaching corresponds to Pañcarātra. Also the *smṛtis*, like Manusmṛti are [valid means of knowledge], since they too are in agreement with [them].

In all these texts the supreme sovereignty of Viṣṇu is conveyed, nowhere is the supremacy of some other [being] stated. Therefore, one should meditate only on these [texts], never, however, on the other [texts]. Other works have been composed only [by Rudra] under the command of Hari in order to deceive [the Asuras]. Therefore, one should not accept, what has been taught there, because they direct the Asuras to the [eternal] darkness. Since they have been composed by Śiva on the command of Viṣṇu, one need not reject [all] what is taught there, so far as they are not in contradiction to the [teaching of Sadāgamas]. Even the Vedic statements, which [seem] to contradict the absolute sovereignty of Viṣṇu, they should be in every case properly interpreted in agreement with the sovereignty of Viṣṇu."[327]

Analysing these statements closely we come to a very surprising conclusion. On the one hand, Madhva does not reject the Śaivite Āgamas (= *mohaśāstrāṇi*) completely: Firstly, because they contain textual passages, which are not in contradiction with the *pañcamaveda*, and secondly, because the Śaivāgamas have been composed on the command of Viṣṇu by Rudra. On the other hand, Madhva admits, that there are passages in the Veda, which apparently do not teach the absolute sovereignty of Viṣṇu. Both points of view are clearly inconsistent with the statements Madhva made on Sadāgamas and *mohaśāstrāṇi*, for the Sadāgamas proclaim *per definitionem* and on the basis of self-evidence (*svataḥprāmaṇya*)[328] the meaning of the eternal Vedas and the *mahātātparya* of the absolute sovereignty of Viṣṇu.

---

[327] MBhTN I 30-36. Interestingly enough that Madhva presents in ChUBh (p. 445,10-11) a fictitious passage ascribed to BrahVP, which corresponds partly with the statement of Bhaviṣyatparvan (cf. above n 119). According to it, the Brahmasūtras serve as a criterion for the interpretation of Vedas and other texts:

> *brahmasūtrānusāreṇa vedādyaṃ sarvam eva ca /*
> *yojyaṃ na brahmasūtrāṇi dṛśyamānārthato 'nyathā //*

= Bhaviṣyatparvan (MBhTN I 44ab):

> *tasmāt sūtrārtham āgṛhya kartavyaḥ sarvanirṇayaḥ.*

A similar hermeneutical principle we come across in Rāmānuja's Vedārthasaṃgraha (crit. ed. J.A.B. VAN BUITENEN. Poona 1956, p. 142,16-17): *anyāni sarvāṇi purāṇāny etadavirodhena neyāni / anyaparatvaṃ ca tattadārambhaprakārair avagamyate / sarvātmanā viruddhāṃśas tāmasatvād anādaraṇīyaḥ* (*ibid.* p. 84,11): *śodhakavākyāny api niravadyaṃ sarvakalyāṇaguṇākaraṃ paraṃ brahma bodhayantī.*

[328] Cf. above n 225 and also the self-statement of Madhva in MBhTN I 59-60:

Likewise, the position of the Śaivāgamas in this context is clear, too. In agreement with VarP, these texts go back, but only indirectly, to Viṣṇu, since they have been composed on his command by Rudra. Their main purpose is to deceive the Asuras. On this reason, it can be excluded that the Śaivāgamas praise Viṣṇu as the supreme God. Besides, the very definition of *mohaśāstrāṇi* as works of cheat, illusion as well as of repugnant and forbidden practices (*kuhakam cendrajālāni viruddhācaraṇāni*) and also as texts, which are in contradiction to the *sarvottamatva* of Viṣṇu (*duḥśāstraṃ tadvirodhi*), has been accepted by Madhva and sharply criticized by him on other occasions.[329] It is, therefore, very strange that Madhva, in fact a 'fanatic of Viṣṇu', takes here a very liberal position with regard to the Śaivites and attempts to interpret their scriptures under the scope of inclusivism.[330] We can be sure that it is not a casual remark of Madhva,

---

na ca vaiṣṇavaśāstreṣu vedeṣv api hareh paraḥ /
kvacid ukto 'nyaśāstreṣu paramo viṣṇur īritaḥ //
nirdoṣatvāc ca vedānāṃ vedoktaṃ grāhyam eva hi /
vedeṣu ca paro viṣṇuḥ sarvasmād ucyate sadā //

cf. BĀUBh p. 268,24f.; above n 325. Madhva proves this point of view with the help of PadP (VI 71,114-116) = MBhTN I 53-56 :

paramo viṣṇur evaikas tajjñānaṃ mokṣasādhanam /
sāstrāṇāṃ nirṇayas tv eṣa tadanyan mohanāya hi //
jñānaṃ vinā tu yā muktiḥ sāmyaṃ ca mama viṣṇunā /
tīrthādimātrato jñānaṃ mamādhikyaṃ ca viṣṇutaḥ //
abhedaś cāsmadādīnāṃ muktānāṃ hariṇā tathā /
ityādi sarvaṃ mohāya kathyate putra nānyathā //
uktaṃ pādmapurāṇe *ca śaiva eva śivena tu* /
yad uktaṃ hariṇā pūrvam umāyai prāha tad dharaḥ //

329 Cf. above n 316f. Elsewhere, Madhva criticizes this position in accordance with the teaching of Maitrāyaṇyupaniṣad (cf. above n 205f.).

330 For the concept of inclusivism, see Inklusivismus. Eine indische Denkform, ed. by G. OBERHAMMER (Publications of the De Nobili Research Library [Occasional Papers 2]). Vienna 1983 and W. HALBFASS, India und Europe. An Essay in Understanding. New York 1988, p. 403-418. However, in opposition to his opinion above, Madhva quotes a fictitious passage ascribed to Brahmatarka (BĀUBh p. 311,14ff.), commenting that in the disputation one should cite only from the Sadāgamas and not from the Durāgamas:

for there is also another even more clear statement in connection with this subject matter, namely:

> skānde *'py uktam śivenaiva ṣaṇmukhāyaiva sādaram /*
> *śivaśāstre 'pi tad grāhyaṃ bhagavacchāstrayogi yat //*[331]

On further consideration, this observation strengthens our previous statement, that Madhva reshaped textually a certain passage from SkaP, proclaiming Viṣṇu as the supreme God for the purpose of incorporating it with his typical doctrine of *pañcamaveda*.[332] The quotation above calls for special attention to the position of SkaP and implies that the teaching of sovereignty of Viṣṇu, put forward there, is in complete agreement with the view of Sadāgamas (*bhagavacchāstrayogi*), and, therefore, should be accepted as a valid teaching (*grāhya*), despite the fact that it is a Śaivasāstra. Madhva presents this view again, when he asserts:

> *na ca vaiṣṇavaśāstreṣu vedeṣv api hareḥ paraḥ /*
> *kvacid ukto 'nyaśāstreṣu paramo viṣṇur īritaḥ //*[333]

> *pṛṣṭena prathamaṃ mānaṃ vaktavyaṃ vādinā śubham /*
> *vedāḥ sarve śubhaṃ mānaṃ setihāsapurāṇakāḥ //*
> *sapañcarātramīmāṃsāḥ smṛtayaś cāpy anantaram /*
> *tadanyad aśubhaṃ proktaṃ na prayojyaṃ kathāsu ca //*
> . . .
> ityādi brahmatarke.

331 MBhTN I 52. Similarly, it cannot be accidental, that Madhva in MBhTN (II 101-102) makes two significant textual changes [put below in heavy type] in the citation from MBh (XII 337, 63-64ab), specially adding half a *śloka* (*sāṅkhyapāśupatādiṣu*) in order to adapt it to the above mentioned interpretation: *sarveṣu ca nṛpaśreṣṭha jñāneṣv eteṣu dṛśyate / yathāgamaṃ yathā jñānam* . . . :

> *pañcarātrasya kṛtsnasya vaktā nārāyaṇaḥ svayam /*
> *sarveṣv eteṣu rājendra jñāteṣv etad viśiṣyate //*
> *jñāteṣv eteṣu rājendra* **sāṅkhyapāśupatādiṣu** *//*
> **yathāyogaṃ yathānyāyaṃ** *niṣṭhā nārāyaṇaḥ paraḥ //*

In (Anuv p. 88,22) however without these changes!

332 Cf. above n 272f.

333 MBhTN I 59; cf. above n 305f.

In this very context a citation in guise ascribed to Bhaviṣyatparvan, which is divided in two parts, fits rightly.[334] The first part proceeds with the subject matter broached here and supplements in a special way the teaching in the Bhaviṣyat-parvan, which has been already introduced above. The second part, dealing with the peculiar doctrine of Madhva, that he descends on earth as an *avatāra* of Vāyu, has been already discussed above.[335] So we can turn to the first part:

> bhaviṣyatparvagaṃ *cāpi vaco vyāsasya sādaram* /
> *vāsudevasya mahimā bhārate nirṇayoditaḥ* //
> *tadarthās tu kathāḥ sarvā nānyārthaṃ vaiṣṇavaṃ yaśaḥ* /
> *tatpratīpaṃ tu yad dṛśyen na tan mama manīṣitaṃ* //
> *bhāṣās tu trividhās tatra mayā vai saṃpradarśitāḥ* /
> *ukto yo mahimā viṣṇoḥ sa tūkto hi samādhinā* //
> *śaivadarśanam ālaṃbhya kvacic chaivī kathoditā* /
> *samādhibhāṣayoktaṃ yat tat sarvaṃ grāhyam eva hi* //
> *aviruddhaṃ samādhes tu darśanoktaṃ ca gṛhyate* /
> *ādyantayor viruddhaṃ yad darśanaṃ tad udāhṛtam* //
> *darśanāntarasiddhaṃ ca guhyabhāṣānyathā bhavet* /
> *tasmād viṣṇor hi mahimā bhāratokto yathārthataḥ* //

„And the Bhaviṣyatparvan contains the honoured statement of Vyāsa: In [Mahā-] Bhārata the glory of Vāsudeva is firmly stated. And all stories [in this text] have this meaning. The glory of Viṣṇu has no other meaning. Whatever appears opposed to this is not intended by me. In this [work] three [kinds of] speeches have been revealed by me. The glory of Viṣṇu is [there] namely described by Samādhi[-speech].[336] In some places, Śaiva stories following Śaivadarśana have been narrated. Whatever has been stated by Samādhi[-speech], should be absolutely accepted. And what is stated in the [Śaiva-]system should be accepted,

[334] MBhTN II 112-117 ; II 118-123; cf. below n 297.

[335] Cf. above n 69ff.

[336] Cf. Vādirājatīrtha's commentary Bhāvaprakāśikā on MBhTN (quoted in PANDURANGI 1993: 122): *viṣṇumahimāpratipādakabhāṣā samādhibhāṣā / samāhitamanasā cittaikāgratayā kathitatvāt samādhibhāṣā*.

[only] if it is not contrary to Samādhi [-speech]. Darśana[-speech] is that, what is stated [in Śaiva-system] and in other philosophical systems [and] what is in contradiction to the [absolute sovereignty of Viṣṇu taught] from the beginning till the end [of MBh].[337] The hidden speech conveys [a meaning that is not articulated expressly in the text and is] different [from the literal meaning].[338] Therefore, the glory of Viṣṇu is indeed proclaimed in [Mahā-] Bhārata in accordance with the truth."

---

337 Cf. the teaching of an unknown source Bhāṣāviveka in BhāgTN p. 767,11f. and MBhTN II 66:

> *ādyantayor ity avadad sa yasmād vyāsātmako viṣṇur udāraśaktiḥ /*
> *tasmāt samastā harisadguṇānāṃ nirṇīyate bhāratagā kathaiṣā //*

cf. also Vādirājatīrtha's commentary Bhāvaprakāśikā on MBhTN (in: PANDURANGI 1993 l. c.): *ādyantayor viruddhārthapratipādakaṃ darśanam / ādāv uktakṛṣṇamahimākhyaprameyasya ante vakṣyamāṇakṛṣṇotkarṣarūpaprameyasya ca viruddham / darśanāntarasiddhaṃ vaiṣṇavadarśanaviruddhapāśupatādidarśanāntarasiddhaṃ yat kṛṣṇasya śivārcakatvādiprameyaṃ madhye yad ajñajanamohanāya kathyate taddarśana bhāṣayoktam ity arthaḥ.*

338 Vādirājatīrtha understands *anyathā* as different from both other two speeches: *gūḍhārthakapadaracanayocyate yā bhāṣā sā guhyabhāṣā / anyathā darśanabhāṣāto anyathā samādhibhāṣāto anyathā yad bhavet sā guhyabhāṣā* (Bhāvaprakāśikā, in: PANDURANGI l. c.). This passage refers to the literary device used by Madhva frequently (cf. above n 134f.), which allows him to attribute to Viṣṇu all quotations in disguise composed by him. In this sense, he ascribes directly to Vyāsa-Viṣṇu (*mayā saṃpradarśitāḥ*) the hermeneutical principle regarding the three levels of the speeches in respect to the absolute sovereignty of Viṣṇu. We have here a reminiscence of Gī (XV 16-20), where the revelation of Viṣṇu-Kṛṣṇa as *puruṣottama* is introduced as the highest mystery of God: *iti guhyatamaṃ śāstram idam uktaṃ mayā* (cf. above n 142). As a matter of fact, Madhva adduces elsewhere the above mentioned reference from Gī together with two other fictitious quotations, ascribed to Paiṅgīśruti and to VarP (VTN p. 19,6f.) respectively as a proof, that all canonical scriptures convey the highest meaning of the absolute sovereignty of Viṣṇu (*viṣṇoḥ sarvottamatva eva mahātātparyam āgamānām*) and that all other meanings are subordinate to it (*avāntaram tatparatvaṃ tadanyat*). In ChUBh (p. 442, 25-26) this is attributed to BrāṇP:

> *mahātatparatā viṣṇor utkarṣe 'vāntarā tataḥ /*
> *anyatra sarvavākyānaṃ yuktīnāṃ ca viśeṣataḥ //*
> iti brahmāṇḍe (unidentified).

The point is, that everywhere in MBh (*ādāv ante madhye*) the absolute sovereignty of Viṣṇu is taught.[339] In this sense, Madhva says in the disguised quotation from Bhaviṣyatparvan: *tadarthās tu kathāḥ sarvā nānyārthaṃ vaiṣṇavaṃ yaśaḥ* or in his self-statement: *tasmād viṣṇor hi mahimā bhāratokto yathārthataḥ*. In order to achieve this goal, Madhva differentiates three speech levels. With the help of this literary device he attempts to explain that even a passage with an opposite literary meaning does have a hidden purport, which has not been articulated by the author expressly, which, however, is intended by him (*gūḍhārtha*), namely the absolute sovereignty of Viṣṇu. This hermeneutical principle corresponds to the technical term *yojya* mentioned also in a fictitious citation from Bhaviṣyatparvan:

> *viṣṇvādhikyavirodhīni yāni vedavacāṃsy api* /
> *tāni yojyāny ānukūlyād viṣṇvādhikyasya sarvaśaḥ* // [340]

---

cf. also below n 340.

[339] Cf. the *śloka* (cf. above n 59; 266) from the Harivaṃśa (III 132, 95) quoted by Madhva very frequently:

> *vede rāmāyaṇe caiva purāṇe bhārate tathā* /
> *ādāv ante madhye ca viṣṇuḥ sarvatra gīyate* //

[340] Cf. above n 237f. A similar hermeneutical principle is attributed in VTN (p. 19,13-17) to Paiṅgiśruti and VarP by Madhva:

> *sarvotkarṣe devadevasya viṣṇor mahat*
> *tātparyaṃ naiva cānyatra satyam* /
> *avāntaraṃ tatparatvaṃ tadanyat*
> *sarvāgamānāṃ puruṣārthas tato 'ta* /
> iti paiṅgiśrutiḥ
> *mukhyaṃ ca sarvavedānāṃ tātparyaṃ śrīpateḥ paraṃ* /
> *utkarṣe tu tadanyatra tātparyaṃ syād avāntaram* /
> iti mahāvarāhe
> *yuktaṃ ca viṣṇoḥ sarvotkarṣe mahātātparyaṃ sarvāgamānām.*

The fictitious quotation from the Paiṅgiśruti appears with slight changes (*naiva cānyatra dṛṣṭam*) in GīT (p. 4,23f.), however as an anonymous *śruti*. As a matter of fact, we have here a hermeneutical principle developed in the Mīmāṃsā, which divides the whole Veda into two parts. The main part consists in precepts (*vidhi/codanā*) The rest is subordinated to it as an explanation of the meaning of the precept (*arthavāda*) or as a supplement to the

This is now a guiding principle for the inquiry of other two passages, which Madhva assigns to two known sources, namely to NārP and to BhavP, and is a weighty complement to our investigation so far:

kutsitāni ca miśrāṇi rudro viṣṇupracoditaḥ |
cakāra śāstrāṇi vibhur ṛṣayas tatpracoditāḥ ||
dadhīcyādyāḥ purāṇāni tacchāstrasamayena tu |
cakrur vedaiś ca brāhmāṇi vaiṣṇavān viṣṇuvedataḥ ||
pañcarātraṃ bhāratam ca mūlarāmāyaṇaṃ tathā |
tathā purāṇaṃ bhāgavataṃ viṣṇuveda itīritaḥ ||
ataḥ śaivapurāṇāni yojyāny anyāvirodhataḥ |
iti nāradīye.[341]
bhaviṣyatpurāṇe ca—
ṛgyajuḥsāmātharvākhyā mūlarāmāyaṇaṃ tathā |
bhārataṃ pañcarātraṃ ca vedā ity eva śabditāḥ ||

---

precept (*vidhiśeṣa*) (cf. MSū I 2,1-30). Giving a new interpretation to this twofold division of the Veda, the Advaitins propounded that the sole purport of the Vedas was the undivided-whole Brahman (*akhaṇḍārtha* or *abheda*), and consequently all other meanings are to be subordinated to this truth. In opposition to both of these views, Madhva asserts that the absolute sovereignty of Viṣṇu alone is *mahātātparya* of all canonical scriptures and all other meanings are subservient to it (VTN p. 19,5f.): *ataḥ sarvapramāṇaviruddhatvān nābhede tātparyaṃ vākyasya | kiṃtu viṣṇoḥ sarvottamatva eva mahātātparyam āgamānāṃ* (cf. above n 59). In support of this view he adduces the above mentioned citation from Paiṅgiśruti and VarP. Elsewhere in VTN (p. 15,19-23), while criticizing the opinion of Prābhākara-Mīmāṃsā, Madhva puts forward again a fictitious citation, which he ascribes to NarP: *prasiddhaṃ ca vyākaraṇaniruktādīnāṃ siddhamātre prāmāṇyaṃ sarvavādīnāṃ | tadanaṅgīkāre ca sarvaśabdavyavahārāsiddhiḥ |*

uktaṃ ca nāradīye –
sarvajñaṃ sarvakartāraṃ nārāyaṇam anāmayam |
sarvottamaṃ jñāpayanti mahātātparyam atra hi |
sarveṣām api vedānām itihāsapurāṇayoḥ |
pramāṇānāṃ ca sarveṣāṃ tadarthaṃ cānyad ucyate |
iti.

341 GīBh p. 35,22-36,2.

purāṇāni ca yānīha vaiṣṇavāni vido viduḥ |
svataḥprāmāṇyam eteṣāṃ nātra kiñcid vicāryate ||
yady eṣūktaṃ na dṛśyeta pūrvakarmātra kāraṇam |
nāprāmāṇyaṃ bhaved eṣāṃ dṛśyate hy adhikārataḥ ||
itaḥ prāmāṇyam anyeṣāṃ na svatas tu kathañcana |
adṛśyoktau tatas teṣām aprāmāṇyaṃ na saṃśayaḥ || [342]

For a better understanding of both these pieces, it is specially significant to compare them with the passages from Bhaviṣyatparvan. The comparison shows that each of the two fictitious citations above comprises separately one principle discussed in Bhaviṣyatparvan. The NārP contains the inclusivistic explanation of the Śaivapurāṇas, namely that the contradictory propositions in the Śaivapurāṇas should be put in tune with the contents of Sadāgamas, or that they should be interpreted according to Sadāgamas (*śaivapurāṇāni yojyāny anyāvirodhataḥ*). The BhavP unfolds for its part the principle of *svataḥprāmāṇya* of Sadāgamas, however, with a small variation. In harmony with the context of the BSū (II 1,5) this principle is supplemented by an addition that the reason for the failure to have a valid knowledge does not lie in the Sadāgamas, but in the *karma* of a person, since the results of *svataḥprāmāṇya* sometimes fail to take place due to *karma*.

In this way, we can see that both those quotations are in perfect harmony with the teaching of Bhaviṣyatparvan, not only regarding the enumeration of the texts together with Mūlarāmāyaṇa belonging to *pañcamaveda*, but also with regard to the proof of *svataḥprāmāṇya* of the fifth Veda and with respect to *aprāmāṇya* of Durāgamas. It is noteworthy, that in Madhva's

---

342 BSūBh p. 60,3-8.; cf. also BĀUBh (p. 268, 15-17):

vedāś caivetihāsāś ca purāṇaṃ bhāgavataṃ tathā |
mūlapramāṇam uddiṣṭaṃ mīmāṃsā ca tathottarā ||
eteṣām avirodhe tu mānam anyad udīritam |
eteṣāṃ tu viruddhaṃ yad apramāṇaṃ vido viduḥ ||
iti vyāsasmṛtau (unidentified!).

opinion the Durāgamas too can convey a valid knowledge, but on the condition that their wrong meaning is corrected in agreement with the absolute sovereignty of Viṣṇu. Through this inclusion of Śaivāgamas in the doctrine of Śabdaprāmāṇya, Madhva accepts that practically they too belong to the Sadāgamas[343], although they are known in the tradition of Purāṇas as *mohaśāstrāṇi*.[344] From all the observations discussed above we can surely conclude, that the redactional style and

---

[343] It is, therefore, not astonishing that Madhva does not polemize against Śaivites in his works, like VTN. This is strange in view of the fact that in the Viśiṣṭādvaita it builds up a fixed subject within the proof for the supremacy of Viṣṇu (cf. Yāmunas Puruṣanirṇaya in: ĀP p. 88,4-101,8; Vātsya Varadaguru: Tattvanirṇaya, Hrsg. S. STARK [SbÖAW 570 = Beiträge zur Kultur- und Geistesgeschichte Asiens 4]. Wien 1990, Teil 1: p. 94, 17ff.). Possibly, Madhva shares *mutatis mutandis* the opinion, as, for instance, Jayantabhaṭṭa held in NM (p. 241, 31ff.; for details see OBERHAMMER 1974: 67ff.), when he differentiated between two groups of Āgamas. The first one is in complete contradiction to the Veda, like the Āgamas of the Buddhists (*kāni cit sarvātmanā vedavirodhenaiva pravartante bauddhādivat*) and for this reason, they should be rejected. The other group is in harmony with Veda, like the Āgamas of the Śaivites and Vaiṣṇavites. These Āgamas should be accepted as authoritative (*kāni cit tadavirodhenaiva śaivādivat / tatra śaivādyāgamānāṃ tāvat prāmāṇyam*); cf. the part-citation from Bhaviṣyatparvan (BĀUBh p. 269,1ff.):

> . . .
> *pratyakṣāder viruddhatvāt saugatādyā durāgamāḥ /*
> *bahvāgamavirodhāc ca duṣṭatvaṃ teṣu saṃsthitam //*
> *prāmāṇyaṃ svikṛtaṃ yais tu vedānām āgamā hi te /*
> *śatakoṭayaḥ pañcarātraṃ purāṇaṃ tāvad eva ca //*
> *rāmasya caritaṃ tāvat tāvad anyac ca sarvaśaḥ /*
> *anantāś ca tathā vedāḥ sāṅgopāṅgāś ca sarvaśaḥ //*
> *sarvādhikyaṃ yatra viṣṇos tātparyāt samudīryate /*
> . . .

cf. also above (n 157f.) the quotation from NārP.

[344] PadP (VI 236, 18):

> *mātsyaṃ kaurmaṃ tathā laiṅgaṃ śaivaṃ skāndaṃ tathaiva ca /*
> *āgneyaṃ ca ṣaḍ etāni tāmasāni nibodha me //*

cf. MBhTN X 83; above n 57; 325.

shape and specially the contents of the fictitious passages let know that Madhva himself is their literary author.

SUMMARY AND FINAL REMARKS

At the end of this investigation the most important results achieved in the course of this study will be summarized with the help of a passage from Bhaviṣyatparvan, which in Madhva's view is the second in the rank among his fictitious works, after Brahmatarka. Both present almost all the peculiar doctrines of Madhva.[345] Since this passage is a literary composition of Madhva, and fits well in the scenario of his unknown sources, it is best qualified to illustrate in an exemplary manner the fictitious frame of the unknown sources as a literary device to introduce the original doctrines of Madhva. The passage is intimately associated with his doctrine of Bhakti (*tatprītyaiva ca mokṣaḥ prāpyas tenaiva nānyena*), based on KathU[346]:

---

[345] Cf. n 34; 51; 76; 91; 121; 138; 192; 219; 238; 326; 327; 334; 338; 340; 342f. The close relation between both these texts is attested also by Appayadīkṣita who mentions them together in his list, cf. above n 33.

[346] KathU II 23 = MuU III 2,3 (= MBhTN I 77):

> *nāyam ātmā pravacanena labhyo na medhayā na bahunā śrutena /*
> *yam evaiṣa vṛṇute tena labhyas tasyaiṣa ātmā vivṛṇute tanuṃ svām //*

In sequence to this verse follow 22 *ślokas*, which are assigned to Bhaviṣyatparvan (*ibid.* I 78-99). It is divided in two parts. The first part (I 78-85) gives a list of Madhva's typical doctrines described as the path of the deliverance, while the second part (86-99) deals with different classes among the individual souls (*jīvasaṅghāḥ*), alloted according to their innate ability (*yogyānusareṇa*), namely to *muktiyogyāḥ*, *sṛṣṭiyogyāḥ* and to *tamolayāḥ*. Most probably, Madhva is following the Pañcarātra-view, which accepts four types of individual souls: *muktāḥ*, *muktiyogyāḥ*, *nityabaddhāḥ* and *tamoyogyāḥ* (cf. SCHRADER 1973: 99). Madhva makes use of these descriptions elsewhere (cf. TV v. 6-7; MBhTN I 18; TS p. 60,6f.). Madhva uses the same fictitious frame work, when he presents his Bhakti doctrine in VTN (p. 19,17-20,10) and in BSūBh (p. 5,57). He establishes this doctrine in two steps, namely that the release is the highest object of human pursuit (*mokṣo hi sarvapuruṣārthottamaḥ*) and that it is based unconditionally on the grace of Viṣṇu (*mokṣaś ca*

viṣṇur hi dātā mokṣasya vāyuś ca tadanujñayā |
mokṣo jñānaṃ ca kramaśo muktigo bhoga eva ca || [78]
uttareṣāṃ prasādena nīcānāṃ nānyathā bhavet |
sarveṣāṃ ca harir nityaniyantā tadvaśāḥ pare || [79]
tāratamyaṃ tato jñeyaṃ sarvoccatvaṃ hares tathā |
etad vinā na kasyāpi vimuktiḥ syāt kathaṃcana || [80]
pañcabhedāṃś ca vijñāya viṣṇoḥ svābhedam eva ca |
nirdoṣatvaṃ guṇodrekaṃ jñātvā muktir na cānyathā | [81]
avatārān harer jñātvā nāvatārā hareś ca ye |
tadāveśāṃs tathā samyag jñātvā muktir na cānyathā | [82]
sṛṣṭirakṣāhṛtijñānaniyatyajñānabandhanān |
mokṣaṃ ca viṣṇutas tv eva jñātvā muktir na cānyathā || [83]
vedāṃś ca pañcarātrāṇi setihāsapurāṇakān |
jñātvā viṣṇuparān eva mucyate nānyathā kvacit || [84]
māhātmyajñānapūrvas tu sudṛdhaḥ sarvato 'dhikaḥ |
sneho bhaktir iti proktas tayā muktir na cānyathā || [85]

---

viṣṇuprasādaṃ vinā na labhyate). By the fact that Madhva takes only *mokṣa* as the highest object of human pursuit, he devalues the other three (*trivarga* : *kāma, artha, dharma*). Before him, Śaṅkara has taught this radical dichotomy, possibly based on ViṣP (I 17,19; cf. SDS p. 272,20-25 and MESQUITA 2000: Ü. n 168) though in the context of his Advaita idealism, (cf. W. HALBFASS, Menschsein und Lebensziele. Beobachtungen zu den *puruṣārthas*. In: Hermeneutics of Encounter. Essays in Honour of Gerhard Oberhammer on the Occasion of his 65th Birthday, edd. FRANCIS X. D'SA and ROQUE MESQUITA [Publications of the De Nobili Research Library 20]. Vienna 1994, p. 131ff.). While accepting this dichotomy, Madhva rejects in all strictness Śaṅkara's idealism. He refrains also from the view of other philosophical schools, like Nyāya-Vaiśeṣika, which divides the objects of human pursuit, in *dṛṣṭa* and *adṛṣṭa* or, like other authors, in *laukika* and *pāralaukika*. According to this opinion *kāma* and *artha* belong to the first category, while *dharma* and *mokṣa* belong to the latter (cf. HALBFASS l. c.). In opposition to it, Madhva defines the first three as *anitya* and *mokṣa* as *nitya*. As reference he quotes from Bhāllaviśruti and from MBh. Both citations are not to be located and they give rather the impression that Madhva composed them *ad hoc*. In order to prove the second aspect of his doctrine about Mokṣa, which could be established by many references found in the Sanskrit literature, especially in Gī, Madhva brings forward, besides two citations from KathU (II 23 = MuU III 2,3) and from Gī (XII 7) four other unidentified passages assigned by him to Paiṅgiśruti, SkaP. And two of them are in *iti ca*-quotations. All four should be literary compositions of Madhva.

„Viṣṇu bestows liberation, so does Vāyu by his command. Liberation, knowledge, as well as enjoyment in the liberation will be granted to the subordinates according to their [respective] rank by the grace of the higher in rank [and] not otherwise. Hari is the eternal governor of all [beings]. [All] other [beings] are subordinate to him. Therefore, one should acknowledge the hierarchy [among the subordinates], as well as the absolute sovereignty of Hari. Without this [knowledge] no one can attain liberation in any way. One can achieve liberation only after knowing the fivefold difference and the absence of internal difference in Viṣṇu,[347] after knowing that he is free of imperfections and full of [infinite] attributes. And in no other way [it can be obtained]. After knowing the *avatāras* of Hari and those, who are not his *avatāras*, as well as after knowing correctly those of them, which Hari has taken possession of, liberation takes place. And in no other way [can it be obtained]. After knowing that creation, sustenance, destruction, knowledge, destiny/guidance, ignorance, bondage and liberation are caused by Viṣṇu alone,[348] liberation takes place. And in no other way

---

[347] Cf. above n 195ff.; 228f.: *asatyaḥ svagato bhedo viṣṇoḥ*; ChUBh p. 393,8: *svagatabhedo bhagavati nāsti*; above n 42; 234; 239. For details see MESQUITA 2000: St. n 524f.

[348] Cf. VTN p. 20,6-8:

> *utpattisthitisaṃhārā niyatir jñānam āvṛtiḥ |*
> *bandhamokṣau ca puruṣād yasmāt sa harir ekarāṭ ||*

iti skānde = BSūBh p. 8,11-12; cf. also Anuv p. 8,19-20; ChUBh p. 442,21-22; TS p. 61,3-5. In VTN (p. 40,5f.) it has been handed down as the teaching of the Paramaśruti:

> . . .
> *sargasthitikṣayayatiprakāśāvṛtibandhanam |*
> *sarvakṣaraṇām ekaḥ sa kuryāt sāttvikamokṣaṇam |*
> *sargasthitiyatijyotirnityānandaprado 'kṣare |*
> *ceṣṭāpradaś ca sarveṣām eka eva paro hariḥ |*
> *tasya nānyo 'sti sargādikartā nirdoṣakaś ca saḥ |*
> iti paramaśrutiḥ.

Cf. above n 169.

[can it be obtained]. By knowing that the Vedas, Pañcarātras along with Itihāsas and Purāṇas have Viṣṇu as their purport, liberation takes place. And in no other way [can it be obtained]. Very intense love, which surpasses all [other beings], and which is deeply rooted in the knowledge of supreme majesty [of Viṣṇu], is called Bhakti. It causes liberation. And in no other way [can it be obtained]."

A close scrutiny of these statements shows that they are very significant in two respects. First, they present us a synthesis of all the important doctrines of Madhva. Secondly, they are introduced singly in a definitive way, with the help of an adverbial negative expression (*na cānyathā*), each time as unconditional presuppositions for the achievement of *mokṣa*. In this sense they make up the religious plan of Madhva school.

It should be emphasized that Bhaviṣyatparvan is a source devised by Madhva himself, which he attributes to Viṣṇu (*uktam bhagavatā bhaviṣyatparvaṇi sphuṭam*).[349] A comparison between the above mentioned statements of this source and other fictitious passages, which Madhva uses to establish his peculiar teachings, shows clearly that they have the very same literary structure. All these textual passages, as I have documentated in the course of this study, have been composed by Madhva as befitting to the occasion and have been assigned sometimes to the known work-titles and sometimes to fictitious work-titles. From time to time, he has reworked the literary passages handed down in the tradition in accordance with his doctrine. And this procedure corresponds to the critical evaluation brought forward by Veṅkaṭanātha: *keṣucid aprasiddheṣu vā naṣṭakośeṣu vā anirūpitamūlāgreṣu vā purāṇeṣu prakṣipya paṭhanti* and *vākyāni saṃpratipannaśrutismṛtiṣv adṛśyamānāni* respectively.[350] This becomes obvious on account of our analysis of the fictitious passages with respect to *pañcamaveda* and to the Bhakti doctrine

---

349 Cf. above n 34f. and n 118.

350 Cf. above n 29 and Appayadīkṣita: *atyantāprasiddhānām eva vacanānāṃ sākṣitayopanyāsaḥ* (above n 32f.).

(v. 79ab, 84, 85) based on KathU,[351] with regard to the hierarchy (*tāratamya*) of Gods (v. 79 cd-80)[352] and to the teaching that all worldly developments, such as creation etc. are caused by Viṣṇu (v. 83),[353] with respect to the fivefold difference (*pañcabheda*) and to the absence of internal division (*abheda*) in Viṣṇu (v. 81)[354] and finally with regard to the typical doctrine of *avatāra* (v. 82). While formulating this doctrine Madhva is following the Pañcarātra tradition, which makes a distinction between primary and secondary *avatāras* (=*aṃśāvatāras*). The latter, in oppostion to the former, are not identical with Viṣṇu, however, Viṣṇu is fully present in them through *āveśa* and *jñānadīpana.*[355] For this reason, Madhva can appear under the guidance and accreditation of Viṣṇu as the reliable author of all literary texts.[356] This fact entitles Madhva to attribute to Viṣṇu (*uktaṃ viṣṇunā sākṣād* etc.)[357] all his literary compositions. It implies that the charismatic influence of Viṣṇu not only applies to the stimulus to act, but also to guidance at the composition of the texts in all phases, so that one can say that the literary compositions of Madhva comprise all what Viṣṇu actually wanted to reveal. In this construct of ideas Madhva reshapes the traditional thought patterns and fits them in his new frame work.[358] In the same way, Madhva was not the first to use the *avatāra* theology in order to establish the authenticity of religious traditions. Some Vaiṣṇavite circles had developed long before him a thought pattern, which

---

351 Cf. above n 267.

352 Cf. above n 312.

353 Cf. above n 169; 348.

354 Cf. above n 195; 228f.

355 Cf. above n 73ff. and n 122f.

356 Cf. above n 105ff. It is very significant that Madhva puts a special emphasis in this connection on the fact that the correct knowledge about his *āveśa* is absolutely necessary for Mokṣa: *tadāveśāṃs tathā samyag jñātvā muktiḥ*; cf. MBhTN (I 82cd; I 137) and above n 117; 128.

357 Cf. above n 134ff.

358 Cf. above n 80f.

made possible to secure a permanent acceptance of these traditions. According to this pattern Viṣṇu descends as *avatāra* due to his omnipotence in different ages and with different human bodies and proclaims the doctrine of salvation under different names.[359] In this case too, Madhva reshapes this principle, since he uses it not to prove the legitimacy of traditions well known for their long traditional antiquity and continuity, but to establish his new system without any traditional link. However, in order to exclude, in case of his unknown sources, every suspicion of a modern literary composition Madhva employs another old traditional pattern that all traditions are beginningless:

> *anādikālato vṛttāḥ samayā hi pravāhataḥ* |
> *na cocchedo 'sti kasyāpi samayasyety ato vibhuḥ* ||[360]

A more detailed explanation of the infallible authority of his canonical scriptures is attempted by him again with the help of another thought pattern put forward, combining *vedamūlatva* with *īśvarapraṇītatva*, by Vaiṣṇavite authors. According to this pattern, all sources of Madhva have their origin in the eternal Vedas, as far as they are resting in the intellect of Viṣṇu (*viṣṇubuddhigāḥ*). The role of the Ṛṣis and that of the *guruparaṃparā*, as canals for transmitting the Vedic knowledge, is belittled in a great degree in this thought pattern, for the Ṛṣis do not have the full knowledge of Vedas (*bhāgenaiva na sarvaśaḥ*). Madhva's sources, on the contrary, have the advantage that they are based on the Veda as it is known in its fullness by Viṣṇu since eternity, and which he reveals at the beginning of each creation. In this way they are in agreement with the entire Vedas.[361] Exactly in this context the view of the fifth Veda (=

---

[359] Cf. OBERHAMMER 1974: 85ff.; above n 123 and n 132; cf. also Abhinavagupta's Tantrāloka, chapter 35, where he refers to the meeting of religious traditions (*śastrāṇāṃ melanam*), since these traditions are parts of the original divine revelation.

[360] Anuv p. 71,24; cf. NM 5,10-11: *ādisargāt prabhṛti vedavad imā vidyāḥ pravṛttāḥ* ; cf. above n 12 and n 176.

[361] Cf. above n 254f.

Sadāgamas) is tied up. Its original frame work, restricted solely to Itihāsas and Purāṇas, is widened in order to include not only the Pañcarātrasaṃhitās, all traditions (*smṛtayo 'khilāḥ*), Brahmasūtras and Sāṅkhya-Yoga, but also 'works' or 'work-titles' of Madhva, like Brahmatarka or Bhaviṣyatparvan.[362] The reason why Madhva puts forward his fictitious quotations side by side with traditional sources, definitely transmitted and acknowledged by the *śiṣṭāḥ*, is to emphasize that they are equally matched to the traditional sources. The common characteristics of Madhva's sources are that they all deal with his peculiar doctrines, which proclaim to be the only means of *mokṣa*.[363] And the fact, that all of Madhva's sources are ultimately grounded on the eternal Vedas have a specific aim to express the doctrinal antiquity and continuity of his system. Madhva follows a particular procedure while quoting from his unknown sources, for these are introduced only after he had brought forward his point of view by a self-statement. The aim of this procedure is to show that the particular doctrine is definitely embedded in an existing tradition.[364] It is remarkable that there are no cross-quotations from Madhva's works!

Taking into consideration the 'unfinished shape' of Brahmatarka which surprisingly, does not refer to his *avatāra* doctrine, we should assume that all the unknown sources of Madhva are not 'finished products', but merely 'work-titles', which Madhva employs as a loop to hang up his literary compositions. Sometimes, Madhva uses for this purpose also the well known sources, like Purāṇas. And very often the fictitious passages are quoted anonymously with *iti* or *iti ca*.[365]

The analysis of the fictitious passages has shown that Madhva himself composed them as befitted the occasion. For it is highly unlikely, that the text of Purāṇas read differently as it was

---

362 Cf. above n 150f. and n 153f.

363 Cf. above n 333f.

364 Cf. above n 95ff.

365 Cf. above n 17.

opportune to Madhva, in order to support his new doctrines. At any rate, the Purāṇatext-additions introduced by Madhva in agreement with his doctrines did not find any acceptance of the *śiṣṭāḥ*. Even the followers of Madhva seem to have acknowledged the loopholes in the sources of Madhva with some uneasiness. For, soon after the demise of Madhva, several myths began to take shape, in order to explain these lacunae. For instance, the author of Sumadhvavijaya, Nārāyaṇapaṇḍitācārya, son of Trivikramatīrtha, who was an immediate disciple of Madhva,[366] reports that the Māyāvādins plundered Madhva's library[367] or he relates that Madhva, while searching for the rare manuscripts in Northen India, was always ahead of his disciples thanks to his athletic constitution.[368] The purpose of this tale was to explain, how only Madhva was aware of rare manuscripts and could seize hold of them.

Nevertheless, we can exempt Madhva from the accusation of 'literary forgery' (*svamātrakalpita* or *svakapolakalpita*)[369] raised against him by well known and respected persons of the local tradition, as Veṅkaṭanātha, Appayadīkṣita and Nirvāṇa. For, Madhva is sincerely and firmly convinced that he was acting on the command of Viṣṇu. Madhva articulates this sense of mission through a phrase, which he repeats very often, namely: *viṣṇuprasādāt*[370] or *viṣṇvājñayaiva* or even more through his

---

366 Cf. SIAUVE 1968: 7f.

367 Cf. Sumadhvavijaya XII 40-42; ZYDENBOS 1994: 173.

368 Cf. Sumadhvavijaya VI 49-53; ZYDENBOS 1994: p. 172.

369 Cf. above n 30f.

370 Cf. Abhinavagupta, Tantrāloka XIII 286cd-287ab:

> *prasādo nirmalībhāvas tena saṃpūrṇarūpatā /*
> *ātmanā tena hi śivaḥ svayaṃ pūrṇaḥ prakāśate /*

cf. also Jayaratha's Tantrālokaviveka: . . . *tenātmanā tattatsaṃkucitātmāvacchedaṃ parigṛhyāpi pūrṇaḥ prakāśate pratyāvṛtta pūrṇadṛkkriyāsvabhāvo bhavet.*

statement as the third *avatāra* of Vāyu: *pūrṇaprajñas tṛtīyas tu bhagavatkāryasādhakaḥ.*[371] He expresses this conviction also in his appearance as a self-confident teacher of all canonical scriptures (*sadāgamāḥ*) in the *kali* age with the help of an over-subtle assertion that there can be no revelation without him: *amunā vinā na vinirṇayaḥ.*[372] In this context the names taken by him as *pūrṇaprajña* and *ānanda* [*-tīrtha*], which have a close relation to the divine attributes of Viṣṇu (*pūrṇānandajñānaśaktisvarūpa*)[373] become more meaningful. And in this very frame the self-statement of Madhva suits to the point, namely that he is an 'omniscient teacher' (*sarvajñamuni*) or that he is an 'all-knowing solar deity' (*sarvajñasūrya*).[374]

The results achieved here are not a mere working hypothesis, but a definite finding with regard to Madhva's authorship of the unknown sources. It is based on several individual observations and on Madhva's decisive self-statements. Although

---

371 Cf. above n 81f., 117.

372 Cf. MBhTN XXXII 159cd; above n 105f.; cf. also Madhva's similar expression in regard to the authorship of Viṣṇu (VTN p. 14,7f.): *nityā vedāḥ samastāś ca śāśvatā viṣṇubuddhigāḥ / sarge sarge* 'munaivaita udgīryante *tathaiva ca / . . .*

373 Cf. MāṇUBh p. 513,7.

374 Cf. MVD (in: VTN, Kolophon):

> *iti sarvajñamuninā māyāvādatamo 'khilam /*
> *nirastaṃ tattvavādena satāṃ saṃśayanuttaye //*

MVUD v. 18:

> *māyāvādatamovyāptam iti tattvadṛśā jagat /*
> *bhātaṃ sarvajñasūryeṇa prītaye śrīpateḥ sadā //*

MBhTN II 171:

> *pūrṇaprajñakṛteyaṃ saṅkṣepād uddhṛtiḥ suvākyānāṃ /*
> *śrīmadbhāratagānāṃ viṣṇoḥ pūrnatvanirṇayāyaiva //*

BĀUBh p. 341,28: . . . *pūrṇaprajñasvarūpatvāt vijñānamaya īryate*; *ibid.* p. 342,16f.: *pūrṇaprajñānusāreṇa* . . . ityādi ca mahāmīmāṃsāyām; cf. above n 8.

these observations rest on limited materials, nevertheless the philological scrutiny of individual fictitious quotations has shown that Madhva not only composed new literary passages, but also that he has reshaped, enlarged and interpolated the existing ones, for instance, textual passages from the Purāṇas. The critical method employed here, as well as the redactional criteria worked out on the basis of critical philology should be supplemented in many points through the analysis of other fictitious quotations in Madhva's works. For this purpose, some preparatory studies and several working cycles are required. For instance, a collection of all fictitious passages found in his works. So far, only one collection of all 'quotations' assigned to Brahmatarka has been prepared. Other collections of similar passages ascribed to other work-titles and arranged under the different doctrinal topics, should be subjected to a critical examination.

Taking all these facts into consideration, I should say that the present study is only a beginning, which should be continued, employing other complementary procedures, for instance paying close attention not only to the peculiarity of Madhva's doctrine, but also to his language, style and selection of words. I do expect earnestly that the present monograph will supply necessary impulses to further research and contribute to foster this rather neglected field of Indian Philosophy.

BIBLIOGRAPHY AND ABBREVIATIONS

ABORI — Annals of the Bhandarkar Oriental Institute.

AiU — Aitareyopaniṣad.

AiUBh — Madhva, Aitareyopaniṣadbhāṣya, s. Anuv.

Anuv — Madhva, Anuvyākhyāna. [Works of Sri Madhwacharya]. In: Sarvamūlagranthāḥ – Prasthānatrayī, sampuṭa 1,ed. by B. GOVINDACHARYA. Udipi 1969.

ĀP — Yāmunācārya, Āgamaprāmāṇya, ed. M. NARASIMHACHARY [Gaekwad's Oriental Series 160]. Baroda 1976.

BĀU — Bṛhadāraṇyakopaniṣad.

BĀUBh — Madhva, Bṛhadarāṇyakopaniṣadbhāṣya, s. Anuv.

BGD — Parāśarabhaṭṭa, bhagavadguṇadarpanākhyaṃ śrīviṣṇusahasranāmabhāṣyam, ed. by P.B. AṆṆAṄGARĀCĀRYA. Kancheepuram 1964.

BhāgP — Bhāgavatapurāṇa with Sanskrit Commentary Bhāvārthabodhinī of Śrīdhara, ed. by J.L. SHASTRI (M. Banarsidass). Delhi 1983.

BhāgTN — Madhva, Bhāgavatatātparyanirṇaya. [Works of Sri Madhwacharya]. In: Sarvamūlagranthāḥ — Purāṇaprasthāna, sampuṭa 3, ed. by B. GOVINDACHARYA. Udipi 1980.

BHANDARKAR 1913 — R.G. BHANDARKAR Vaiṣṇavism, Śaivism and minor religious Systems [Grundriss der Indo-Arischen Philologie und Altertumskunde, hrsg. H. LÜDERS und J. WACKERNAGEL, III. Band, 6. Heft]. Strassburg 1913.

BhaviṣP — Bhaviṣyatpurāṇa, ed. by KH. KṚṢṆADĀSA (Nag Publishers). Delhi 1984.

BrahP — Sanskrit Indices and Text of the Brahmapurāṇa by P. SCHREINER and R. SÖHNEN [Purāṇa Research Publication, Tübingen, ed. by H. VON STIETENCRON, Vol 1]. Wiesbaden 1987.

BrahVP — Brahmavaivartapurāṇa, ed. by J.L. SHASTRI (M. Banarsidass). Delhi 1983.

BrāṇP — Brahmāṇḍapurāṇa, ed. by K.V. SARMA. Varanasi 1983.

BSū — Brahmasūtras.

BSūBh — Madhva, Brahmasūtrabhāsya, s. Anuv.

CHANDRA-VASU 1910 — Chhandogya Upaniṣad. With the Commentary of Madhvāchārya, transl. S. CHANDRA VASU. [Sacred Books of the Hindus, ed. by B.D. BASU, Vol. III, Part II]. Allahabad 1910.

CHANDRA-VASU 1916 — The Brihadaraṇyaka Upaniṣad. With the Commentary of Madhvāchārya transl. S. CHANDRAVASU. [Sacred Books of the Hindus, ed. by B.D. BASU, Vol. XIV]. Allahabad 1916.

ChU — Chāndogyopaniṣad.

ChUBh — Madhva, Chāndogyopaniṣadbhāṣya, s. Anuv

GarP — Garudapurāṇa, ed. by KH. KṚṢṆADĀSA (Nag Publishers). Delhi 1984.

GHATE 1981 — V. S. GHATE, The Vedānta. A Study of the Brahma-Sūtras with the Bhāṣyas of Śaṃkara, Rāmānuja, Nimbārka, Madhva, and Vallabha. [Bhandarkar Oriental Research Institute: Government Oriental Series Class B, No.5]. Poona 1981.

Gī — Bhagavadgītā.

GīBh — Madhva, Bhagavadgītābhāṣya, s. Anuv.

GīT — Madhva, Bhagavadgītātātparya, s. Anuv.

GK — Gauḍapādakārikā.

GLASENAPP 1992 — H. VON GLASENAPP, Madhva's Philosophy of the Vishnu Faith, transl. by SH.B. SHROTHRI, ed. by K.T. PANDURANGI [Dvaita Vedanta Studies and Research Foundation]. Bangalore 1992.

GRIFFITH 1987 — R. T.H. GRIFFITH, Hymns of the Ṛgveda. Translated with a Popular Commentary, Vols. I-II (complete rev. and enl. ed.). New Delhi 1987.

HACKER 1960 — P. HACKER, Zur Entwicklung der Avatāralehre, WZKSO 4 (1960), p. 47-70.

HEIMANN 1922 — Madhva's (Ānandatīrtha's) Kommentar zur Kāṭhaka-Upaniṣad. Sanskrit-Text in Transskription nebst Übersetzung und Noten, hrsg. BETTY HEIMANN. Leipzig 1922.

ĪśU — Īśopaniṣad.

ĪśUBh — Madhva, Īśopaniṣadbhāṣya, s. Anuv.

KANE 1962 — P.V. KANE, History of Dharmaśāstra (Ancient and Medieval Religious and Civil Law in India) Vol. V/2, [Government Oriental Series, Class B, No. 6]. Poona 1962.

KathU — Kathopaniṣad.

KathUBh — Madhva, Kathopaniṣadbhāṣya, s. Anuv.

KāvM — Rājasekhara, Kāvyamīmāṃsā, ed. by C.D. DALAL & R.A. SHASTRY, Rev. and enlarged by K.S. RAMASWAMI SASTRI [Gaekwad's Oriental Series 1]. Baroda 1934.

KeU — Kenopaniṣad.

KeUBh — Madhva, Kenopaniṣadbhāṣya, s. Anuv.

KhN — Madhva, Khaṇḍārthanirṇaya, s. ṚgBh.

KN — Madhva, Karmanirṇaya. In: Daśaprakaraṇāni, caturthobhāgaḥ, ed. by ANANTHARĀMĀCHARYA. Madras 1972.

KūrP — Kūrmapurāṇa, ed. by KH. KṚṢṆADĀSA (Nag Publishers). Delhi 1983.

MahānārU — Mahānārayaṇopaniṣad.

MaiU — Maitrāyanyupaniṣad.

MāṇU — Māṇḍūkyopaniṣad.

MārP — Mārkandeyapurāṇa, ed. by KH. KṚṢṆADĀSA (Nag Publishers). Delhi 1984.

MBh — Mahābhārata, crit. ed. by V.S. SUKTHANKAR etc. Poona 1933ff.

MBhTN — Madhva, Mahābhāratatātparyanirṇaya. [Works of Sri Madhwacharya]. In: Sarvamūlagranthāḥ – Itihāsaprasthāna, sampuṭa 2, ed. by B. GOVINDACHARYA. Udipi 1971.

MESQUITA 1990 R. MESQUITA, Yāmunācāryas Philosophie der Erkenntnis. Eine Studie zu seiner Saṃvitsiddhi. [SbÖAW 563 = Veröffentlichungen der Kommission für Sprachen und Kulturen Südasiens 24]. Wien 1990.

MESQUITA 2000 – Madhva, Viṣṇutattvanirṇaya. Der Nachweis des wahren Wesens Viṣṇus. Annotierte Übersetzung mit Studie. Vienna 2000 (*forthcoming*).

MTM Appayadīkṣita, Madhvatantramukhamardana [with Auto-commentary] Madhvamatavidhvaṃsana, [with] Ṭippaṇa Sandarbhavivaraṇa by Chinnasvāmi Sāstri. Kāśī 1941.

MuU Muṇḍakopaniṣad.

MuUBh Madhva, Muṇḍakopaniṣadbhāṣya, s. Anuv.

MVD Madhva, Māyavādadūṣaṇa, s. VTN

MVUD Madhva, Māyāvādopādhidūṣaṇa, s. VTN.

NārP Nāradīyapurāṇa, ed. by KH. KṚṢṆADĀSA (Nag Publishers). Delhi 1984.

NM Jayantabhaṭṭa, Nyāyamañjarī, ed. by S.N.S. ŚUKLA. [The Kashi Sanskrit Series, Haridās Sanskrit Granthamālā, Nyāya Section No. 15]. Benares 1936.

NyāV Madhva, Nyāyavivaraṇa, s. Anuv.

OBERHAMMER 1971 G. OBERHAMMER, Yāmunamunis Interpretation von Brahmasūtram 2,2,42-45. Eine Untersuchung zur Pañcarātra-Tradition der Rāmānuja-Schule.[SbÖAW 274=Veröffentlichungen der Kommission für Sprachen und Kulturen Südasiens 10]. Wien 1971.

OBERHAMMER 1974 – Die Überlieferungsautorität im Hinduismus. In: Offenbarung, geistige Realität des Menschen. Arbeitsdokumentation eines Symposiums zum Offenbarungsbegriff in Indien, hrsg. G. OBERHAMMER [Publications of the De Nobili Research Library 2]. Wien 1974, p. 41-92.

OBERHAMMER 1994 – Offenbarungsgeschichte als Text. [Publications of the De Nobili Research Library. Occasional Papers 5]. Wien 1994.

OLIVELLE 1987 P. OLIVELLE, Renunciation in Hinduism. A Medieval Debate, Vol. II, The Viśiṣṭādvaita Argument [Publications of the De Nobili Research Library 14].Vienna 1987.

PANDU-RANGI 1993 — Mahābhāratatātparyanirṇayaḥ. Translated by K.T. PANDURANGI, [First Volume: First three Chapters] S.M.S.O. Sabha Publication No. 21. Chirtanur 1993.

PadP — Padmapurāṇa, ed. by KH. KṚṢṆADĀSA (Nag Publishers). Delhi 1984.

PL — Madhva, Prāmaṇalakṣaṇa, s. VTN.

PP — Bhāvasena, Pramāprameya, ed. V.P. JOHRAPURKAR [Jīvarāja Jaina Granthamālā No. 18]. Sholapur 1966.

PraśU — Praśnopaniṣad.

PraśUBh — Madhva, Praśnopaniṣadbhāṣya, s. Anuv.

PUTHIADAM 1985 — I. PUTHIADAM, Viṣṇu the ever free. A Study of the Mādhva Concept of God. Madurai 1985.

RAO 1960 — C.R.K. RAO, Madhva and Brahmatarka. Udipi 1960.

ṚgBh — Madhva, Ṛgbhāṣya. [Works of Sri Madhwacharya]. In: Sarvamūlagranthāḥ – Śrutiprasthāna, sampuṭa 4, ed. by B. GOVINDACHARYA. Udipi 1973.

SCHRADER 1973 — F. O. SCHRADER, Introduction to the Pāñcarātra and the Ahirbudhnya Saṃhitā, Adyar Library. Madras 1973.

SDS — Mādhavācārya, Sarvadarśanasaṃgraha, ed. by U. S. SHARMA [The Vidyabhawan Sanskrit Granthamala 113]. Varanasi 1964.

SHARMA 1960 — B.N.K. SHARMA, A History of the Dvaita School of Vedānta and its Literature, Vol. I: From the Earliest Beginnings to the Age of Jayatīrtha (C. 1400 A.D.). Bombay 1960.

SHERIDAN 1992 — D.P. SHERIDAN, Vyāsa as Madhva's Guru. Biographical Context for a Vedāntic Commentator. In: Texts in Context. Traditional Hermeneutics in South Asia, ed. by JEFFREY R. TIMM. New York 1992, p. 109-125.

SIAUVE 1968 — S. SIAUVE, La Doctrine de Madhva. Dvaita Vedānta. [Publications de l'Institut Francais d'Indologie 38]. Pondichéry 1968.

SIAUVE 1971 — –Les Hiérarchies Spirituelles. Selon l'Anuvyākhyāna de Madhva. Textes choisis et traduits par S. SIAUVE [Publications de l'Institut Francais d'Indologie 43]. Pondichéry 1971.

SINGH 1958 — S. SINGH, Vedānta Deśika: His Life, Works and Philosophy. [The Chowkhamba Sanskrit Series Studies 5].Varanasi 1958.

SkaP — Skandapurāṇa, ed. by KH. KṚṢṆADĀSA (Nag Publishers). Delhi 1986.

SULLIVAN 1990 — B.M. SULLIVAN, Kṛṣṇa Dvaipāyana Vyāsa and the Mahābhārata: A New Interpretation. Leiden 1990.

TaiU — Taittirīyopaniṣad.

TaiUBh — Madhva, Taittirīyopaniṣadbhāṣya, s. Anuv.

TS — Madhva, Tattvasaṃkhyāna, s. VTN.

TSāS — Madhva, Tantrasārasaṅgraha, s. VTN

TU — Madhva, Tattvodyota (=Vāda) [Daśaprakaraṇāni tṛtīyo/ caturtho bhāgaḥ. Madras 1971/72, s. KN.

TV — Madhva, Tattvaviveka, s. VTN.

Ukh — Madhva, Upādhikhaṇḍana [with] Ṭīkā by Jayatīrtha [Daśaprakaraṇāni, prathamo bhāgaḥ, ed. by P.P. LAKSHMINĪNĀRĀYANA UPĀDHYĀYA. Madras 1969].

UkhṬ — Jayatīrtha, Upādhikhaṇḍanaṭīkā, s. UKh.

Vāda — Madhva, Vāda (= TU), s. VTN.

VarP — The Varāha Purāṇa, crit. ed. by A.S. GUPTA. Varanasi 1981.

VāyP — Vāyupurāṇa.

VENKATA-SUBBIAH 1986 — A. VENKATASUBBIAH, The Māṇḍūkyopaniṣad and Gauḍapāda. In: The Indian Antiquary. A Journal of Oriental Research, ed. by E.A.W. OLDHAM and D.R. BHANDARKAR, Vol. LXII (1933). Swati Publications. Delhi 1986.

ViṣP — Viṣṇupurāṇa [mit dem Kommentar] Śrīviṣṇucittīya, ed. by P. AṆṆAṄGARĀCĀRYA. Kañcipuram 1972.

VL — Madhva, Vādalakṣaṇa, s. VTN [misquotation for Kathālakṣaṇa, s. UKh].

VTN — Madhva, Viṣṇutattvanirṇaya. [Works of Sri Madhwacharya]. In: Sarvamūlagranthāḥ – Saṅkīrṇagranthāḥ, saṃpuṭa 5, ed. by B.GOVINDACHARYA. Udipi 1974.

VTNṬ Jayatīrtha, Viṣṇutattvavinirṇayaṭīkā [Daśaprakaraṇāni (dvitīyo bhāgaḥ), ed. Śrīmanmādhvarāddhantasaṃvardhanī sabhā]. Madras 1969.

WESSLER 1995 H.W. WESSLER, Zeit und Geschichte im Viṣṇupurāṇa. Formen ihrer Wahrnehmung und ihrer eschatologischen Bezüge, anhand der Textgestalt dargestellt. [Studia Religiosa Helvetica Series Altera, ed. by PHILLIPE BORGEAUD u. a. Bd. I]. Bern 1995.

ZYDENBOS 1991 R. J. ZYDENBOS, On the Jaina Background of Dvaita-Vedānta, JIP 19 (1991) p. 248-271.

ZYDENBOS 1994 – Some Examples from Mādhva Hagiography, in: According to Tradition. Hagiographical writing in India, ed. by W.M. CALLEWAERT/R. SNELL (Khoj – A Series of Modern South Asian Studies). Wiesbaden 1994, p. 169-189.

INDICES

The indices follow the order of the Roman alphabet. The numbers after the entries refer to footnotes. In a number of cases they point out also to the respective pages of the monograph, where the footnote reference occurs. Index locorum refers only to the quoted passages in the text or in the footnotes. The subject index lists a selection of important terms.

A) INDEX OF NAMES

1) List of Authors

2) List of fictitious titles cited in the Madhva's works

3) List of fictitious passages and references attributed to Purāṇas

B) INDEX LOCORUM

1) Index locorum in Madhva's works

2) Index locorum in other works

C) SUBJECT INDEX